SPYING IN G

William Shaw is the author, with Richard Lowe, of *Travellers:
Voices of the New Age Nomads* of which the *Sunday Times* said,
'Books as good as this one are evidence that we should not give
up hope completely.' He is a feature writer for the American
magazine *Details* and contributes regularly to many British
publications, including *Select* and *Mojo*.

SPYING

IN

GURU

LAND

INSIDE BRITAIN'S CULTS

William Shaw

FOURTH ESTATE · *London*

For Francesca

Author's Note
To research this book I became involved with several British cults, often closely. Most had no idea I was writing about them. Therefore while names of cult 'leaders' I met and descriptions of the events that took place are unaltered, in the interests of ordinary cult members' privacy I have sometimes changed their names and identifying details.

Contents

INTRODUCTION

Holy John

1

Near the westernmost tip of England, just a few miles north of Land's End on a headland called Kenidjack, is a derelict stone quarry, a horseshoe carved out of the cliff face. After the tourists leave at the end of the summer, it becomes an abandoned landscape, full of Iron Age tombs, prehistoric standing stones and deserted industrial remains. Ten minutes' walk to the north, Geevor, the county's last working tin mine lies empty, shut down in the 1980s. In winter a curious smell of cabbage fills the air, from the crops grown in nearby fields; the locals and the migrant workers who harvest them boast of being able to take home £38 in a day if they work flat out, which they say isn't bad money in these parts.

The quarry is an inhospitable place, maybe a hundred feet above the Atlantic, a flat bare floor, sheltered on three sides by steep rock. When the mist descends on it, as it does sometimes for days at a time, the foghorn starts its regular mournful booming to warn ships off the rocks below.

For two years in the late 1980s a small community of people lived here largely unnoticed, waiting for an Arthurian city called Lyonesse which they believed was going to rise out of the sea and herald the birth of a great and magical neo-Celtic civilisation that would be led by them and their leader, a man called Holy John. They were a collection of misfits, hippies and new age travellers who saw themselves as the dispossessed of Britain.

One of their primitive huts remains, defiantly rebuilt by somebody after the local council had demolished the site and evicted the inhabitants. It's an intricately constructed circle of stone, broken by a low chimney, out of which a metal stack pipe rises. The roof is made from a tarpaulin strapped over bent sticks. It looks like part of a prehistoric outpost, or something from an archaeological reconstruction of life two thousand years before. A few years ago there was a hamlet of these huts here.

Holy John is in his fifties now. He still lives locally in the small cottage which became the headquarters of the mysterious millenarian cult he called into being, whose followers lived on the cliff. A middle-class man, whose parents ran a hotel, John had worked as an antique dealer for some time. While serving a prison sentence that had resulted from a minor drug possession offence, John had an extraordinary vision that changed his life. A great earth goddess called the Lady, and her consort Pan, were going to return to rule Britain and save us from impending ecological disaster. There would be floods and some of the land would be lost for ever, his dream told him. All cars would be claimed by the waves. The unjust would scatter. The old world would perish and a new Arthurian age would dawn. The vision told him to go west, where this new age would begin when Lyonesse rose from the sea. The vision changed his life.

One day in Easter 1985 John arrived out of the blue from London in a van, accompanied by several followers who had already become drawn to his prophecy, having travelled as far west as he could. Holy John was impressed by the name of the nearby town of St Just. The town soon became woven into the prophecy. When the old world was swept away, the houses would be left empty and the just, the dispossessed, would make this their capital.

John cut a striking if strange figure, a tall spindly man, with a long face, big long teeth and long dark hair. He wore loud waistcoats, baggy shirts and silk trousers. Sometimes he carried a large stick with him that had the faces of Egyptian gods carved into it. 'He was like Mick Jagger on a bad acid trip, dressed as an Apache,' recalls a local who saw him when he first arrived. John was a karate teacher. Sometimes he would stride around the local lanes wearing his white robe and black belt. When no one would rent this outlandish-looking figure a local hall to teach karate in, he started to give classes outdoors, in a field near the house he lived in. The strange sight they made may have startled passing ramblers, but his karate pupils became the core of his disciples.

John brought with him his collection of books on the occult and oriental mysticism. There were titles by Aleister Crowley and Madame Blavatsky. Much of the cosmology of his visionary world might have been inspired by Robert Graves's poetic interweaving of Greek and Celtic mythology, *The White Goddess*. But John dismissed the books as young man's stuff. Although John believed the stream the cottage was built over was a holy one, it made the house he had moved into damp. In the back room he kept them in, the books slowly began to rot. He wrote his own dreams and visions in a big book of his own, carefully illustrating it with his own drawings of the gods and goddesses he had seen.

The cult revolved around a commune who lived in John's house, and the outpost of travellers waiting for the goddess on the cliff. They would sit in his house and he would talk to them late into the night, by candlelight after his electricity had been cut off. He told them when the new age came there would be no fixed marriages and all women would be shared, and that the homeless would all be given homes. 'And everybody believed this stuff,' say those who, for a while, did. He introduced many of them to 'astral travelling'; in mild trance states they would 'leave their bodies' and return with more dreams and myths to add to the growing lore of the cult. Holy John would interpret their visions for them.

'It all seemed to fit into the collective consciousness,' one of them recalls. ' "Oh yes. I've known about it all along." ' As the intensity of belief grew, people began witnessing strange things. They saw mystical ships or submarines floating off the coast; they saw UFOs. For about two years, disbelief evaporated and was replaced with faith in John's phantasmagorical world. 'It was like living in a legend,' one of them says.

It didn't last. It's not easy to work out exactly what went wrong. I stumbled on Holy John's cult of the Lady while visiting locally. Fascinated, I spoke to several of the people involved, but when they talked about what had happened, six or seven years ago, it became hard to disentangle what actually had gone on from the myths and visions that had become as real to the members as their dole cheques. What's clear is that many of the followers started to resent the rules that had begun to emerge, sometimes delivered by Holy John, sometimes by his lieutenant, a man known as Black Steve. Relationships between members were sometimes disapproved of. Communal work, like chopping wood for the huts' stoves, became a chore. 'John would say he was the octopus and we were his tentacles. Ultimately it all became too strange, and there were constraints on what people could say or do.' John's knowledge of karate also gave him physical power over his followers. Sometimes he dominated them by force. There were arguments and fights. Some were forcibly thrown out of the commune.

But the biggest disappointment of all, was that when the declared time of the millennium arrived one spring, the city of Lyonesse failed to break through the waves. For a while the sect remained in the area, reluctant to abandon their vision; but gradually over the next year the followers dispersed, disillusioned. The cult failed. The world carried on, much the same.

Not long after Waco went up in flames, killing twenty-nine Britons, I joined my first cult. The absurd siege in the desert in Texas had burst violently on to our TV screens just a few weeks after I had chanced across the remains of Holy John's following. Though both are cults that died, one very publicly and brutally, the other inconspicuously and uneventfully, they left me astonished by the extremes people seem capable of when they come to believe things most of us would find fantastic.

Curious, I decided to join cults myself to try to find out how people allowed themselves to be lured by what appeared to be such obviously self-destructive beasts. I was fascinated by what happened to converts once they were inside. How easy was it to maintain belief in something the rest of the world saw as plainly mad, abusive or exploitative? Maybe I would even take part in their ceremonies and rituals if necessary to try to understand how they affected the believers.

Cults have a reputation for deceit. If I let the cults know why I was joining there would be room for me to suspect what I saw, or still more importantly, for others to cast doubt on what I reported, so it often seemed simpler not to tell the gurus and their followers that I was writing a book about them.

The abrupt fame of Waco gave us a vision of cults as nightmarish, sexually abusive death traps. When the dust settled, after the cack-handed but lethal forty-five minute gunfight that ensued when a US government agency raided the Branch Davidian compound on the last day of February 1993, four government agents and six cult members lay dead or dying. A fifty-one day siege began. Over a hundred people were caught inside the ranch, and to the incredulity of UK commentators, over a quarter of the followers of this guru – who preached with a certain ironic accuracy that the end of the world was nigh – were British. There was a sense of surprise that good British people had become tricked into joining something so evil and so absurd.

For two months the papers were full of Waco. If you look at their grim reporting of the stand-off in the Texas desert now the dust has settled, you'll notice that their headlines are strangely, even comically similar. 'Sacked preacher lured Brits to bloodbath cult. He hypnotised my lad Winston' (*Daily Star*); 'Zombies – Freed British children have been brainwashed by Jesus cult' (*Today*); 'In the grip of Jesus Monster – Lust for virgins' (*Daily Mirror*); 'Mesmerised by Messiah of death' (*Daily Mail*). The genteel broadsheets were only marginally less colourful: 'Cults feed when the soul lies empty' (*Daily Telegraph*); 'Cult recruits brainwashed' (*Guardian*). The archetype was astonishingly consistent. Each headline might have come from a script conference for a George Romero film. They all replayed the same plot. Young, innocent and vulnerable victims are suckered into giving up their money, homes, lifestyles and families to satisfy the thirst of a power-crazed devil, an evil sexual predator, who will eventually lead them to their doom.

The press presented absurd visions of an incomprehensible world. Reporting of cults presents us with the things we're most afraid of in them, rather than giving us any idea of what really goes on inside. Cults are dark monsters, come to invade our mind, steal our children and inflame strange sexual passions in us. Their leaders are powerful, and unbelievably cynical.

Holy John's millenarian cult failed slowly; maybe it never even really got going. David Koresh's was brought to a more abrupt end. It's hard to see any connection between the demise of an obscure hippie sect on the cliff in Cornwall and the violent public news drama of what happened in Waco. Most conspicuously, the people who lived on the cliff didn't talk about being zombies, being mesmerised or being brainwashed as we were told the disciples in the desert were. Though for a while they accepted Holy John as their guru, they acknowledged that they were all in some way actually responsible for what went on. One woman I spoke to even talked in a way that suggested that it was the followers, as much as Holy John, who called the dream into being. The week before he arrived in his van, she remembered praying she would meet someone who felt the same way about the mysterious landscape of Cornwall as she did. 'A lot of people who had come to Cornwall already felt there was a mysterious purpose in why they had come here,' she said. 'John put this into focus. He crystallised their mystery, he gave it a mythology, and he made it seem right.'

If the inhabitants of Waco weren't the zombies portrayed by the press either and had also been in some way equally responsible for the strange nightmare world of David Koresh, then maybe I would find cults to be altogether different monsters from the ones the headlines conjured up.

I wandered up and down past shaven-headed Hare Krishna book distributors on London's Oxford Street hoping they'd notice me. I lurked outside the Scientology headquarters on Tottenham Court Road imagining someone would offer me one of the question-naires they use to recruit new members. I plucked stacks of leaflets from the shelves of health-food shops and alternative bookshops, scanning them for any that appeared to be conspicuously odder than the rest. In the first few weeks, when I was thrashing around trying to join a cult, but with pathetically few ideas of how to go about it, I went to all sorts of meetings, and I found a lot of people who told me they were 'searching'. In the new age ministry of the Church of St James Piccadilly, I was surprised to find about 1,000 well-heeled people turning up to pay £5 a head to hear the best-selling Christian guru and mystical psychotherapist M. Scott Peck speak, and on a midweek afternoon too. Having learned about the talk from a pink photocopied sheet advertising a series of new age lectures titled 'Alternatives', I had expected one of those small meetings where there was an embarrassing 'Any questions?' pause at the end. Sitting in the gallery still taking in the scale of this English tidal wave of spiritual enthusiasm, I heard a tall, smartly-dressed man in his forties turn to his neighbour and say, smugly, 'Just think, twenty years ago you could have only got this many people to turn up to a political protest.'

For concrete-footed agnostics like myself there's a horror in the idea of people inventing ever-stranger ways to turn their backs on the world as the millennium approaches. For us – rightly or wrongly – cults become a spectre of a millenarian lemming plunge away from the twentieth century; a mass revolt against secular-ism, science, politics and modernity.

This is a book about the time I spent in this world of seekers, misfits, devotees and dreamers, not a work of methodological research. The cults covered are simply the ones that I became fascinated by.

At the time of the Texan siege, many of the articles about it quoted a cult expert called Ian Haworth who runs an organisation called the Cult Information Centre. I tried to call him a few times to ask if he could help me get inside this world, but his line was usually kept busy by journalists and concerned families asking his opinion about the events that were unfolding. (Under the headline 'Could you be lured by evil maniacs who run the cults?' (*Daily Star*), I read, 'There are more than 500 of these mind-bending movements in Britain, says the Cult Information Centre.') When I finally got through to Ian Haworth he first advised me to read a book called *The Secret World of Cults* ('Exposes the con men behind the cults and reveals the horror of the world-wide Satanist revival. Who are the self-styled gurus behind these movements? Are they in it for profit – or perverted pleasure?'); it's a compendium of horrific testimonies of ex-members. Naively, I told him I was more interested in joining cults myself to find out what really happened in them, than in relying on a second-hand view from the outside. I wondered if he could give me some tips on how to get inside them.

The other end of the phone line went quiet for a second.

'If you're thinking of pursuing such a, well . . . foolhardy course, I'm not sure whether I should be talking to you at all,' he said eventually. His voice was full of concern, but I could also hear a weariness, as if he was tired of people like me blundering idiotically into this territory he had spent years of his life studying.

He told me a story about another journalist – Canadian I think – who thought he could keep his objectivity in Guru Land but he joined up and went round the twist. Haworth had identified twenty-six separate techniques of mind-control which cults use over their victims. Used together, he said, they can be 'a very dangerous cocktail'.

'Being intelligent and well educated, one is even *more* vulnerable,' he warned. 'And even when one goes in knowing what – or thinking one knows what – to expect, it still doesn't stop the techniques from working.'

His concern for my sanity was real enough, but his self-assured manner irritated me. What he was saying seemed to boil down to this: cults were so dangerous that the only way to understand them was to talk to experts like himself. I protested, saying that I wanted to find out for myself how cult members came to believe the things they did.

'A judge doesn't have to actually *witness* a murder in order to dole out a sentence,' Haworth scoffed. 'It's like drinking poison to find out if it's poisonous. It's absurd.'

I considered this, worried about whether he was right, as he harrumphed a few more times. 'It's like playing Russian roulette with your mind.'

Academics prefer to ignore the term cult completely, backed against the wall by a vocal anti-cult movement who have made the term their own. They use the lumpy phrase 'New Religious Movement' instead (worse, 'NRM'), a dry device which appears too broad to exclude even the Campaign to Keep Sunday Special from its umbrella, and which robs cults of their air of maverick intensity.

The strongly pejorative meaning of the word these academics are trying to escape is a relatively recent phenomenon. Much of it stems from a network of self-styled cult experts who, since the 70s, have been warning us of the growing threat cults present, and who dominate how we now think of them.

The anti-cult vanguard defines cults in solely negative terms. The American Steven Hassan, who bills himself as a psychotherapist, wrote the anti-cult book *Combating Cult Mind Control*; his version is: 'An exclusive group that exercises negative uses of mind control, which may be understood as a system of influences that disrupts an individual's identity (beliefs, behavior, thinking and emotions) and replaces it with a new identity.'

Hassan's definition is a classic of much of the skewed, fuzzy-headed thinking that surrounds cults. The idea that there is 'negative mind control' means that there is also such a thing as 'positive mind control' – presumably that includes army training, American history lessons and a good college education. Which means simply it's a cult if he doesn't like it. Or doesn't understand it. If you start out with a negative definition, you'll end up with a negative result.

Cults are a collective spiritual rebellion against the orthodoxy, an us-against-them turning of backs on world. Fuelled by the notion that they alone are the virtuous few, they are also a social club, a sort of esoteric Club 18–30 whose members dream up a type of magic they believe transforms the world around them.

Scale is an aspect in the make up of a cult, too. When today's fringe cult grows into tomorrow's sturdily rooted religion it ceases to appear a threat. To dismiss the Hindu Hare Krishna movement in India as a cult would be as absurd as calling, say, the Quakers a cult in Britain. It's only when shaven-headed British youth dance up and down Oxford Street, robed in saffron, chanting and clanging cymbals, that the shoppers gawk in understandable disbelief and puzzlement. As film director Robert Altman once quipped, 'What is a cult? It just means not enough people to make a minority.'

In other words, they also become cults when we think of them as cults. That's not as circular a definition as it sounds. The presence of a hostile, uncomprehending world is as much a part of cult-dom as a sect's own beliefs.

And that, paradoxically, is exactly what the anti-cult movement has been providing since the 70s.

After my first few fumbling weeks I finally fell into a world of cults, where people in Britain do strange things in living rooms, meeting houses, classrooms, communes, church halls, temples, fields and even on cliffs. There are people who do not believe what they are doing is the slightest bit strange, whatever we may think, and who do not understand why all of us don't join them in their crusades to throw away all injustices and establish a perfect heaven on earth. There were nightmare times when I was acting out a role in as many as four different sects simultaneously, dashing between millenarian Rosicrucianism, Gurdjieffan Hinduism, born-again Christianity and the worship of spacemen, when the world appeared to have become very strange, but what I did learn is that the people who join cults aren't lured to them by Vincent Price or Boris Karloff. They are usually asking quite ordinary questions, like why am I here, why are some people rich and others poor, what happens when I die, why doesn't anybody like me, and so on. The real question is, how come they're coming up with such weird answers?

It can be hard to make sense of your life if you've spent two years faithfully waiting for a millennium that never came. These days Nick lives in a caravan rented from a farmer in a valley a couple of miles from St Just, but a few years before he was living in one of the stone huts at Kenidjack.

He has long hair and a neat beard. The caravan is decorated with a few of his paintings, dark and skilfully executed local landscapes. Since leaving the cult his life has been erratic. The caravan he's in now is plush compared to some of the places he's stayed since. It's on the electric. But in April he has to move out of the caravan and find somewhere else to live. At first, he's reluctant to talk about his time at Kenidjack, about what he now considers to be the lowest point of his life. One local tells me that some of those who were Holy John's followers still believe he has powers, and are anxious not to cross him.

After leaving art school, Nick had gone on the road, growing dreadlocks and joining the new age convoys. He arrived in Kenidjack one day in a brightly painted truck, looking for somewhere to stay while he and his friends did the round of the summer festivals.

'I was asleep when we got there, but I woke up when we arrived and my first thoughts were, "Bloody godforsaken place, this." It was the end of the world.' When the rest of the people he was travelling with met Holy John, they thought the man was crazy, but Nick was intrigued. To Holy John the arrival of the new age travellers was confirmation of his prophecy.

Soon, Nick was caught up in Holy John's dreams and visions. He too began to experience things which he is still unable to explain. He says that one night, in particular, he had a vision of extraordinary clarity while standing on the cliffs. The moonlight suddenly filled the sky, and he saw a family tree, with his parents at the bottom, and a strange succession of historical figures spreading up through the sky. Some figures he recognised – Jesus Christ, King Arthur, Hitler, Gandhi, Richard the Lionheart – a few he guessed were figures from mythology, and others were monstrous figures. He seemed to hear a voice telling him, 'All these faces, all these people lived so that this moment could happen.' The thought terrified him. The voice continued, 'Be a light and a hope and a heart.' It was perfectly real to him. Even now he can't explain it.

The next day he found Black Steve and burst into tears. 'I don't know what's going on. I can't cope with this.'

Steve told him, 'Pull yourself together. You know exactly what this means. It's why you're here.'

Nick began to resent both the responsibility of his mystical role in the would-be future, and the more present mundane drudgery of survival on a cliff. People told him he wasn't pulling his weight. Life seemed to revolve around fetching water. They asked him, 'Have you done your hour on the saw-horse to make sure everyone's got enough wood?' Increasingly paranoid, he started getting up earlier to chop logs to show that he was trying as hard as he could. They bickered over who had eaten whose porridge. To make matters worse, the council evicted them a couple of times, bringing JCBs to demolish their huts.

As things turned sour for everybody, it was the sense that he was an essential part of a mythic history that made it impossible for Nick to leave the cult. By then he really wanted to leave, but he didn't feel capable of breaking away. 'It was a sort of guilt thing,' remembers Nick. 'You're here for a reason and you're meant to be here, and we *need* you, and if anything changes, and one of us goes, then *nothing* will be the way it should be. You're altering the course of history by going.'

But his life was miserable. After Lyonesse failed to appear, all the excitement of their quest evaporated. When Nick joined, he had not worried about leaving his friends behind, because when Holy John had built his new world, he had felt sure they would join him in their heaven on earth. He lost touch. Now he realised that the only people he knew were also caught up in Holy John's dream. Other travellers steered clear of Kenidjack because they had heard rumours of the cult that lived there. The believers had become isolated in their belief, and by it.

Eventually the decision about how to leave was taken away from Nick. In one of the bouts of infighting that were now gripping the site, he was thrown out. He had no idea what he was suppose to do next. Dazed and unsettled, for a while he lived rough around St Just. After a couple of years living on the cliff, he looked a mess. His hair was matted into thick dreadlocks. He had forgotten how to lead a normal life. 'I just didn't know that you could go and rent places,' he says, as the rain pelts down on to the caravan roof. 'The way I looked I suppose I thought that nobody who lived in a house would want me.'

Over the past few years he's led an uncertain, hand to mouth life, trying to get back into the world the rest of us live in, trying to shake off the past. The first house he lived in after years in caravans and shelters was a small rented flat in a nearby village that he shared with another ex-member who was also trying to rebuild her life. He has given up drugs and does odd jobs, though there is very little work locally. A lot of the time he works on improving his painting technique. His dark, rainy watercolour landscapes, full of local standing stones are tacked to the caravan walls. He dresses neatly now, and dreams of setting up a local art gallery. But he talks like a man woken after a long sleep who is struggling to unravel the meaning of the strange dreams he just had. 'I'm trying to get my life together now,' he tells me, rolling a cigarette. 'I still want to build this new world, but . . .' He still can't make real sense of what happened. He smiles. 'There were grains of truth in what John said, possibly a lot of truth, but it shouldn't have happened. It got into the wrong hands.' He's still trying to work it out.

ONE

Chrisemma

1

They appeared in Totnes three years ago calling themselves the Chrisemma Foundation. Emma Lea, who wears pink lipstick and bleaches her hair, announced, 'I am God.' She was an Enlightened Master. So was her boyfriend, Chris Orchard. As one they were Chrisemma: one higher spiritual force that operates through creating the perfect sexual and spiritual relationship in their followers. 'The dynamic of Chris and I being together is the latest God technology,' said Emma.

For five hours once a week the pair sit on a sofa in a small upper room in Totnes High Street and deliver their philosophy of eastern self-denial and western sexuality to the twenty or so who have joined their fledgling cult. The Enlightened Masters give them advice on how to pursue their personal relationships to reach the giant void of true consciousness. Sometimes they are given guidance on business, or on emotional problems. Sometimes they are told to sleep with their partners, sometimes they are told not to.

The Chrisemma Foundation teaches how the soul can be freed by the correct practice of love, relationship and sex.

Emma has well-manicured nails and carefully plucked eyebrows; today her lips are salmon pink and her tan is a rich brown. She looks like one of the young women who work behind the cosmetics counters in Harvey Nichols. But in spite of her worldly appearance, her state of enlightenment is so deep that she has become unordinarily detached from the ordinary world. She hardly ever speaks, and sits instead with her legs tucked under her on the sofa, staring with beautiful vacancy at the carpet tiles on the floor for hours on end in a theatrical demonstration of her elevated consciousness. Chris is thirty-three, dresses in smartly fashionable jackets and thin ties, and does all the talking, often on her behalf.

Outside the room, shoes are neatly piled. A notice requires you to abandon them before entering the small upper floor of the office building. People bring their own cushions and lounge on the floor at their Masters' feet. Contributing my £10 entrance fee, I join them for my first meeting. By the sofa, two bottles of mineral water await Chrisemma. When, after half an hour of waiting, they sweep into the room in stockinged feet, a hush descends on the disciples, who sit, backs propped against the white walls, adopting spiritually distant, meditative expressions that will stay on most of their faces for the entire five hours.

The windows are open. It's a hot day in late summer. Chris looks up and smiles widely at his followers, clears his throat like a C of E vicar, and starts on his opening sermon.

'The other week,' commences Chris, 'Emma went fishing. For mackerel.' He pauses and smiles at us. 'It's something she likes to do, probably because she used to do it as a child . . . ' He is talking about Emma as if she is not there. Her face remains blank, as if not caring or even registering that she is being discussed. 'She told some of you last week that she had caught a fish. Afterwards, several of you came up and asked the same question. You all asked, "How did you kill it?" All of you wanted to know exactly the same thing.'

Around the room, everyone copies Emma's expression of languid detachment. It is the total opposite of other cults I will join. Instead of ecstasy, these people have cultivated sublime boredom as the outward expression of their spirituality. Disciples of Chrisemma must become empty. They must, as Chris repeatedly tells them, 'die'. The death he talks of is that death of attachment to the physical, emotional world, but he uses the word with obvious relish.

'Everyone asked the same question. How did you kill it? Later, I talked to Emma about it. The thing is, it was of absolutely no concern to her *how* she killed it.'

Emma appears to have selected one particular carpet tile as the object of her attention.

Chris continues. 'I suppose there are two ways of killing a fish, aren't there? You can either leave it to drown in air, or you can give it a brain haemorrhage. But the thing that *you* were interested in was how did she put it out of its suffering. And Emma didn't care. It didn't matter to her at all because she has reached a different level of enlightenment. What does it matter to her how the fish died? It's a fish, and dying is doing the fish thing. It is what fish do,' says Chris, smiling happily.

'But we want to stop that fish suffering. Now, we have to ask, who is suffering? You or the fish? Do we *know* that the fish is suffering? No, we don't. It is *us* who are doing the suffering, because we want to interfere with the fish which is doing the fish thing.'

The listeners take on the crazy teacher logic, the world turned upside-down, cross-legged on the floor, slumped around the walls. 'It is a very human thing to want to interfere. We hear about people in Bosnia or wherever, and we want to help them. We want to interfere. But by interfering, we create our own suffering. We suffer for them. Out of our own suffering we create the conflict.'

The war in Bosnia is a product of our own psyche. If we banish our own suffering, we shall banish the suffering of others.

Chris Orchard was studying at Coventry College of Art when he took his first steps on the road to enlightenment. Finding the Graphics course he had signed up for too conservative, he changed to Fine Art, and started painting abstracts which he says were about 'uncovering the taboo around the fear of the unconscious'. From the age of twenty-three he began to study oriental religions, seeking out Living Masters, eastern teachers who claim to be so enlightened they are no longer bound to this earthly life, but who stay here to teach the higher way. It was a disturbing time. Chris became fascinated and at the same time terrified by the horror of the idea that one should let one's personality 'die' in order to achieve the calm Absolute. He finally became one of the followers of the Hindu meditation teacher Sri Chinmoy, and though Chinmoy's teachings didn't produce the sense of panic he had initially experienced during his spiritual conversion, Chris's life became austere. He became isolated from his peers, had few close friends and attempted to practise a life of strict celibacy to follow his spiritual quest for God.

Then in 1990, when he was thirty, he suddenly claimed to have discovered 'self-realisation' in the form of the twenty-three-year-old blonde-haired Emma Lea. His celibacy came to an abrupt end and he developed a new set of ideas that linked finding the Absolute with surrender of male and female to each other. His world somersaulted a second time. This time Emma became the manifestation of the solution to everything: 'This woman before me was saying that she was the very form of this so-called God or Guru that I had been looking for,' Chris wrote later. 'It was hard to believe that it could be present in the body of a twenty-three-year-old English girl with absolutely no spiritual credentials whatsoever . . .'

A child who never enjoyed the company of others, Emma Lea claims to have realised what she calls 'The Truth of Being Alone' at the age of three. She claims that relationships with her parents were difficult. Her mother, she has said, placed excessive demands on her. Her father, a management consultant, regarded her as a failure, she believes. She doesn't get on well with them.

By eighteen she was practising her own spiritual philosophy which revolved around the belief that to understand the 'truth and mystery of life' one had to learn to acknowledge 'the pain of being alone'.

In early 1993, the newly formed Chrisemma Foundation produced a magazine to advertise themselves to the world: *The Final Discovery – The First Chronicle of the Enlightenment of Chris and Emma*.

It was edited by a former lover of Emma who became one of the early disciples of the new gurus. The magazine is full of photographs of Chris and Emma together, taken by Emma's ex-boyfriend. Many feature the guru-goddess Emma lips parted and breasts braless in a thin cotton top. The photographs are a strange act of worship from a former lover who had gone out with Emma before Chris, the guru, arrived. The relationship between Emma and her former lover is typical of the convoluted intensity of relationships that exist among the Chrisemma following. In its typed pages the disciple confesses his own pain as he watched his own relationship with the bleach-blonde guru disappear as her relationship with Chris began: 'When she met Chris,' he penitently wrote, 'the sheer deviousness of my need still perpetuated the obsessive idea, in spite of the pain I felt as I lost her, that she had transferred her manipulative need on to him and still secretly wanted me. This psychic affair has persisted in me for six years and it is only now that I am seeing the depth of the games I have played, believing I could get Love from outside of me, and the amount of abuse and blame I have transferred on to Emma.'

Such is the flagellant self-abasement of the true Chrisemma disciple.

By some act of common consent, based on geography, ley lines and myth, certain British towns have become capitals of the new age. Glastonbury is the most famous, full of druids, crystal vendors and soothsayers. The small medieval town of Totnes in Devon is gaining a similar reputation. Postcards in newsagents' windows advertise Colour Therapy and Astrological readings.

Many of the people who join Chris and Emma are people who have been searching for years. Some are guru junkies. Several used to number themselves amongst the thousands of disciples, or Sannyasins, of Osho, the bearded, multiple Rolls-Royce owning guru formerly known as Bhagwan Shree Rajneesh. Rajneesh abandoned his lectureship at the University of Jabalpur to travel round India, and then the world, running courses in Meditation, Bodywork, Zencounter and Neo Tantric Orgasmic Undoing. When he died in 1990, many of his Sannyasins were bereft. Some – notably a Sannyasin called Paul Lowe – set up their own groups. Others drifted, looking for a new guru.

One of Chris and Emma's early converts was Terri, a Sannyasin who had spent eleven years in Poona. She had been there with Osho when he died. When a friend told her of the two new gurus who had arrived in Totnes, she thought, 'So what's new? It happens all the time in Totnes. Gurus are two a penny.' After Osho's death she had experienced what she called 'so-called Enlightened ones' like Paul Lowe, whom she says were only into power. She had come to Totnes to be herself, not to get involved with any more gurus.

But she went to a meeting in December 1991 in a friend's living room and was impressed by what she calls 'the ordinariness, the emptiness and the incredible depth of being of this young man and woman sitting on the sofa'. She felt she had found something incredibly rare.

She wrote an account in *The Final Discovery*. 'And so, there and then my journey and seeking ended. I realised that I could not find the Guru within until I had totally been with, and destroyed, the Guru without and here it was presented to me. Fifteen months after that first meeting I am still with Chris and Emma. I will never leave them, for what is happening around them, and to me, is the most real and true of anything I know. I am eternally grateful.'

Like Terri, Ron is an ex-Sannyasin of Osho. After Osho's death, Ron felt lost. He didn't know what to do with himself, until a friend told him about these new gurus. Now he goes to the meetings every week. Today, after Chris has finished the monologue about Emma and the mackerel, he turns to Ron, who sits patiently in bottle-green trousers, neatly pressed, and asks: 'How are you, Ron?'

'OK.'

'And how are things between you and Gina?'

Gina is younger than Ron. She wears a pair of men's white thermals as leggings, and has her long legs tucked up under her chin.

'Well, um,' says Ron quietly. 'It's been quite fraught. There has been a lot of friction between us . . . and it's been quite depressing.'

Each disciple has to make a little offering to Chris, surrender a piece of their personal life.

It turns out that Gina has decided that she and Ron are no longer going to have sex. Ron says he is trying to go along with her decision, but 'it's been very hard work'. He complains: 'She has an idea of an ideal man, and I feel that she's just waiting for the ideal man to come along.'

Chris stares impassively at Ron from the sofa. 'Have you been blaming her for this?' he prompts, when Ron dries up.

'Yes. There have been quite a few occasions when we've blamed each other for it . . . we've had some pretty tense arguments.'

Chris turns to Gina. 'And Gina. How do you feel about this?'

The young, dark-haired woman clears her throat and starts talking in a quiet voice. 'Well, listening to Ron just now, I was rather hurt, actually. I don't think I have been blaming him for what has been going on.'

'You've decided you shouldn't sleep together,' says Chris, eyeing them both.

'Yes,' says Gina.

'Tell me why.'

Pause. Gina starts hesitantly. 'I just think that there is something else. I *do* have a vision of an ideal man, and I don't feel there is any meeting with Ron on a spiritual level. I can't talk to him about things like that.'

They lay their relationship out before Chris and Emma in excruciating detail. In exchange Chris starts to deliver his own prescription for their life. He says Gina is making a mistake. It's no use chasing after another man. All men are Ron. The truth is to realise the pain of relationship. Elsewhere she will only repeat the mistakes she made with him. Until she realises that, she will be unfulfilled. He is telling her that even if she doesn't think she loves Ron any more, even if he repels her, she must stay with him because there is only one love.

'I know,' says Gina, 'but . . .'

Chris: 'What do you feel when you think about sleeping with Ron?'

Gina, quietly: 'Horror.'

Chris pauses, then tells her she must overcome this. Chris tells her they must go home and sleep together, following a sort of eastern Tantric yoga prescription. Ron must insert his penis in her and must lie perfectly still. He must not go any further, or try to reach orgasm. They must contemplate themselves in that position. This is a road to learning the truth of relationship. 'Will you do that?'

Gina says, quietly, 'Well, I can say yes here, but the thought of going back to our place after this and . . . sleeping together still fills me with horror. It's like . . . rape.'

Chris repeats his request, unmoved. She and Ron should sleep together. All the disciples remain silent, staring blankly at the floor with the bored expressions of martyrs in medieval paintings. No one interrupts and contradicts Chris, or lends Gina any support. No one opens their mouth to suggest that asking a girl for whom sex feels like rape to sleep with a man is a cruel, possibly even dangerous thing to do. Myself included.

For the first time I feel uneasy in my role as silent observer. I intended to pass through the cults I would join in the same way that tourists visit new foreign countries; curious about their exotic customs, but not over-eager to dabble too closely in them. When I set out I told myself that I wouldn't argue with the beliefs I encountered, I would accept that they were sincerely held, however odd they were to me. There's an undignified absurdity in attempts to disprove religious faiths. At some time all of us have committed the ghastly mistake of attempting to contradict the re-born Bible thumper on the doorstep. It doesn't work. In the end your arguments end up sounding just as weird as theirs. Besides, I have never once heard a Jehovah's Witness say, 'You know, you're absolutely right? Maybe everything in the Bible *isn't* literally true.' And it wasn't the doctrine I was interested in as much as how and why people come to accept it. So I would just go along and act the part of convert to observe what was going on. I'm not responsible for what goes on here, I'm just watching. But it's beginning to occur to me that my non-interventionist stance isn't really very far from those ex-cult members who say, I wasn't responsible for what I did while I was in the cult, I was just obeying the mind control of the bad guru.

Chris continues to tell Gina she is deluding herself looking for an ideal man away from Ron. Like Bosnia, this is a problem of consciousness. 'We're all the same man,' he says. 'Even if you were to sleep with me, the Master, it wouldn't be any different because the problem is within you. If I were to put my saggyworm inside you, it would still be the same . . .'

The ludicrous image of the Master having a 'saggyworm' for a penis, bursts the tension and everybody laughs. Chris moves on to counsel another young couple: a handsome goatee-bearded Frenchman called Jan and his beautiful dark-haired girlfriend called Alison, who looks like a dolorous American Indian squaw and who manages to adopt a perfect expression of gloomy introspection throughout the meeting.

Alison has been suffering extreme vaginal pain during sex with Jan, but she reports back this week that everything is much better now. Last time they talked, Chris told her that the pain was simply 'mind', and she was to ignore it. Her vagina still hurts when they have sex, but the pain, she reports contentedly, isn't important any longer. Chris smiles at her and nods, lovingly.

Later, as the meeting closes, Chris turns back to Gina. 'And you're going to try what I said?'

'Yes,' says Gina.

2

Next Sunday, when Emma's nails are painted a cool pink and her hair sprouts from a purple headband on the top of her head, Gina turns up again with Ron. After Chris has finished his opening monologue, Emma sips her mineral water slowly as he turns to Gina and asks, 'How are you feeling?'

'Fine,' answers Gina, with a little smile.

'And have you been doing that thing I asked you to do last week?'

'Yes,' Gina answers quietly.

'And is it good?'

'Yes.'

When asked, she explains that she still has her reservations. Sometimes, she tells us, Ron tries to act more sexually, which isn't so nice, but yes, she's much happier now. I am astonished. When asked, Ron says that he is trying hard to be close to her. 'Good,' smiles Chris. 'That is because you are becoming closer to me, to the way and the truth and the life that is me . . .'

*

9

Chris's grand theme plays on a sort of spiritual *double entendre*. All men are one, as the oriental notion of Absolute self announces. Therefore for a woman to love a man is for a woman to love all men. And for a woman to love all men is for a woman to love him, the Master. His followers love the Master.

Each couple that attends the weekly meetings Chris leads has a strange, triangular relationship with him. I am conspicuous in the meetings as the only single person. Everyone else turns up in a pair, usually sitting next to each other. I tell Chris my partner doesn't want to come, which is quite true; Chris tells me that might mean she's not fully committed to our relationship. Maybe she's getting ready to walk out on me.

A middle-aged woman with short black hair glows with love for Chris. Her name is Frances. Today, her offering to Chrisemma is a story about her stepdaughter, who has begun to talk to her about death. Frances is happy that for the first time the girl is showing an interest in things that are deeper, and more spiritual. Chris always talks about how we must face death.

Today, instead of praising Frances for her spirituality, he abruptly scolds her for speculating about the girl. 'What does it matter to *you* what she's doing? It's all *mind*.' Frances is interfering. We must learn not to interfere, with fish or with Bosnia.

Frances nods sadly. Sometimes the path to enlightenment seems long and hard. She looks at Chris with sad puppy eyes and says, 'I was on the beach the other day, looking at the sea, and I felt so old, and so tired . . .'

Chris grins. 'It is because you *are* old, and tired. You are dying,' he says happily.

Tears begin to pour down Frances's face. 'I just feel so empty and tired sometimes . . .'

'That's good,' says Chris, smiling. Frances gulps silently for air. Her own grief and horror is welling up within her, pouring out as an offering before the Master.

Seated next to her, Alison peers with woebegone eyes into empty space, a perfect disciple. No one goes to comfort Frances as she weeps unceasingly, as Chris talks of the need for all of us to die intellectually and materially to leave our souls unencumbered. Chris returns gleefully again and again to this need for a death in all of us. But Frances appears grateful for the catharsis of the tears. 'I see,' she says, 'Yes.' She smiles damply.

Chris turns to Alison and Jan. Today, Jan's problem is that he is unhappy about something that Chris has been telling him in previous weeks; that he should not seek work because work is unimportant. 'I have never worked in my life,' protests Jan. 'I feel I want to.'

'That's because you are full of poison,' Chris scolds him. 'Alison has a little bit of the poison in her, but *you*, you are full of poison.'

Beside him, Alison too is crying now, small silent submissive tears falling on to her dress. Crystals dangle in the windows catching the summer sun and refracting it on to the white walls.

At the break, earnest Ron turns to me quietly and whispers, radiantly pleased with the way things are going, 'It's a very powerful meeting.'

Chris drives a Ford Fiesta. He believes that we must detach ourselves from the self-importance of the world, the hurry to get irrelevant things done. He drives his car no faster than fifty-six miles an hour, even on motorways. If he finds himself going any quicker he slows down.

I miss a few meetings, then Chris and Emma are away on holiday, so I miss another week too. (What *do* gurus do on holiday?) The next meeting I go to is in October. Today, after he's sat in silence for two minutes, Chris begins with an opening sermon – one of the long, pausing monologues that can last up to an hour. Today it is about mastering what he calls the psyche, the worldly part of our thought process that confuses us, and distracts us from the other higher mystical calling. 'What we're trying to do is to get back to another world, or to realise another state within us that we are,' he says.

'The psychic world,' the savant tells us, 'is an incredibly tricky world. The psychic world involves poisoning each other. And games. And war. A lot of mini wars. It involves guilt. It's what religions and priests rely on. All governments rely on it.'

Today, our guru talks to us about one aspect of psychic poisoning: what happens when men look at other women, a typical Chris topic; stirring up an issue that is already full of sexual guilt and confusion. 'When a man looks at another woman, he's looking at the psyche. The psyche of the many choices, infinite possibilities.'

The problem is in the messed up way in which we look. Chris wants to teach us to be able to look at women, to make love to women, without the psyche, without guilt, without complication.

'*I* look at other women, don't I?' He stares at the women in the room, one by one. 'I'm looking at Frances now. I'm always looking at other women. But that is not the problem. It's the implication or the psychic load that's put on to the *mind*, that's put on to looking. I'm loving prior to looking. That is because of the realisation that I have of the masterful consciousness behind the psyche. I've extracted myself from the psychic beliefs and psychic cords that you lot believe in – you lot of the psychic mankind.'

There is absolutely nothing wrong with a man looking at women. As long as that man is Chris. We must not forbid ourselves to look. Rules are for religions. Instead we must learn to look as the Master does.

Chris says, '*I've* extracted myself out of that psyche, to know myself and . . . just love.'

Outside, through the room's two windows, you can see the drizzle falling on the grey slate roofs of Totnes. Everyone in the room looks divinely, subserviently bored, caught in conundrums.

'Purify your consciousness. This is the position of the Master. Remember,' the Master says, 'you don't need to know what consciousness is. I don't know what consciousness is. I don't know where consciousness is going or where it came from. Nor do any of the Masters. They just are. Consciousness. Life.'

The Master beside him takes a sip from her mineral water, leaving pink lipstick on the rim of the glass.

It's all a giant paradox, which we should not engage our psyche in. All we need is love. 'What we are all trying to do is get someone, to know that we are loved. Prior to discussion, I love *you* for what you are. I don't want you to be anything. Before my works, before my thoughts, before my explanations about truth and reality, before my clever tricks, I want you to just say yes to me.'

A pigeon is sheltering under the eaves of the house opposite. It can't get its footing and keeps sliding off, flapping one wing to keep balance.

'I want you to treat me like God. Like I'm the only being in existence. And I don't have to do *anything* to get that respect. I don't have to show you anything. I want you to love and honour me when I am just blob. Zero. And that will be unconditional love.'

Today, as he does every week, Chris turns to Ron and Gina and starts to ask them about their relationship. Chris's sessions provide a sort of alternative soap opera; we get to peek into the distressed private lives of everyone present. Ron answers he has been over-working, becoming obsessive. Chris admonishes him to become more 'robotic' instead. There is no point becoming obsessive about anything, we are all unimportant.

'Nobody,' Chris tells him, 'is required. The machine runs without you. *You are not required.* Robert Maxwell can steal all the pensioners' money and it doesn't make any difference. The pattern of the world still runs. What you really need to do,' he tells earnest, hard-working, friendly, humble Ron, 'is to disengage.'

Then he turns to Gina, the quiet and willowy, dark-haired younger partner. 'And how are you, Gina?' Chris smiles.

Gina tells him she is unhappy again. She feels she is working hard to love Ron, but it is one sided. She complains, 'I have to create the love.'

Ron answers, in his own defence, that he feels she is attacking him. 'I tend to pick up on the anger and get quite hard and just say, "Look, you're attacking me. If you're going to fight, I'm going to fight." And then it's like Gina is nearly always the one that gives up the fight first. She feels the pain and gets upset and I get hard.'

We spiral into yet another strange, free-form counselling session, with the guru entering the relationship in a strange troilism. Chris comforts Gina, 'I am in relationship to Ron in exactly the same way as you. I have to do most of the work too.'

Gina answers, 'I don't know whether I should accept that, just carry on loving, or . . . do something.'

'I would do both,' Chris replies, with characteristic ambiguity. 'Your very being is a problem for him,' he tells Gina, 'your very *non*-being – your very stillness – makes him have a problem. That's very interesting, isn't it? You can't really understand it, it's so profound, so utterly *profound*. The void makes us seem neurotic. But you embody that as woman. You just present him with a problem. One day,' says Chris, 'you will spontaneously want to give him everything. That's natural. That will arise in you.' And their relationship will reach the mystical perfection of the void.

There is a long pause.

Chris looks at Gina, silent. 'Are you all right?'

The pause stretches. Eventually Gina looks up at Chris, the Master, and says in a small voice, 'I just want to say that I love you.'

A long, heavy silence fills the room. Chris smiles back, and I begin to wonder, when she sleeps with Ron, as Chris told her to, who does she think about?

Several women in the group appear to have taken Chris's demand for devotion to heart. They deliver the unconditional love he asks for.

After another long wait, Chris asks, 'Why do you love me?'

Gina's answer is a whisper. I can't make out what she's saying. The other faces in the room remain impassive. A heavy silence descends. The sound of every car that drives up the medieval street outside sounds ridiculously loud. Gina clears her throat and says, 'I feel like I've pushed you away in the past.'

Chris shifts on the sofa and says, 'That's all belief. That's all psychic. There's no such thing as not loving me. You can't push me away because I am not out there. I'm within you. The love that never leaves you. So how can you push me away?'

In *The Final Discovery* there is a poem written about Chris by one of the women: 'You made me feel my pain, No sunshine only rain. You said There is no hope, And you're just a great big dope, I don't know how I can cope. So thanks for all the sorrow, And ending my tomorrow, As I look into the horror.'

One day one of the followers, Iain, arrives quarter of an hour after Chris and Emma have taken their place on the sofa. 'Why are you late?' demands Chris sternly.

'I'm sorry,' says the man, handsome, thin haired, older than Chris.

'I asked you a question, *why are you late?*'

The man repeats his apology.

'No. I asked you *why?*' Chris raises his voice.

Chris glares at him, until Iain explains that he was delayed leaving home. The flow of Chris's opening talk has been interrupted. He is furious.

A few weeks later at one of the regular meetings Chris rounds on Iain again. Iain runs a printing company. When it comes to Iain's turn to talk to Chris, Chris starts discussing some unspecified business they have together. Iain announces that it might be a good idea to talk about it on Tuesday, or another day.

Chris interrupts him, suddenly furious. 'That's your arrogance. That's your silly little arrogance speaking there. How the hell can you talk like that? You don't even know that you're going to be there, so how the hell can you talk like that? You don't know what's going to happen on Tuesday and *you're* giving *me* your *guaranteed* word that you're going to be there on Tuesday. You could have a heart attack in the next five minutes! You could go insane in the next five minutes. You don't know what's going to happen in the future. So to suggest you do, and to be so confident about it, means that you're a very *dangerous* person to be around.'

Other disciples still maintain their invincibly distant expressions as the exchange becomes a public dressing-down from the guru. 'I'll trust *you* when you know you're a dangerous person to be around,' Chris froths at him. 'You need to look into that. It's like saying to a woman, "You know I love you. I don't need to show it." You need to create love.'

Some days Iain plays tennis with Chris. But the guru doesn't even find favour with his tennis, today. 'One example of your untrustworthiness is you don't turn up for tennis on time! You're always *late*. You're busy *organising*, to get things together, to get everything together. You're spending a lot of time in all sorts of states of fragmented mind. You don't see anything as more valuable than anything else. So you're just a mind. So you're late for everything. Are you hearing what I'm saying?'

'Mmm,' answers the disciple truculently.

'You're *late*,' continues Chris relentlessly, 'because I'm not any more important than any other factor in your life. You're going to learn that I'm *not* just another factor in your life. Can you see that?'

Tight-lipped, Iain answers, 'Mmm.'

Chris's teachings follow the discontinuous logic of dreams. The only fixed point is Chris himself. The territory he inhabits is built from a hotch potch of oriental doctrines learned from his gurus, about the need to destroy the 'psychic' process by which we identify ourselves with our illusory emotions and the material world that produces them. To free ourself from this process will be to free ourself from the unhappiness of the world. But the rest comes from somewhere deep and dark inside him. It is a world where we have to love, but where love always creates pain. He has bound the one to the other: relationships always break down and fail, just as the body breaks down and dies. We must resign ourselves to the great inevitability. Sometimes, listening to Chris's despondent creed it's hard to imagine why these disciples return week after week.

Every Sunday we break for lunch. Our £10 also entitles us to a salad of greens, nuts and carrots, and slices of wholefood bread. The gurus withdraw to another room and the disciples chomp the meal, supplemented by crinkle-cut crisps from the news-agent across the street, and swap chat about who's doing what. 'Your partner still not coming?' I'm asked every week. Two handsome fair-haired brothers turn up regularly each week with their partners. Like Ron they are ex-Sannyasins of Osho. Today they're talking about their mother who has recently become severely ill. She's in a lot of pain, they say. Someone asks, 'Has she had a diagnosis yet?'

'It's a tumour,' one replies. 'Is that cancer?'

The doctor has apparently told her to smoke and drink all she wants to, which sounds ominous. He says that he'll give the full prognosis next week.

While we eat, the brothers start discussing which pieces of furniture they will keep when she dies. One claims an old corner-cupboard. 'Who wants the car? I don't. Well, we should sell that then.' Others in the room, sitting cross-legged on the floor over

16

their salad bowls, laugh uneasily at the brothers' apparent callousness, unsure if it's shock or just a pure expression of the spiritual detachment of the kind advocated by Chris.

'Which one of you is going to have her dog?' someone asks.

One brother replies, 'I think I'll have it for about a week, give it a good time, and then I'll have it put down.'

This produces more incredulous laughter.

'I want the pleasure of the dog,' he says by way of self-justification.

'I can't *believe* it,' one of us howls in horror. Someone else tries to warn them. 'It will affect you more than you think it will.'

The mood changes. The brothers start to address our shock seriously. One tells us, 'She's in pain, but I'm sure her pain is going. You see, all her life she has felt, "I can't believe my kids are not what I want them to be." I think she's glad to die. None of us have had family backgrounds. We got involved with the Bhagwan. I think she's glad she's dying. She can get out of it. Forget the lot.'

The gurus came to Totnes. Now they're leaving.

The last meeting I go to is going to be one of the last they hold in the small Devon town. Chris and Emma have recently moved to Bristol, and now travel down for the day at 56mph in their Ford Fiesta.

A lot has changed since I last attended. The session now costs me £40 instead of £10, though they're held less often. The set up is smarter, more like a professional therapy session than just a guru surrounded by cross-legged followers. Instead of cushions on the floor, there are now chairs. People are now allowed to wear shoes in the room. The Chrisemma Foundation has changed its name to the Chris Orchard Foundation, and is offering public courses in 'Self-realisation', and 'The teachings of Chris Orchard'. Emma, the silent guru, still sits on the sofa, but her role as the divine partner seems to have withered.

It's not just the gurus who are leaving. The followers are moving too. After almost four years in Totnes, they've reached a point where they have to move on. Totnes is too small.

Ron and Gina, and the two brothers are moving too. I turn to a woman sitting next to me; it turns out she's going to Bristol as well. She came to Totnes to get away from the world but is now looking forward to moving to the city. 'It is time to re-enter the world,' she says.

How many of you are moving to Bristol with Chris and Emma, I ask. Everybody?

She looks round the room. There are about twenty people there. 'Mmm. Not all at once. But yes. We all decided to move.'

The entire group is uprooting its life and moving. As we wait for the gurus to arrive after lunch, the two brothers are reading each other letters they sent to their mother from boarding school, gasping and giggling over the stupid things they wrote. Has she died now? I'm not sure.

Chris returns with silent Emma and sets off over now familiar ground, delivering the strangely bleak creed of relationship that has paradoxically held them together for three years: 'Relationship never works. It always breaks down. Your relationship fails. Your body fails. You can't get away from the death. The death of relationship. But you can make it conscious. Which is what I've done . . .'

TWO

Leo and the Maze

1

The Festival Of Mind, Body And Spirit is a huge annual bring and buy sale of new age faiths and therapies held in London's Royal Horticultural Halls. On stage, a singer and a flute player perform. 'This is about humpbacked whales,' the flute player says, by way of introduction. The next song is about 'the female Buddha energy'.

The large glass-roofed hall is full of stands advertising a thousand therapies, new solutions to ancient problems and allegedly ancient solutions to new ones. At the back of the hall stand number 47 is advertised as 'The Eminent Theatre Journey'. Unlike other stalls piled high with candles and crystals, it's difficult to discern exactly what they are trying to market here. The only things that appear to be on sale are a book and a tape of music. The book is called *A Second Chance at Life*. Leaflets, fanned out in a neat pile, offer a course called 'The Search for Truth'. I pick one up and struggle with its dense language: 'We believe that there are high purposes for all human life, and our journey and dedication is to discover and join these purposes as best we are able,' it reads. 'Our response and arising is in part due to the state of today's world, for within this we see that the human race is now demonstrating symptoms of an ending epoch closing in upon it, whilst in turn the onset of a new epoch for human and planetary life heralds the call for new and in-simile response.'

'Response and arising'? 'Ending epoch'? 'In-simile response'?

I ask one of the people on the stall, a pointy-faced young man with short black hair, what Eminent Theatre Journey means.

Pleased by my interest, he answers earnestly: 'Well, yes. That's a good question. It's hard to answer simply. You have to do it to understand it. We are on a journey of discovery of higher worlds,' he says. 'And we use theatre as a means of discovery . . . and eminent . . . is because we're on an eminent journey to higher things. Do you see?'

An older man is displaying a pack of strange-looking tarot cards to a middle-aged couple. They have pictures of monks, wizard figures, naked women, lions, palaces and occult symbols on them; they look like abandoned pieces of artwork for a 70s progressive rock album.

'I'm not saying there's not something in other tarot cards, but they're usually just used for entertainment. In the Eminent Theatre Journey, we have our own tarot pack, much, much more subtle than others, based on more ancient laws that have been forgotten about.' He writes the word 'Taro' on a blackboard.

But he loses the struggle with the couple. The woman tugs the man's sleeve and they wander off to peer at another stall peddling aromatherapy cures. The man with the tarot pack turns to me and says, 'Are you interested in the unseen worlds?' His name is Matthew. He gives me a printed invitation to an open night at the Eminent Theatre Journey Centre.

He promises, 'You'll get a lot out of it.'

The Eminent Theatre Journey Centre turns out to be a gloomy old Welsh Chapel school set back off Willesden Lane, made gloomier by the evening's steady drizzle: big old letters fastened to the red brick Victorian gable end read CAPEL CYMRAEG. I am just about to lock my bicycle to a drainpipe when a man holding an umbrella looms up to me in the car park, asks me if I've come for the meeting, and says, 'No, leave your bike here.' He points under a large tree. 'It'll be drier.'

'But,' I say, 'there's nowhere to lock it.'

'Don't worry. Nobody will steal it. There are good energies here.'

I'm sure he's trying to be helpful, but I'm reluctant to leave an expensive bike in the care of good energies.

He insists, smiling. 'I'm here all night, keeping an eye out. I'll look after it.' I leave him under his umbrella in the rain, puzzling as to exactly why he'll be standing there all night.

Inside, a young squat man called Dave crushes my hand warmly and asks eagerly, 'Have you ever felt an aura?' An athletic type with long hair greets me too. 'I'm Jeff,' he grins. 'I've only been coming here a couple of months, but the changes I have felt have been *incredible*.' He has a bright over-keen intensity. Seven of us have come to the open night. In a small kitchen, the members of the Eminent Theatre Journey offer us tea and biscuits and smile brightly at us before tonight's introductory session begins. 'Hi! What's your name?' Their enthusiasm is prodigious.

A piece of pseudo-psychological new-speak dreamed up in the 70s by those who set out to prove that cults are uniformly evil floats into my head: 'love bombing'. It's a great anti-cult phrase: all their ardour for you to join in is no more than a disguised lethal weapon. These people's shiny glow may be so strong that it almost seems a parody of what I expect of cults, but it is also far too guileless to be a cynical exercise. Maybe I'd find it easier to understand if these people *did* just cynically want me for my money or my unquestioning devotion. But it's far stranger than that. As far as I can make out, they desperately, genuinely, burningly want me to join their club.

After tea we move to the Chapel hall where the introductory talk is to take place. The hall has been prepared for our arrival. The exact number of chairs are already laid out in a semicircle for us and our four or five ever-smiling welcomers. Facing us behind the stage is a strange giant painting: a woman with huge angel wings. Her left breast is exposed. And then a young man called Paul in a khaki shirt sweeps in and starts to talk.

We may not know it but each of us, he says, has an aura. The ancients knew about them, but we, somehow, have forgotten. Paintings of angels' wings, he points behind him, are ancient people's attempts to picture the auras radiating around us. Our auras are all different colours. You might have a red aura if you were being aggressive. Or a blue aura if you were feeling peaceful.

'Here in the Eminent Theatre Journey,' he says, 'we like to be practical. So we're going to try a little experiment.' Paul produces a blindfold, ties it round the eyes of one of my fellow newcomers and manoeuvres him on to a circle of red paper on the floor. He doesn't know what colour his feet are on, but the colour, we are told, will affect him, and each shade will produce different changes in our auras. 'Tell us exactly how you feel.'

The man stands on the disc, soaking in the vibrations of the red. His hands flex. He sways, uncomfortably: 'I feel anxious. Trembly. I feel tight in my chest. I can't breathe. Can I get off?'

Yanking off the blindfold, he sees that the disc he has been standing on is red. 'Isn't that amazing?' says Paul.

The man nods, amazed.

'Red is a very powerful colour,' Paul says. 'You have to be very careful when you use it.'

A woman tries the blindfold test next. Again, she begins to sway. She shivers. 'I don't like it. There's a tightness, in my chest.' She jumps off the circle, unable to bear it any longer. This time though, the disc turns out to have been blue.

'Well,' says the teacher, 'different colours have different effects on different people.'

Next we are to feel auras ourselves. Paul tells us that with practice we can develop great sensitivities. 'You can tell a lot from someone's aura,' he says. He goes up to one listener and holds out his hand, palm flat, in front of him, sensing the ether. 'I can tell from your aura, you're like this.' He makes little stabbing motions in the air. 'You make little jabs at the world and then withdraw.' He turns to me. 'And you,' he samples my auric emissions, 'are like this.' He holds his hand in front of his face and peers out behind it. 'You are hiding behind things. You don't like to give everything away.' I experience an unexpected wave of paranoia: maybe he really *can* read my aura, and from it he can tell that I'm a counterfeit. No. Absurd.

In pairs we try feeling auras ourselves. It's a bit like postman's knock, but without the postman. Or invisible man's buff. Jo, a cheery redhead in her early thirties, walks towards me tentatively, holding out her palm to sense the edge of my aura. 'It's like a balloon,' says the teacher. 'You'll feel it give just a little resistance.' Jo stops about three feet away. 'It's here, I think.' She prods the empty air.

Teacher shakes his head: 'No, it's closer.' And, with authority, holds his hand about two inches closer to me. 'Here it is, see?'

When it's my turn, I make a wild guess and stop about the same distance away from Jo. 'Yes,' teacher nods. 'That's right.' I smile proudly at my classmates.

Jo is impressed and excited. Tonight is a revelation to her. She has always known that there is another world out there, and sensed that she could see things that were invisible to others. Now, for the first time in her life, here are a group of people who seem to be confirming something she's had to keep to herself for years. The only reason she came along tonight was because her friend Jeff, who had joined a couple of months before, had changed his character so dramatically. He used to spend his days lying around the house, smoking dope. Now he seems full of enthusiasm and energy. It is so unlike him. She was suspicious of his sudden change of behaviour and wanted to check out that he wasn't getting involved in something bad. Now she thinks she's found something herself.

Later, on the way out to collect my well-protected bicycle, Jeff, Jo's friend, the athletic, enthusiastic convert shakes my hand firmly again. He wants me to believe in it too. 'You have to come back,' he says. 'This is just scratching the surface.'

Jeff is right. This is just scratching the surface. There is a great deal which has not been told to us on our first introductory evening. The first four letters of the curious title Eminent Theatre Journey actually spell out a hidden word 'Emin'. A guru called Leo, who dreamed up this enterprise, says 'Emin' is an ancient word meaning 'faithful one'. The Emin is also the name of the cult he established in North London in the early 1970s. Anti-cult groups, who tirelessly monitor cult activity, can supply you with files of incriminating material on most sects, but they draw a vague blank on the Emin. They admit they know little about it. It's described in anti-cult literature as 'highly secretive and exclusive'.

Despite its obscurity, the Emin is one of Britain's most successful home-grown new age cults; though numbers in the UK have always remained only in the hundreds, they have spread surreptitiously throughout the world and have claimed a steady global membership of around 2,500 for the last ten years.

These followers of the Eminent Way inhabit a strange and invisible universe, different from the one the rest of us live in. At the centre of their beliefs is the notion that they have established contact with a vast, powerful 'unseen world' that the ancient civilisations knew about, but which we have lost touch with because of our blind reliance on science, rationality and industrialisation.

They're not too sure what all of it looks like but they know it's there. The unseen world has two aspects. First, there are our own unseen auras, which can be detected through sensing the minute electrical forces that surround us, and which can be influenced to heal us. Second, there are spooky, unseen 'higher' beings who float around us, nameless but all-powerful, which can be contacted by the initiates. Leo has evolved a strange, highly elaborate, system of rituals, disciplines, hierarchies, movements, dances, costumes and thought processes which are intended to allow our unseen energies to come into harmony with this great ineffable cosmos. His ideas aren't greatly different from many other new age faiths. Two hundred years ago Franz Anton Mesmer gained a following amongst the fashionable classes of Paris for his belief that a magnetic force surrounding our body could be manipulated to cure illnesses. He would put patients into a trance – 'mesmerise' them – and announce that in this state they could contact the spirit world and see into the future while hypnotised. But Leo has created a bubbling stew from this tradition of new age ideas, and built a new faith around it.

For new members though, this is too subtle a knowledge to be delivered all at once.

2

I have signed up for a course of ten lessons with the Eminent Theatre Journey, 'The Search for Truth', at a cost of £45. Lessons are twice a week starting at 7.45, finishing in theory around 11pm, but in practice they often go on towards midnight.

The hall is painted pale greeny blue: an auric colour that is supposed to encourage energy and enquiry. The pictures that hang around the walls change each day: sometimes there might be a picture of the Taj Mahal, other times a photo of the pyramids, edifices built by others who shared the knowledge. There are small vases of flowers placed on neat table cloths. A small collection of marbles, or a spiral seashell might be placed on a window ledge. Candles are lit. A tape machine plays new age music until the meeting starts: sometimes it's one of the Emin's own tunes, a pastelly wash of sound especially composed to create the right atmosphere, to summon the right forces from the unseen world; often we are treated to the circular electronic tinklings of 'Tubular Bells II'.

The courses are nearly always taken by a couple: a man and a woman: they sit at either end of a table, and call themselves 'Ushers'. In lesson one, the short squat man, who introduces himself as Simon, does all the talking. The thin, severe-looking woman stays silent, observing him and his students, occasionally making a few notes.

'Have you ever thought about the brain?' ponders Simon, holding up a small home-made grey papier mâché brain for our attention. 'The brain is a marvellous instrument. It can do anything for you. It can count up to a million if you want it to,' he says, pacing around our semicircle of chairs, puffing on a Silk Cut. There are fourteen students starting the course, but several have actually been in the Emin for some time and are here to gee us newcomers along. 'And yet scientists say we're only using ten per cent of it. I don't know about you, but I find that incredible, don't you?'

As we sit there we start to notice odd things. For a start, Simon smokes a remarkable quantity of cigarettes. There are ashtrays placed around the room, by our chairs. And several of the other Emin members smoke too, with an impressive and conspicuously un-new age dedication. And about every half-hour as Simon talks, women silently push open the door to the hall, and appear respectfully bearing trays with steaming cups of tea for him and the silent woman.

'You've heard of the sixth sense? Well there are many, many, many more senses than six,' says Simon.

We start to learn about the different levels of our aura. It turns out there are three different types of aura: on the outside is the 'nerve' aura; then closer is the 'blood' aura, and tight around your body is the 'bone' aura. Every evening we carry out 'practical' exercises, to prove the reality of what we are taught. To contact the outer aura, we are told to extend our arms, and wiggle our hands in the ether, while chanting: 'Nerve, nerve, nerve.' That way, we are instructed, we may put our mind in touch with our outer aura.

Everybody takes up these activities eagerly, however unusual. There is a hunger to believe. I look around: Fourteen perfectly normal-looking people, chanting, 'Nerve, nerve, nerve,' diligently flapping their arms like birds.

Jeremy, holding out his arms with the rest of us to contact his nerve aura, is a talented and successful young record producer. He's worked with mainstream and alternative groups on albums that have sold in respectably large quantities. But after only four years he's lost some of the enthusiasm he had for his career. After the huge international success of one of his groups' debut albums, he found it hard to drum up as much enthusiasm when it came to working on their second. At first he enjoyed life as a relatively high-profile record producer: but after a few years in the business, the shine has worn off.

This is one of the mysteries of the new age, and the huge, and often vastly different welter of cults that have sprung from it. Cults of the past could be sociologically explained as the refuge of the obviously poor and the oppressed. These days it is apparently successful people like Jeremy who join, suffering another, obscurer discontent.

Like Jo, he has his reasons for coming here. In winter 1992 he took a skiing break in Switzerland. New Year's night, high in the Alps, turned out to be a turning point in his life. In the first hours of 1993 one of the chalet girls, drunk out of her skull, got on a toboggan, slid down the mountainside and over a drop. A rock dislodged in her fall crushed her to death. Jeremy and his friends called the emergency services and waited for them to arrive, the dead girl still pinned under a rock. They didn't show until four in the morning. In the long night wait, he became convinced that a dream he'd had just a few nights before had been a cryptic prediction of the death he had just witnessed. He had always believed in the supernatural, but those few hours before the emergency services arrived to lift the rock from the dead girl crystallised a belief that predestination did exist.

Like me, he found the idiosyncratic stall at the Festival Of Mind, Body And Spirit, and became curious. He realised later he must have been searching for something to help him make sense of the feeling that all of our lives followed higher destinies, the feeling that had affected him so strongly the night the chalet girl died.

The course progresses. A few weeks in we have not yet been told of the existence of the Emin, but things are definitely starting to get, well . . . stranger. We have been tacitly encouraged not to talk about what we do at work. That is a separate world. It must be kept at arm's length. 'I've known some people in this organisation for years,' says Simon. 'And you know, it's *strange*, but I've never even wondered what they do at work. Incredible, isn't it?'

Work pollutes. We are being prised away from our attachment to the mundane. But even if he's not so bound up in his job as he used to be, Jeremy is still proud of his work. He complains to me during a tea break: 'I don't know why we're always being told not to talk about our work. Our work is important.'

At a tea break one of us beginners, Mandy, a loud Yorkshire hippie in brightly mismatched clothes, discovers that Jeremy is a record producer. 'What have you done then?' she challenges him.

He has a fashionably clipped goatee beard and long hair. He mentions the name of an album that became one of the major successes of the Summer of Love dance scene the year before.

'Oh my *God*, did you? That's one of my favourite albums of last year.'

A few Emin look round at her, spooked by her loudness.

*

One of the other strange things that you notice after a while is that there is always someone standing outside, on guard, like the man who kept his eye on my bicycle, to discourage unwelcome intruders while we are performing our strange ceremonies inside the hall. Some carry rape alarms. What, I wonder, are they guarding us from? Maybe somebody once tried to 'kidnap' a child who had got caught up in the Emin. Or an eager vicar burst in, proclaiming them to be Satanists.

By week four we have been told of the existence of the natural laws of the planet. They are a mystical system of numbers and colours, a curious net of significances laid over everything, which appears to explain the universe. The Law of Two, for instance, is the law of opposites – night and day, soft and hard, pitching and yawing, red and blue, action and response. The Law of Three is the law of relationships – mother, father, child; mind, body and spirit. And so on. It's a semiological playground. For the Emin it becomes a hierarchy by which they can classify all phenomena. If anything can be made to fit the laws, it is further proof that the laws exist.

On a Wednesday night I get an ominous phone call from a woman who tells me I must wear 'loose clothing and soft shoes' for tomorrow night's lesson because 'We are doing Electrobics.'

When I get to the hall, I ask a young, eager Emin who tells me his name is Lance, to tell me exactly what this electrobics is. It is a direct question; a mistake. The mystery is too fragile for that blundering approach. Lance avoids my query: 'When you ask that, we're in the Law of Two.'

'What?'

'The Law of Two. You're pitching, and I'll yaw.'

'So if I ask, I'm pitching?'

'Yes,' he smiles annoyingly, 'and I'll yaw.' I smile thinly at him.

We learn that tiny feelings we have noticed all our lives, and dismissed as ordinary, are in fact magical. To 'sensitise' our hands, so they are capable of detecting the unseen, we perform a limbering up exercise. Arms extended, we rapidly flex our fingers as if playing invisible pianos for a minute or more until our arms wilt with fatigue. 'Now give them a little shake,' says Simon, 'and let them hang down by your side . . . Can you feel them prickling? Can you feel the energy in them?' To me this pins and needles feeling is no more than physiology, perhaps the sensation of blood rushing back to the hands. But to the Emin, this is magic. It's something I encounter again and again in the cults I join; the creation of a robust magical world from such apparently ordinary and insignificant events. Magic is conjured out of the blue.

Electrobics turns out to be a strange, T'ai Chi-like series of motions, which the Emin use to clean the system of 'bad' electrical forces that are clogging up our delicate machine. With your hands, you gather the bad electricity from around the different parts of your body, and then fling it outwards, into space. People in the group are now regularly claiming to be able to see these strange unseen forces around us as colours floating round our bodies. It is nothing to have someone say: 'I can see a lot of yellow around you today.' 'Really?'

Bad electricity gathers at our elbows and our knees. Following a strict series of motions we all silently and solemnly gather the invisible forces in our hands as instructed and flick them out into the ether with our fingertips, as if we're shaking dirt from our hands. 'When you flick,' Simon tells us, 'be careful not to look at your fingers. Otherwise the electricity is just going to come straight back round and stick on you again. I've seen it happen.'

Tonight I am using electrobics to clean my ears of bad electrical impulses, twisting my arms around my head as if removing an invisible pair of headphones, as I've been told to, when Simon approaches. 'It's amazing. I can see lines just shooting out of your head. Can anyone else see them?'

A few others pause from busily cleaning their ears and say they can see them too.

At the end of the night, Simon sits us down and tells us that we are a special group. We smile, proudly. Of course we're a special group. 'Even before you arrive here, I can feel the atmosphere in the room changing. You see, when you come here, you bring your own unseen helpers. You may not feel them yet, but I know they are there.'

Then, for the first time, he tells us about Leo. He paints a picture of the great mystic with powers that none of us come close to who shares this secret knowledge with us. He has written thousands upon thousands of words of wisdom, which form the basis of their group, which, we are finally told, is called the Emin.

The genesis of the Emin came, we're informed, when Leo was working in London for a security firm. He used to sit in the back of an armoured car, and it was there that he wrote his first book, *Dear Dragon*, a mystical volume of dense musings and *bons mots*. 'Just imagine that. Isn't that *incredible*?'

Simon asks us what we've made of it all so far. Mandy announces, 'It's wonderful. I have been to a few things before, but this . . . it just feels like coming home.'

'Yes,' agrees Simon, pleased. 'A lot of people feel that.'

3

Among the pictures that are displayed on the walls every meeting, one of Leo now makes its appearance. He is an elderly man, impressively tall, with a perfectly bald, domelike pate and a small, pointed beard. Seated behind a desk, he smiles enigmatically at the camera. His eyes positively twinkle. Underneath the photograph he has written in smooth, flowing pen: 'Yes! I hear what you are saying. But –' signing his name with a flourish and the astrological sign for Leo. It is a typically, almost comically enigmatic touch. But what?

These days Leo lives distantly and aloofly in Florida; members are encouraged to buy fragments of his meditations from the Emin archive, but few have direct contact with him. He is spoken of as if a demi-god.

Details of his early life are sketchy. He was born around 1925 as Raymond John Schertenlieb, the son of a hotel waiter, though he gives his real name as Raymond Armin. He grew up in working-class North London.

There are clues to his character and his early obsessions. In 1993, the Emin added a book called *The Nightwatchman* to their huge library, which may provide a couple of clues to the man. The book is published anonymously by the Emin-run publishing house, but followers say it's a compilation of cryptic stories Leo used to tell about his life before he formed the Emin. It begins: 'Imagine the feelings of desolation and bleakness in the dark streets of a run-down city. Can you imagine how, within this poverty, I as a small boy sought to make my way? Then you can begin to picture the cold, long nights, when I was touched by the harshness of that desolation.'

Fragments of his youth emerge from between the lines – placing him in a more ordered, pre-war Britain, where he used to spend a lot of time in street markets, soaking in the sales banter of the traders. After the war he used to drive past the Cenotaph in a double-decker bus, and all the men on board would take their hats off as they passed. He mourns the loss of that civility. Much of his teachings are an attempt to restore this vanished *politesse* to the world.

In a chapter called 'The Sacred Dance', he describes how as a nine year old, he was overwhelmed by a sense of failure. Other children at school were praised and rewarded by their parents, Leo was called stupid. He relates how his parents beat him, and tried to force him to study. Instead, he would go roller-skating down Eversholt Road, round the back of Euston Station. Roller-skating became an obsession. For four years he skated three or four hours a day, setting off when the lights turned green, and skating furiously down the road to see how far he could get before the lights turned through red, amber and back to green again. 'I did this,' says Leo, 'not because of a fascination with skating or traffic lights. It was because, unable to find an identity in the culture where I always failed, I had to create an identity for myself. This is where it began!' he writes, 'My first Sacred Dance with life.'

After the war Leo was sent to India as part of his national service in the RAF, and developed a fascination with oriental cosmology. Even then he appears to have lived as an outsider. He claims he was able to arrange his duties so that he could take regular three-week breaks. Rather than socialise with his colleagues, he says he would put a knife in one boot, a revolver in the other and wander off 'into the Bush'. The descriptions of holy men he met there may be accurate or fictionalised, but it is clear that his tales of life in India clearly impressed the early hippie disciples he was later to make.

Returning to England he worked for a while as a house painter and then a salesman. Like Werner Erhard, the Californian founder of the yuppie life-reprogramming organisation *est* – Erhard Seminars Training – Leo became an area manager for Encyclopaedia Britannica. Some, cynical of the motives of gurus like Leo and Erhard, speculate that they adapted the 'psychological' hard-sell techniques that were becoming fashionable at the time to lure followers. In the mid-60s, teams were sent out to drive home to prospective buyers their desperate need for this new 'home educational programme'. Salesmen were told in training literature to 'Go out and get 'em. There are thousands of orders lying out there. They are ripe and ready and rosy – and they are going to be collected by someone. Are you going to be one of them?'

But it appears that Leo wasn't particularly successful at going out and getting 'em. He couldn't get his own sales business off the ground. In 1965 he was declared bankrupt in Nottingham. Then in the early 70s, the change came. The story that the Emin tell about how Leo founded the organisation relates that Leo's son, John, was working as an ambulance driver when he picked up a woman who had collapsed. When he saw she was carrying a book of Sufi tales, he said, 'You should meet my father, he reads books like that.' The two met, and Leo started to assume his role as a guru among her hippie friends. 1972 was the official year of the foundation of the Emin – the start of Leo's immense outpouring of mystical texts, and the genesis of a leadership structure that now has its headquarters in Florida, where Leo lives with his wife Violet, known by the Emin name of Ruth, and his 'secretary' or helper Deborah McKay, known as the Lady Ethra. Since the early days, the three have formed a group known as the Trio; a strange holy trinity who have remained the leaders throughout the years.

Leo was a heavy smoker: he smoked roll ups. It explains the ashtrays I noticed that first night. Even though he now lives several thousand miles away, the spell of the guru is strong. Many smoke. As a man in touch with higher worlds, smoking was no longer harmful for him. He informed his followers, 'I'm just *processing* the smoke.'

Leo's knowledge gave him hidden powers. He believed he had learned how to heal people. He announced he could cure leukaemia and bone-marrow cancers. One ex-Emin member, who remembers him as a pleasant, if roguish figure, 'a rough diamond', also recalls walking home each evening after meetings with a young girl from Kentish Town who had been diagnosed with cancer. Leo said he had cured it. 'He used to tell her that the cancer was shrinking. I didn't believe it, but she did. She died of it in the end. Maybe it helped her to believe him,' she says, sadly.

In earlier days, rumours circulated among his more zealous followers that Leo also had darker occult powers. When a *Private Eye* journalist wrote a series of exposés about the cult accusing Leo of being a huckster, he received a letter from one such believer: 'Seven of our society's enemies, to my knowledge, have died so far of medically diagnosed cerebral haemorrhage, cancer and heart failure.'

One curious glimpse of the early cult was given in the *London Evening Standard* for Friday 11 February 1977, headlined, 'On The Trail Of Leo's Astral Trip'.

'The sect has about 500 members, most of them in their teens and twenties – its turnover has grown from a few hundred pounds to £15,000 in the past year. At the centre of the Emin is Raymond John Armin, known to his followers as Leo. A charismatic six-foot Cockney with a shaven head and goatee beard, he left his job with Security Express three years ago to work full time for the Emin. He now earns £12,000 a year and lives with his wife and American secretary in a flat in a remote house at Newbury, Berkshire.

'Leo claims to have healing abilities based on the use of an "electrical force" within our bodies. And he claims that it is possible for the mind to leave the body and astral travel. Both he and his son say they have done it.

'If there is a core to Emin thinking it was expressed in a statement from Leo. For eight years, he claimed, he spent his Saturday mornings underneath an oak tree on Hampstead Heath until he finally fathomed the first of the laws of life. "There had to be definite laws that govern everything, absolutely everything. And I thought to myself, if you can find those laws, seeing as everything comes from them, they must explain everything. And I found them, I found them."'

The piece portrays him as a genial nutcase. A smiling photo of Leo accompanies the piece, captioned, 'Leo . . . Saturday mornings under an oak tree on Hampstead Heath.'

4

A message appears on my ansaphone telling me to meet on Sunday, 27 June at 8am at Heston Services, and telling me to bring walking shoes. Being in the Emin fills your life and squeezes everything else out. You get phone calls, cryptic messages delivered down the telephone tree to which your name has been added, that give you a time and a place, and a hint of the activity you're being summoned to. No one says you have to go, but people turn up. The Emin is an adventure playground for people in their twenties and thirties.

I get to Heston early. The first person to arrive that I recognise is a thin twenty-two year old called Oliver who lives with his mother in Hillingdon. He was at the first meeting I went to, and has diligently appeared at every session since. We buy tea at the counter and wait, unsure what we've let ourselves in for. Oliver is excited by our mysterious summons.

As I eat my scrambled eggs, Oliver chatters. He tells me he's starting a drama course at university in the autumn. It was the word 'theatre' that attracted the thespian in him to the Emin stall at the Festival Of Mind, Body And Spirit. Before college starts he's working to earn spending money selling adverts in a trade paper.

It's called 'blind calling' he tells me. 'Good morning. Have you ever considered how use of display advertising can affect your business?' He has to ring up different regions each week. He regards it as training for his career as an actor. Last week, when he was ringing up Wales, he concentrated on pronouncing all the names correctly. One Welshman told him he wished he could pronounce English as well as Oliver did his Welsh, he tells me proudly. Recently though, Oliver's been ringing round offices in the City. Unlike Wales, no one there gives him the time of day. He only gets as far as, 'Hello. I'm from . . .' before they slam down the phone on him. It's hard work.

Every Friday the managers encourage the staff to turn up in fancy dress to relieve the boredom. Oliver, ever the joiner, says he's been turning up in some really *outrageous* stuff in the last few weeks. He turns up to work dressed as a clown, or as a vampire. It's like acting. He's a sweet-natured boy; when he smiles, his mouth forms an almost perfect U-shape.

While we talk a few others arrive at the motorway service station: Simon and the stern-faced woman who sits next to him at meetings. Her name, it turns out, is 'Mero'. The penny is starting to drop amongst us newcomers that Emin members all adopt strange names. The squat person who introduced himself as Dave at the first meeting is now calling himself Sky. The happy, athletic person who greeted me on my first night at the Emin Centre called himself Jeff back then. Now he is calling himself, peculiarly, Stone Bear.

Oliver, eager, enthusiastic and friendly, continues to chatter. He confides: his sister and his mother are getting concerned about these evening classes he's been going to twice a week. He comes home and he tells them how exciting all the new things he's learning are. 'They hear about the tarot and things like that and because they've only heard about it as something bad, they're worried. They're worried I've ended up in a *cult*,' he smiles.

The day, it turns out, is a magical mystery tour. Only a few know where we're going. We climb on a coach, three-quarters full of Emin from around the south of England. There's a pretty, slightly bossy woman called Opal I've seen before who smiles incessantly. Her parents were in the Emin back in the early days. She goes out with Lance, the super-keen boy who yawed while I pitched. They are an Emin dream couple.

Matthew, the man I met at the Festival Of Mind, Body And Spirit, stands up and does a class in numerology as we travel west on the M4. He grins at us, like the school teacher who wants to be mates with his pupils, jokey and laddish, all at once and tells us about our 'route' numbers. By progressively adding the numbers of our birth date we reach a number between one and nine. 'Route' number is a typical Leo play on words – it's both our root number, and the route our lives will take. He is a man obsessed with multiple meanings.

Opal helps me work out my number. It turns out to be one: which means I am an initiator, a direct person, like the figure one, a straight line. I like the sound of that. The day's 'route' number is one too. People nod sagely. Significance hangs in the air. Someone tells us that one way of finding out about what our number signifies is to draw the figure in the air, in our auras, to see how it makes us feel. I start to draw the figure one in front of me until Matthew stands up at the front of the coach and contradicts the last speaker. 'You can't feel something as *sensitive* as electrical detection on a motorway going at seventy miles an hour,' he tells us. Of course you can't, people laugh. How silly we are. This hidden looking-glass world starts to wrap around everybody.

I am wondering what on earth the portly, grizzled coach driver with mutton-chop sideboards makes of all this. One day football fans, the next tarot readers. He maintains a bored professional inscrutability.

At Barbury Castle, a 2,000-year-old hill fort high on the Marlborough Downs, we disembark and perform another weird ritual – not unlike the electrobics I have already learned. It is to sharpen our 'colour' senses. Each part of our body is associated with a different colour. The exercise is designed to focus our mind on this association. It's still Sunday morning. I could be in bed reading the papers. Instead, I'm standing on my right leg, with my head bowed and my hands folded behind my back chanting, 'Blue, blue, blue,' with forty-one other people. Occasionally one of us topples over into thistles. Day trippers peer, understandably puzzled. Starlings flock over a copse of beech trees.

We are here to use our Emin powers to 'detect' the forces that still inhabit the ancient castle. Everything is a clue from the unseen world, everything, as Leo has taught us, has multiple meanings.

'Barbury Castle,' says Matthew, peering at us through his gold-rimmed glasses. 'Think of the word. Bury. Maybe something is buried here? A bar? A bar of what?' With Mark, one of the 'watchers' who often stands guard at our meetings, and a hippie girl called Mandy, I wander round the old circular ramparts and ditches that are all that remain of the hilltop site, 'detecting' the energies. Mark stops on top of a rise. 'Do you feel silver, very . . . fast?' Yes yes, we answer. Mark nods, sagely. The grass, he says, is silvery. A minute later: 'Poppies,' he says. 'That might mean that there has been bloodshed.' Of course.

Mandy is dressed in a pair of baggy shorts. On the inside of her right calf she has a tattoo – a red star outlined in blue. She is smiling happily. The sun shines warmly. This is great. It's just like coming home.

It's hot. We start to sweat. Flies buzz around us. 'What do flies mean?' asks Mandy. 'Are they silver, too?'

'I don't know,' says Mark, thrown by the question. 'Possibly.'

In the afternoon, we men are segregated from the women. It's the first hint of the range of sexual roles that we will gradually be allocated in coming weeks. The women are led away to learn Emin songs. 'Right,' says Matthew, 'we're going to do some exercises to reawaken the warrior in you.' I blink, horrified.

He lines us up in pairs and teaches us three marches, which he says come from ancient Iran. The first is called 'The March of the Friendly Negotiation', the second 'The March of the Alert Mind' and the third, 'The March of the Black Immortals'. Despite its name, the first turns out to involve stamping our feet hard on the soil in a most unfriendly fashion. The last time I marched was when I was six, in the playground of my junior school, when a craze of militarism broke out. The idea of marching for an unseen world strikes me as absurd, even sinister. But as the strains of the girls' voices reach us, we march, stumbling, out of step, while Lance bangs a drum to keep our raggedy steps in rhythm. 'Think like an ancient Persian,' Matthew barks at us. 'One, two, one, two. About turn.' A couple, pushing a pram and eating ice cream, watch us, puzzled, as we stamp our feet up and down on the grass for Matthew. The grimly named 'March of the Black Immortals' is an absurd Chaplinesque waddle. 'Turn your leg and foot out at each step,' orders Matthew, 'like this.' He demonstrates, marching stiffly alongside us, flinging his arms out sideways with each step. A pair of young punks gawp. I think I can hear them laughing. I wish they would go away and leave me alone with this humiliation.

As we copy Matthew, I catch Stone Bear's eye. He's wearing shades and a string vest which shows his muscles. I can see he thinks this is as inane as I do. I strongly suspect we're not the only ones. But no one – out of all of us – dreams of protesting. I wonder what would happen if one of us stopped dead and said, 'I really don't like doing this?' But no one does. As I parade up and down in the baking mid-summer heat, I realise I am acting out a fundamental, depressing lesson about how cults operate. Once the collective has been formed, no one dares break ranks and say, 'Hold on. What we're doing is really stupid.' Once you've started tearing up reality, and rebuilding it in a different shape, you don't want to step out of line or the whole precarious structure will crumble.

The women finish their singing practice. They come over and before they sing us sugary new age chants with words like, 'In the weakness of ourselves/Is a strength that nothing can bind,' they stand and watch us perform our shambolic marches one last time. Up and down we tramp, ashamed. Afterwards, I hear a Canadian woman saying, 'Didn't they look like *men*, when they were marching?' And a tall Scandinavian girl approaches and tells me, 'You all looked very manly.' I scan her face for any trace of irony, but there is none.

Later, thankfully, Jo tells me that we looked ridiculous.

The strange bus trip continues. In nearby Savernake Forest we are split up into groups. Those who have only been in the Emin a short time are led off to a small clearing in the woods and played a tape of Leo speaking. Oliver, Jeremy, Mandy, Jo, Stone Bear and a few others lie back on dry leaves, and stare up at the sun through the leaves. 'This tape,' says Simon, 'is called *Growing Up A Second Time*. Which is a pretty incredible idea if you think about it.'

It's the first time I've ever heard Leo's voice. He speaks – for twenty minutes or so – in a measured drone, still with a hint of North London in his accent, about how we can realise our lives fully. We gaze up at the beeches and young oaks above us. It's a simple message. There is more to life than work, pub, sex, work. Recognise the unseen world and your life will change. You will reach a new maturity. 'It's up to you,' says Leo. 'You can carry on, living your life from one day to the next, making the same mistakes over and over, or you can be *different*.'

An ant is crawling up my trouser leg. I rustle on the leaves, uncomfortable and disappointed. I had expected something far more mysterious, something more obviously life changing, instead of this simple message. Stone Bear appears to be sleeping, leaning back against a sapling. But then I look over at Mandy and she is wearing the brightest, widest smile on her face.

On the bus back everyone sings more songs with names like 'Dedication', chanting the words from the Emin Songbook One. Lance strums a guitar, still full of energy. I am exhausted. Oliver tells me that the talk by Leo affected him. 'I'm going to have to work out how to keep this going when I go to university,' he says. He doesn't want to be ordinary. He wants to be different.

Somewhere around Junction Three, Mandy stands up and turns in her seat to face the rest of the coach. 'I've got an announcement,' she shouts. The coach quietens for a minute. 'I've decided to change my name . . . to Freedom.' And the whole coach starts cheering wildly, happily. 'Hello Freedom!' we shout back.

Back in the real world, when I tell my friends about the Emin, they listen goggle eyed. 'Go on,' they hoot. 'Do The March of the Black

Immortals for us.' It becomes a party piece. They love my ungainly waddle. 'Aren't you afraid it's going to get to you? You'll suddenly disappear and never come back?' they ask me. 'How can you keep a straight face?'

In the beginning I had worried that however well I played the part, I would be spotted as an impostor. My lack of belief would betray me. Instead, I am discovering that in many ways it is easy to exist inside a cult. You are welcomed with open arms when you show the slightest interest. Cult members' beliefs are absolute and real. They can't understand why *everyone* isn't doing it. As for keeping a straight face, one of the miracles of the collectively weird behaviour of cult members is how quickly it starts to look commonplace. It is curiously easy to go along with it as long as everyone else around you is doing the same. My friends sometimes worry that if I spend too long in a cult, the beliefs somehow will rub off on me: but it's not that that I'm finding unsettling. Whatever the doomy warnings of Ian Haworth, I'm still finding myself disappointingly impervious to their alleged 'mind control'. But what I am finding stranger, day by day, is the in-between life I lead. At the next meeting, after my friends have giggled and stared at my performances of The March of the Black Immortals, I feel guilty for making fun of my fellow Emin marchers, who greet me with increasing warmth at each meeting. After all, I am betraying their secret world.

After the Emin day trip, everyone simultaneously comes down with a heavy mid-summer cold, eyes streaming and heads thick. I am sleeping badly, partly because of a temperature, but also because for two nights I have wild nightmares. In them the Emin have the invisible powers they claim and really can see into the darker cavities of my soul. I am repeatedly unmasked as a low impostor, about to betray precious Emin secrets. 'How could you do this to us?' they plead, hurt, one night. I try to argue back in dream illogic, telling them these powers don't exist.

It's affecting us all in different ways. Our ordinary world is gradually transformed. At the start of the next meeting I overhear Jeremy, the goateed record producer, telling someone: 'In a few weeks, it's completely changed my life. I'm more sensitive to everything around me.'

Now everybody calls Mandy by her new name, Freedom. The change was easy. You'd think it would be impossible to say, 'Do you want a cup of tea, Freedom?' In the meeting Simon starts telling us why it's important to change your name. He draws a line on the blackboard and tells us, it's a question of crossing the line from one side to the other, and a new name is like a flag planted in new, uncharted territory. But he warns us not to get carried away with our new names. They are only to be used amongst ourselves. 'People out there would get confused if you went about changing your name all the time, wouldn't they though?' says Simon. Everyone guffaws loudly.

At the next meeting Oliver stands and smiles his semicircular smile: 'I've decided to change my name to Patience,' he tells us. 'Hello Patience,' we boom back. It's a quality he desires. Emin names are vaguely mythological, vaguely new age: Listen, Hope, Morgan, Nature, Infinite, Aspire, Peleas, Neo. You can change your name as often as you want, as often as you want to change yourself. It gets confusing, so people wear self-made badges saying 'Grit' or 'Success'.

Another week, Jo chooses Keep as a new name. 'Hello Keep.' She is loving the meetings. All her life she's known that there are other forces out there waiting to be contacted, but thought she was the only one who felt like that. Now she's surrounded by others who seem to think like her. After each meeting she goes home to her flatmate, a photographer who is always up in the small hours, developing prints, and gabbles for hours about the things we've done. She's tried talking about it to other friends but they don't understand. They tell her she's getting into some hippie nonsense. So in the end she doesn't talk to them about it any more.

Jeremy is next. He changes his name to Sol. 'Hello Sol,' we chorus. It's easy. They cross the line, one by one. I realise I have a definite, prudish resistance to changing mine.

One time, Simon is about to address me at a meeting, but he forgets my name. He apologises and says, 'Tell me, at the moment I forgot your name, were you thinking about choosing a new one?'

*

A table full of Leo's tracts has started to appear at each meeting. Some are just single photocopied sheets. Others are books. A single photocopied sheet will cost 55p. A set of three books including the first that Leo wrote in the back of his Security Express van, *Dear Dragon*, costs £37.50. We are encouraged to buy these writings regularly, to take them home and study them. They are the collected wisdom of Leo. The more we read, the more we shall understand.

He writes in imposing sentences that tumble with biblically dense, arresting sub-clauses, foggy with mysticism: all through history 'recorded and before', he writes in one early pamphlet called 'The Emin', there have always been a few dedicated individuals reaching towards 'that which was, is now and not seen, and always will be, but never put into bondage'. Verbose and syntactically eccentric, the document talks of 'a most supreme sense in this fashion' that is 'fashioned by the mighty strength of the upholders of the universe from first to last'.

At the bottom of many of the tracts, even single sheets, there is a stern copyright warning. So many Emin acts ring with mistrust of the outside world. This is knowledge to be passed around only within the Emin circle. The uncomprehending, desensitised outside world won't be able to make head or tail of it.

As far back as 1988 the Emin talked of Leo having contributed over four million precious words to the Emin Archive. It's a constantly changing, constantly expanding web of philosophies, always irreducible to a simple set of statements. In its sheer scale and convolution, the Archive puts Leo on a level with L. Ron Hubbard, founder of the Church of Scientology, who claimed a total of seven million words. There's an extraordinary, if strange, imagination behind these floods of print. L. Ron Hubbard invented a huge and brilliantly bizarre pseudo-scientific vocabulary for his books, full of neologisms like 'engram', 'thetan' and 'Dianetics'. Leo, instead, has a knack for using familiar language but often in strangely unexpected ways, imbuing it with odd new significance. Again, much of the vocabulary is borrowed from science. Leo's various secret methods, like electrobics, are referred to as 'technologies'. We talk about 'researching' into tarot, or colour vision. Instead of saying that something is explained, which it never fully can be in the Emin's strange and visionary world, we talk about how something is 'given location'.

However opaque its meaning, Leo's language is often oddly pretty: works and teaching methods are given surprising titles: The Opal Inbreath, Opal Ramble, Gemrod Call-Over, Cobwebs and Tears, the Amethyst Sigh. Gatherings of followers, called by Leo, are also given wonderful, mystical-sounding names: The Random Emin Keep, the Blue Emerald Classroom, the Quiet Gathering.

As a result, when followers talk, it's as if they're talking in the mythical tongue of a race of futuristic Hobbits. Newcomers only understand a fraction; they can end up with the distinct impression that those who have been in the Emin for years are visitors from a rare secret world.

When Leo is in one of his active phases, missives appear from Florida at regular intervals. The latest are snapped up eagerly. My co-religionists eagerly scan the densely worded papers for some inkling of a sign, some hope of a new way forward. Sometimes, sections of them are read aloud, in reverent wonderment. One day one of the senior Emin reads out a passage from Leo's latest outpouring, about the current state of enlightenment of the Emin. 'It has,' the man reads, 'as true development should have, a thunder and a lightning, a tornado and a wonderment, and a disarrangement by stretch, that can then be put together in actual form – inside which was a refuge and a sanctuary of no danger and starting peace . . .'

Whether any of them understand any more of this than I do, I cannot tell, but nodding sagaciously they say, 'Wow.'

Three sayings from *The Teachings of Leo*:

'It is better to be an honest man than to carry sandwiches around in a briefcase.'

'The art of thrusting into lost causes is the terror that offers sanctuary to prevent salvation.'

'Hope by the human, if confirmed by the mother, replaces H with an M and makes a poem.'

*

As our commitment to the Emin becomes more intense and rarefied, so do our duties towards it. As the course draws to a close, we are all individually invited to apply for provisional membership of the Emin sub-group called the Emin Jewels. Our application consists of a declaration that we will keep all the laws of the country, never take drugs, avoid party politics within the group and pay £10 a week. One section of the declaration is headed Medical Details. Question 3: 'Have you had any mental disorders or illness?'

Simon explains our subscriptions to us, how they cover rental of this hall, and heating. He says £10 a week isn't really a way of paying to *become* an Emin. That's something money can't pay for. Later, after six months of meetings, we will cease being provisional members and become full Emin members. Then they will be asking for a £15 weekly contribution.

I sign under the oddly ominous paragraph that reads: 'I declare that I will not hold the Emin Jewels responsible for any health problems or illness suffered during or after my membership.' On the front of the four-page document is a typical Leonine declaration: 'A journey of a thousand miles cannot be accomplished without the first step . . .'

6

A sort of discipline creeps up slowly on us; most embracing it willingly. We are told to bow to Simon and Mero at the start of each lecture. At first we feel sheepish, but we do it.

There is a powerful sense of consensual behaviour at work in the small, tightly knit group of the Emin. A young, bright-eyed, twitchy girl tells me she joined a group in Guildford, but now, because there aren't many members there, the whole network is transplanting itself to London to be near other members. She is supposed to move in a week, but she hasn't got a flat yet. She has no idea where she will be living. She giggles nervously at the prospect. She's not the only one who has relocated to be near other Emin members. Later, I meet a group from Edinburgh who have moved *en masse* so they could come to more meetings.

But while most manage to look miraculously wild with happiness for the four-hour sessions, nodding, laughing hilariously at every tiny joke, I notice other, older members who look tired and red-eyed at the constant round of meetings after a day at work. Are they still enjoying themselves, or do they want to leave, and, like Nick on the cliff in Cornwall, not know how to any more?

Jo, for one, is beginning to have her doubts. She started as one of the most committed members, but the lustre is wearing off. One day she talks to Seek, one of the keenest young Emin members, so enthusiastic he appears somehow to be always leaning forwards, about how she's getting tired of the endless meetings: 'I don't know how you manage to turn up to meetings two or three times a week *and* at weekends. Don't you ever feel the need to take a holiday?'

'The way I look at it the Emin *is* a holiday.'

'But I don't understand how you fit it all in. What if you've got something else planned at the weekend and they ring you up?'

'I try and make sure I don't have anything planned,' he smiles. 'Just in case.'

As far as Jo's concerned, the worst aspect of the Emin is the strange gender roles that have started to appear without warning, little by little. We are told to refer to women as 'Ladies'. It's just a matter of respect, they say. We menfolk are 'Gentlemen'. Then we are all given duties. While it's the gentlemen's duty to change the furniture in the hall, lifting the heavy oak lectern off the stage and laying out the chairs, the ladies are only supposed to prepare food and tea, and to wash up. Jo is becoming twitchy.

Life seems to become full of new ritual. We are taught to 'prepare' the hall for each meeting. A group of us gentlemen perform a synchronised clapping sequence in each corner of the room to disrupt the 'bad' electricities that have accumulated in the corners. Then we walk solemnly clockwise around the outer edge of the room, palms an inch or two from the walls, projecting the colour blue from our minds. This is the blue shield. It protects us from the evils outside. The ladies' part of the ritual is to process around the room, carrying a censer to purify the air with an incense specially chosen to suit the electricities of the day.

Jo works for a theatre lighting company and has enough trouble at work with holding back the weight of gender roles. All this is starting to drive her mad. She asks, 'Why can't *we* shift the furniture too? Why can't we put up the blue shield?' People look surprised. Simon and Mero tell her, of course she can if she wants to. 'We're not trying to make rules,' they say. So one night she doggedly joins the men putting the furniture away. Men approach her and say, 'Don't worry. I'll lift that.' She is furious. It's all going wrong. Even Emin women whisper to her, 'You shouldn't be doing that.'

After each evening meeting, we are taught how to put everything away carefully, to re-create the Christian children's school, just as it was before. I take down the huge Emin emblem – a complex symbolic shield of a rising triangle of colours and inset gems, rising through a grid – that now hangs on the stage and pack it carefully in its packing case. I lift the heavy lectern back on to the dais, and then replace the Bibles on the shelf. This is a man's job. The women get to fold up the coloured linen that decorates the hall.

The Emin regard the Christian symbols we replace with hostility. Even clearing up the room acquires a ritual of its own. Symbolically, the last act of clearing the hall is to replace the plain oak crucifix on the hook where the Emin shield hung. It is the final act of surrendering the place again to the unbelievers. Mark tells me, 'It's really important not to forget to put up the cross, because some people have just left it lying on stage,' he admonishes me. 'They go spare here if we do. It's mumbo jumbo, I know, but . . .' he says, with absolutely no sense of irony at all.

7

And then one day Mero announces she is going to measure us for our Emin costumes. Costumes? But having come this far, we accept anything with equanimity and hand over £10 to her to buy them. Nobody asks why, or what they are going to look like, even though we are all from generations who did all we could to avoid wearing school uniforms. The clothes arrive the next week, packed in polythene. Opal, ever smiling prettily, the child of Emin parents, had spent her birthday sewing them for us.

My name is carefully written in italic pen on a label on one of the packages. We unwrap them, curious to see what we shall now wear to meetings. They consist of a white cotton tabard top and a light blue sash, worn around the waist. A little note falls out. I pick it up and laugh: it is a set of washing instructions, just as if we'd bought these strange ritual garments at Marks and Spencer's. 'Your sash is made out of satin. Warm iron, preferably damp.' We are to wear them over our shirts and trousers, with the sash tied to one side. Great care has been lavished on these garments. Our pale blue sash apparently denotes our group: we are told we are the Turquoise Emin Jewels. Others, more experienced, have different colours. Opal wears a yellow one; Mark's is red. It's like we're spiritual Boy Scouts.

At first it's funny dressing up. In the men's toilets, Jeremy, Oliver and I try ours on for the first time, giggling. Mark tells us to roll up our long sleeves, because we mustn't obstruct the electrical forces that emanate from our elbows. 'Why don't they just have short sleeves?' someone asks, with dazzling logic.

'The ladies' tunics have short sleeves,' answers Mark, matter of factly. 'Ours have long sleeves.'

'Oh,' we answer. Of course. I look ridiculous in mine: 'I feel like an extra in Star Trek,' I snigger.

'I feel like a wine waiter,' grins Jeremy. 'And Patience looks like he's about to start reciting something from Shakespeare.' We snigger like schoolboys trying on our costumes for a school play.

But when we join our fellow Emin in the hall, they are all, for the first time, dressed in tunics with us. Before, they had not worn them. Presumably not to frighten us away until we were ready. Now we are ready. Our joking stops and with the solemn little bow from the waist we have been taught to do, we welcome Simon and Mero as they walk into the room for tonight's lecture.

We sit in a neat semicircle of chairs; this shape has a special electrical conductivity. At bigger meetings the shuffling of chairs to achieve the right shape can take twenty minutes.

We learn that every time we wish to address the meeting we should stand. Sometimes being in the Emin is like being at school again. Lectures, rules, uniforms, blackboards and daytrips. Maybe that's part of the attraction for some people; it's a school you never have to grow out of or leave.

A woman gets a ticking off for wandering out into the car park in her new uniform. We are not allowed to wear our uniforms anywhere where the public might see them.

Today Simon tells us we are doing 'Groundwork'. He writes the word on the blackboard. Groundwork, he says, is something you may have to do a lot of before you get a result, but once you've done it, the results can be amazing. 'It's like the Heinz Ketchup Bottle.' He turn to Mero. 'Mero, will you tell them about the Heinz Ketchup Bottle?'

The usually taciturn Mero says, 'Well, you'll know that when you open the bottle, nothing comes out? So you hit the bottle, and still nothing happens. So you hit it again. And again. And when you hit it the next time, suddenly it *all* comes out.' People laugh. 'It's the same with groundwork. At first you get nothing out, but after a while, you only have to do a little, to get a lottle.'

Mark always seems to be ticking me off for doing something wrong. Once, when I arrive late, I rush to the school toilets which the men use as a dressing room to change into my tunic. He scolds me for hurrying and orders me to calm down before entering the hall in case I disrupt the calm energies inside.

As the meetings stretch ever later into the night I abandon the bicycle and start driving. The first time, after the meeting has finished, I start up my engine to drive away from the school some time around midnight. Mark runs over the tarmac towards me and hisses, 'Turn off the motor! You'll wake the old lady.' What old lady? He points at a window on the first floor. The Emin rent the school hall and various store-rooms from the woman who runs the small Welsh school. She lives in a flat in the old Victorian building. If we disturb her at night, she might kick us out of the hall. Mark tells me we all have to push our cars out on to the main road before starting up the engines.

Leaving the recondite world of a meeting, it's always strange to see the normal, dull suburban streets of Willesden still outside, lit by dull orange light. This furtive way of leaving in the middle of the night, rolling our cars silently down the car park, heightens the sense of space between the Emin and the hostile society around them. The Emin can't afford to lose this hall by annoying the people who let it to them.

In a sceptical world, it's almost impossible for a cult like the Emin to find anywhere to hold their meetings. The anti-cult group Family Action Information and Rescue have passed public warnings to churches that the Emin may try and use their halls. 'Teaching of occult practices would hardly be in accordance with church doctrines,' says one FAIR document. 'In one instance, a hall was booked for a "history lecture", the name of the organisation not mentioned, and the signature was a scrawl. Please check out clients who do not offer credentials . . .'

The Emin are press shy. They know they will be misunderstood. Once, in 1983, they did invite the public to scrutinise them. They stuck their heads above the parapet because they were in danger of losing their permanent centre – a church hall they had leased in Putney. Leo called it his temple. He filled the hall with paintings of silver and gold dragons and installed a fountain surrounded by plants in the middle of the hall. It was a sanctuary. People remember it fondly. Carried away, Leo started to invent church-like ceremonies. Disciples would move to the front of the hall where you were sprinkled with water and offered a wafer to chew on. But locals began to complain of strange goings-on in the hall, of the sound of chanting coming from within, of being woken by cars revving their engines late at night.

Simultaneously, anti-cult organisations who mistrusted Leo's motives had begun feeding stories about the Emin to the press. Reports about the cult started to appear in Cult Corner in *Private Eye* which alleged that Raymond 'Leo' Armin was a fraud, fleecing the gullible. Disastrously, the Emin sued for libel and lost.

David Mellor, the local MP, took up the cause, saying he didn't want people like this in his borough. The local council let it be known that they would refuse the Emin a licence to use the hall when the renewal came up. After weeks of confrontation with local journalists and politicians, the Emin decided to embark on a cack-handed public relations exercise. They had nothing to hide. Everyone would understand their good intentions if only they knew about them. One of their spokesmen was given 1,000 words in the local *Putney Chronicle* to try to explain what the Emin was. What they printed was a dense and baffling attempt at condensing the nebulous Emin creed delivered in magical-scientific Leo-speak. It was, they stated, 'a surveillance upon the Emin Foundation work'. Their talk of electro-magnetic auras was totally incomprehensible to the outsider, of course. Printed next to a sedate article about how Wandsworth had the best chiropodists in the country, the Emin's claims that they could cure cancer did little apart from add to the conclusion that the Emin were obviously a bunch of raving cult lunatics.

Even Leo emerged briefly from the shadows to give what may have been his only real interview to the press: he told a reporter on the *Putney and Wandsworth Guardian* that the members of the Emin were devoted to his teachings. 'Obsession is the weak word for it,' he told the astonished journalist, unguardedly. 'These people would follow me around the world till I die.' The article let slip Leo's extraordinary Svengali-like arrogance. 'I reckon I'm about the most brilliant man you have ever met,' he boasted. 'I must be to have all these people with university degrees following me. I can take a subject and spin a web around you.' There was a picture of him dressed in exactly the same style of white tunic that I dress in. He looked like a runaway madman.

The press campaign was a dismal, if comic failure. The planning application was kicked out. The Emin lost their temple. They retreated into secrecy, convinced that their teachings were far too fragile for the clumsy outside world to understand.

More peculiarly, in his rare press appearance Leo admitted he had actually taken the accusations that he could kill by thought-power seriously. The claims that his more zealous followers had made had obviously unsettled him. He performed a macabre 'experiment' to discover if he really did have these dark powers. 'I caught a mole in my garden,' he told the astonished newspaperman, 'and put it in a jar. I sat and looked at it and tried to give it a cerebral haemorrhage. But I couldn't. If I can't do that to a mole, how can I do that to a human being?'

8

One night, Simon is unbearably excited. He smokes twice as many Silk Cut as he normally does. He paces like a child around the room as he talks, and can hardly contain himself: 'I don't know if you feel it, but the unseen world is changing. It's changed unbelievably already – even since we started this course.' He has a glass full of soluble aspirin on the table by him. His eyes are red and he looks drawn. Mero looks tired too. Leo has written a letter to all the Emin people of the world, in Canada, in Australia, in Israel. All the senior members were summoned to late night meetings to try to fathom the implications. Simon's had little sleep since the letter arrived. He reads us it. He says we probably won't understand much. He's right. It's dated 10 July 1993 and starts: 'To the Emin People, draw near.'

It's a rambling document full of new language. In hurt, betrayed tones, Leo talks of 'lack of take up', a lack of commitment by the followers. But we are in the time of the quickening. He is establishing a new hierarchy. With seven members of the Emin he will establish something called the Acropolis, a committee of Emin, acting under his guidance, who will take the Emin to the next phase.

When he's finished, Simon asks what we, the newcomers, made of the letter. Oliver blurts, slightly shyly, that it had a big effect on him. 'While you were speaking, I couldn't help looking at the shield behind you,' he says. He points to the Emin shield; a triangle pointing skywards, encrusted with coloured glass. 'I felt drawn to it. I felt like it wasn't you reading the letter, it was somehow that picture speaking through you.'

Simon shakes his head, grinning. 'That's really, really incredible. Isn't it Mero?' Mero beams at Oliver.

Opal holds her hand up and points at Oliver. 'I can see a yellow aura around the top of your head, Patience, which wasn't there before,' she smiles. The mystery of the moment is amplified. This is a place where miracles occur, however invisible to most eyes. 'It was really bright,' she says.

By day Opal works for a top international advertising agency.

The Emin exude a pre-millenarian love of impending disaster. The world is corrupt and dying. We are special and have the answer, but people are too blind to see it with their own eyes. But as it descends into further unspeakable chaos the singular truth of the Emin message will become apparent.

One British Emin group publish a magazine six times a year, celebrating the decline of the world and the rightness of Leo's apocalyptic predictions. It's called *Omega*, the last letter of the Greek alphabet, to celebrate our end-time. 'A Herald of World Changes', it boasts. Its glossy cover lines are exuberantly morbid: 'Tropical Diseases . . . Floods on Three Continents'. It's packed with articles culled from newspapers and magazines about the decline of the planet: a sort of *Reader's Digest* of catastrophe. One article dwells on the mounting problem of child prostitution. Another on increased mortality rates from diseases. 'Mounting Crisis in World Leadership' trumpets another. It chronicles gloom with glee. And interspersed in it are Leo's predictions: 'It will become increasingly difficult to keep foods fresh' . . . 'Viruses will lead to new susceptibility to disease to which people used to be immune' . . . 'Bewilderment and disorientation will become widespread.' We said so all along, it seems to merrily say. Alleluia. And the wicked shall perish.

Peleas, one of the upper hierarchy, is addressing us one day. He's a bald man in his forties, dressed in a green polo shirt. He has just returned from a week-long 'Random Emin Keep' meeting with the Trio in Florida. Leo fuels the state of perpetual excitement in his followers by randomly summoning various members to meet him at these gatherings. Anyone can be called out of the blue. Even me, I'm told. When I ask how the Trio would know of my existence, Simon tells me that news of our progress is constantly being passed up to the hierarchy above, and I remember the notes that I see Mero sometimes making during meetings.

Peleas is bouncing with excitement after his encounter with our leader. 'We are not gods yet,' he announces, 'but we have *changed* . . .' He has brought some photographs of the outward expression of the change. The 'before' photo shows a group of Emin delegates from around the world, jetlagged after their long journeys to the Emin headquarters – a small low-ceilinged room in a Florida office block. In the 'after' snaps the delegates are grinning madly, like kids at a funfair, tanned and sparkle-eyed.

Today, after the tea break, Peleas barks, 'Right, everyone stand on their heads.'

We look confused.

'Tea break over! Everyone stand on their heads! . . . You haven't heard that joke?' he says. 'OK. A man goes to hell and he's given the choice of three cells. He looks in the first and everyone inside is standing in shit up to their waists. He looks in the second, and everyone is in shit up to their knees. Oh my God, thinks the man. I don't want to be in either of those. So he looks in the third and they're only standing in shit up to their ankles, and they're drinking cups of tea, smoking cigarettes. Great, thinks the man, this isn't so bad. But as the cell door closes behind him he hears a voice. "Right everyone, tea break's over. Stand on your heads." '

The laughter takes about a minute and a half to die down.

'I'm going to talk about healing,' announces Peleas, more seriously. There is, he says sagely, no such thing as coincidence. It is up to us to find the connections. It is never a coincidence if you are healed, if you pick up a £5 note from the street, or if you think of an old friend one day and get a letter from them the next. It is the work of the unseen worlds.

He invites us to give our healing stories; hands rise. One woman talks of a speedy recovery after an appendectomy. She left hospital only after a day and a half, when the doctors had told her she must wait four days. Another talks of a mysterious back pain, cured by aura cleansing. A small Frenchwoman talks with Gallic forthrightness of a persistent urinary infection which cleared up after joining the Emin. A large woman called Grace talks about how she spilt a cup of hot camomile tea on her infant child, but saved him from scarring by meditating on the right healing colours. 'The doctors were *amazed*,' she says.

We are living in an age of miracles already, only most of us can't even see them.

Grace has another tale for us. When her young daughter was going to primary school, Grace knew that the teacher of the class her child was going to be in was a homosexual. She was appalled. She meditated on the matter, wondering what she could do about it, and realised that she couldn't simply complain about it. But a miracle happened. When the term started, the class turned out to be so large that it had to be divided into two. Somehow, the unseen world had arranged it that her child would be in the care of a new woman teacher. Her offspring was saved from the corrupting influence of a homosexual.

Peleas nods, pleased. Grace's child was saved from the nasty influence of homosexuality. 'It's the unseen world's care . . .'

Right, I think. Everyone stand on their heads.

And then, bit by bit, the people I joined with start to fall by the wayside. One meeting, after we've been learning about astrology and the planets, marching round the room chanting, 'Mars, Mars, Mars,' to see what effect it is having on us, Simon makes an announcement: 'Freedom has decided not to come any more. I don't know why. She's said she's going to write a letter explaining it all.' I realise that I can't even remember Freedom's real name any more. She has a child. Maybe the pressure of coming to all the meetings has been too much for her.

The next to leave is Jo. I give her a lift late one night. Seeing her helping me to push my car silently out of the car park, Mark rushes over to help. 'Ladies' should not push cars. She gets in, incandescent with fury. 'Bloody hell,' explodes an unlady-like Jo. 'I'm not allowed to lift furniture, I'm not allowed to push cars. It's driving me crazy.' She's keeping a list of all the things that are starting to annoy her about the Emin. One is Mero, who takes our weekly subscriptions, who is always breathing down her neck for money. Sometimes Jo finds it hard to keep up the payments. Besides, she says, we never get told what all this money is *for*. And another is the conformity. 'Have you noticed that all the men have exactly the same haircut?' It's true. All the men seem to have the same evenly short hair.

I miss the meeting where Jo makes her last stand. She rises from her chair, as we've been taught to do now when addressing the Ushers and asks, nervously, 'What do the Emin say about same sex relationships?'

Simon is flummoxed. 'We're not here to judge anyone,' he answers, vaguely. 'That's not the point of the Emin. We're not here to say this is right and this is wrong.'

Keep stands her ground. She has discussed it with Sol and Patience, and they said they're unhappy about some of what's been going on recently too. She looks around to see if they're going to back her up, but to her disappointment they're sitting there silently. She ploughs on. 'Yes, but if I sleep with another woman, what do the Emin think about that?'

Simon looks flustered and uncomfortable. 'Well, I would have to say . . . um, that that doesn't happen in the unseen world. In the unseen world, that would be regarded as . . . unnatural.'

Keep sits down again, shaking with nerves and rage, and feeling betrayed. She broke ranks, and no one had backed her up. The word 'unnatural' was the last thing she expected to hear. The Emin had excited her so much in the first weeks. She had met people for the very first time whom she felt understood the world in the same way as she felt about it. But in the end they turn out to have new twists on the same old stupid rules and prejudices of the world outside. She decides, sadly and furiously, not to come again.

The Emin regard homosexuality as abhorrent. Leo laid down his rulings on the matter in the early days. In 'The Poem of the Church of the Emin Coils' he writes, 'At no time will homosexuality, lesbianism, transvestism, nymphonic [sic] or any other unnatural condition or freak practice be permitted.'

It's a curiously dogmatic moment in the loose world of Emin lore. In other respects they have little dogma. But, curiously, this ugly piece of sexual morality is one fixed point in their new age meanderings. Like the exaggerated play on male and female roles, I wonder if it is the product of some dark corner in Leo's psychology. Yet it's also one of the strangely recurrent themes in most of the cults I become a member of; the creation of a safe world of squeaky clean boy-meets-girl sexual roles. That cults should so frequently attempt to make an extreme black and white world of that most renegade of all human emotions – sexual desire – is a depressing consequence of a quest to order a world they often appear to find so intolerably confusing.

Masturbation is allowed, though only once a week and provided that 'no mental associations or mental pictures' are part of the act. 'The action should be entirely mechanical. Excess is sinful and astral deterioration will ensue, by the power of the church Essences. Therefore, use it with care.' You will, it seems, go blind in the spiritual sense.

9

Every last tiny item contains a message. The colour and the shape of trees or flowers all have hidden meanings. The colour of clothes someone wears. The shape of their hands. Even the size of their ear lobes are discussed. 'Have you ever seen statues of Buddha? He usually has long earlobes. They are a sign of spiritual wisdom. Look at that photo of Leo. His lobes are long, too.' Around the room we finger our ears. Mine are obviously sceptical.

Leo's 'technologies' are bafflingly infinite. Every word has a hidden meaning beyond its apparent meaning which can be revealed by breaking it down into its components, its rhymes, or even by anagrammatising it. One night we are studying graphology, but even before examining what our handwriting means we spend half an hour 'researching' the hidden meaning of the word 'graphology'. 'Graph,' someone reads from their Oxford dictionary: 'A symbolic diagram expressing a system of connections.' 'A system of connections! Wow!' Someone else suggests, 'Logy. That's like "Logos", the word of God. So it's like a system of connections to the word of God.' Everyone breathes, 'Wow!'

Matthew, beaming at us as we uncover these hidden secrets, says, 'That's amazing, isn't it? We're just ordinary people. We're just the Mr and Mrs Browns. But look how much we can achieve by looking at just *one word*.'

Every number is trying to communicate with us somehow too; our birthdays, the number of people in the room, or even today's date can be cross-referenced with an ever-unfolding series of meanings delivered by the numbers' shape, or by the letters that make them up, or even by the way they feel when you count them. The figure seven, for example, is especially spiritual. 'Seven,' Simon tells us, drawing the number on a blackboard, 'is made up of a higher spiritual platform, and a line connecting earthwards to us.' Four's crossed lines are said to embody resolution. Leo's curious tarot cards are numbered too. Number four is known as 'the Emin card'. On it there's a picture of a man hanging upside-down from a ghostly tree, which bears a triangle symbol on one of its branches. Out of his pockets pours money. What can it mean? The tendrils of the insoluble puzzle spread over everything.

Like Emin tarot, Emin astrology is subtly different from other versions and claims to go deeper. Mars, for instance, is the fourth planet from the sun. The number is meaningful. And it's red, which plunges us further into the Emin world of colour significances. And we learn that we don't just have one star-sign, but two, because an Emin year lasts nine months. Which means that not only are we all older than we imagine, but we also have a second, more subtle astrological sign. It goes round and round. Everything is a memo from the ineffable. The slightest change of circumstance or even mood can be an indication that the unseen world, beneficial or malign, is trying to contact us or influence us.

In the old school hall, Oliver, Jeremy, Opal, Lance, Seek, Sky, I and several other regulars spend night after night busily cross-referencing one obscure fact with another, under Simon or Matthew's directions, finding strange hints in Leo's texts. Our lives are full. The texts are continually being updated and changed. New documents are said sometimes to invalidate old ones. The Emin creed is plastic, changing constantly. Nothing is fixed. New symbols replace the old ones. As the office in Florida spouts out new documents, the creed expands.

I start to appreciate the weird magnitude of Leo's and the Emin's creation. They have built this vast labyrinth which they can lose themselves in for ever. I realise, to my surprise, that after months in the Emin, I can talk for minutes about the hidden significances of any apparently meaningless object. Even the cup on my desk now has a shape, a name, a colour which can all be woven into this wild jungle of Emin semiology. It's blue, which would denote nurturing, creating. The cup is round which indicates – obviously – 'containment', which is an Emin concept relating again to nurturing, but the shape also forms a zero, or the letter 'O', both of which might produce other meanings. The word cup can be broken down to c-up. Upwards? What does 'c' stand for? Why is the handle yellow? What does the handle's shape signify? And so on, and on, and on.

I wonder, does this sort of ever-fragmenting visionariness denote a sort of madness on Leo's part? At times, at loose in this ultra-complex jungle of signs and symbols, I ponder if this is what a mild version of schizophrenia might feel like – if there is such a thing: the world becomes a highly-developed network of meanings and messages that only you can see, and which separates you from others who don't understand it the way you do. I am curious: in those lonely post-adolescent days when he felt so separate from the world, was Leo suffering from some sort of mental illness, which he resolved into this new system of mystical symbolism?

I call up an American anti-cult worker who carries out 'exit-counselling' with ex-Emin members from the many US groups. He believes Leo has created something extremely harmful. He says he speaks to ex-members who he believes can be 'triggered' by the apparent significance of 'ordinary life events'. He says that one woman he counselled feels that this sensation of triggered meanings still pursues her. It's as if the Emin is chasing her around, long after she left it.

He calls Leo's process 'spiritualising the mundane', a phrase I suspect Leo would have been proud of if only he'd invented it.

When John Levinson joined the Emin in 1977 he had already suffered bouts of mental illness. A Cambridge architecture graduate with shoulder-length hair, he left the Emin in December that year having decided that the organisation was 'quite crazy'. But after quitting he started seeing things. His mother, Dr Mary Levinson, describes his visions as, 'Strange symptoms of seeing everything in vivid colours.' Anyone who has been in the Emin for any time would understand what he saw as part of the world of heightened perception that we were trained to achieve. Those colours would doubtless have had special meanings for John. He also described 'explosions in his head' which he believed were being caused by the Emin. John Levinson was admitted to the Maudsley hospital for psychiatric treatment for three months, then spent time as an outpatient at St Bart's hospital. One night, in November 1978, Mary received a phone call from her son telling her he was going to commit suicide 'unless the Emin let him go'. To try to reassure John, Mary went straight round to the Emin HQ, the hall that they later lost at Hotham Road, Putney. She met Leo's son John Armin there, known in the Emin as Pelle. He told her that they had written to her son to reassure him that he was released from the organisation.

Over the following months, John's search for a cure became more erratic. In an effort to rid himself of the malign influence he believed the Emin still exercised over him, he had himself treated by a Church of England approved exorcist in Swiss Cottage. He visited a faith healer in Letchworth and travelled to Lourdes. At his flat in Islington, even in winter, he would leave the windows open in an effort to try to blow away the Emin's powers.

In May 1979 Mary Levinson and her husband were on holiday in Crete when they received news that John had taken a drug overdose in his flat. The note John left read: 'I'm sorry mum – but I just can't stand it any more.'

The accusation that cults are a trapdoor to insanity comes up over and over again. One article in the *Daily Star* headlined 'The Mind Wreckers' related: 'Fears about the curse of the Emin drove artist John Levinson to suicide. For the 29-year-old graduate could no longer live with the evil hold which he believed the sect had over him. Last night, his heart-broken mother said: "My son would be alive today if he had not joined the Emin." '

*

In a café in Camden I meet a sensible, jolly schoolteacher called Val, now in her sixties, who went to her first Emin meeting in the mid-70s because her son had started going to the meetings. She had heard about groups like the Moonies and was concerned, wanting to find out what they were doing to her son. Much to her own surprise, she was impressed by the polite enthusiasm of members. She was so bowled over she joined too, and for a while thoroughly enjoyed all the impromptu late-night meetings on Hampstead Heath. People would spontaneously say, 'Let's go to the woods and dance and sing.' 'It was madness, but quite nice really,' she tells me over a cup of tea. 'Because I've never been that kind of spontaneous. I've never been a party person.'

We are alone in the café, apart from a waitress who leans over the counter, head in hands, listening in to our odd conversation. Val never got too caught up in the mystical side. People *might* have been able to see auras, they might not, but it didn't matter much to her. She thinks she saw them, but it wasn't a big deal. But the Emin gave her shy son some friends, and helped him cope. It helped her too. At the time she had separated from her husband, but still lived in the same house with him. She realises she was becoming quite erratic in her behaviour before she joined. 'Trying to be bigger than my husband did me a lot of harm, personally,' she says. 'The thing about the Emin is, I learned to clear it out of myself.'

In the end, after three years, when she'd got what she wanted out of it, she left. Some things had annoyed her, especially the way some of the weaker, more dependent members seemed to treat every ceremony in such an absurdly holy way, but mostly she thinks people got a lot of good out of it.

She was a member at roughly the same time as Michael Sellars and Sean Milligan, sons of the Goon Show stars. Spike Milligan's wife Paddy joined too, after she was diagnosed with cancer, but died sadly untouched by Leo's claimed healing abilities. However both Sean and Michael claimed in print that the Emin had been hugely beneficial to them, helping them overcome their drug habits.

The issue of how cults affect sanity gets thrown into the air by anti-cult campaigners all the time, but Val isn't sure you can be too conclusive about it. She left before Levinson died, and doesn't even know if she knew him, because he would have been known by his Emin name. She's neither surprised, nor shocked by the story when I tell her it. 'You've always got to appreciate that there are some people in there who would have got into a state anyway,' she says, replacing her cup on the table. 'It's not the fault of the cult. And that's not to say that it didn't happen because they were in the cult. That's an entirely different thing.' All the same, she has a schizophrenic grandson. She wouldn't like to see him joining. But she can't see the harm in it for most people. She was once invited to join Mensa and went along to a meeting. That, she says, was *far* stranger.

10

I joined the Emin in the spring. It's now autumn. I have spent far longer in this one cult than I calculated I would have to, and I'm worried about how much longer I can afford to spend researching them, but I stay, still hoping to discover something that will help me understand them better. The penny is dropping slowly that I never shall.

On a Sunday in September I am summoned by yet another telephone message to a special meeting in Bishop's Stortford. I don't want to go. I'm resenting the amount of time I'm now spending with them, but I drive up the motorway and find myself in the biggest Emin meeting I have ever been to. I recognise few faces, and I even have trouble getting back inside the hall, because the Emin guard, a tall geeky guy acting as sentry in the lobby, doesn't recognise me and thinks I'm one of the intruders that the Emin seem to believe are perpetually hovering outside.

'Can I help you?' he asks, aggressively.

I reply, absurdly, 'I'm one of you.' He lets me through apologetically.

Today we are going to be addressed by Vital, who is the Emin number two in the UK, and one of the seven members of Leo's new council, the Acropolis. The number one is a man named Regal, also an Acropolis member. The UK is divided into two memberships, one called the Gemrod Petition, which Vital runs, and the other called the Gemrod Endeavour led by Regal.

Despite my neophyte status, I find I am picked to help perform the shielding ceremony for this hundred-strong gathering. Together with three others I carry out today's holy spring cleaning, clapping the bad electricity out of the corners. Before it starts, three singers strum a typically uplifting Emin song in preparation for the meeting. The words are clumsy and earnest, the harmony hesitant. 'Now is the time to be the determinator in what you do,' they sing. I have a headache.

Vital is a youngish man, a natural speaker with a hint of a Scottish accent, a charmer, smartly dressed in casual slacks, wired with a radio mike. This is a pep talk, an attempt to refire the vision. He talks with hurt sadness about those who've left the Emin over the years, whose enthusiasm flared briefly and then burned out because they didn't understand the long-term dedication it really takes. He talks about how important it is not to let the Emin get bogged down, especially now we have to raise money to build a new Emin centre, a permanent home for the Acropolis in Florida. We must always fan the flame of belief. It needs constant feeding.

He tells an anecdote about Leo; how a group of disciples recently went to the cinema with him to watch *The Hunt for Red October*. It's a film in which Sean Connery, sporting a pointed beard much like Leo's, plays the part of an enigmatic maverick submarine commander, mistrusted by the outside world, but with the power to save the planet. I suspect Leo would have identified with the role. He certainly enjoyed it. He sat in the front row, eating a huge box of popcorn, jiggling around with excitement as he watched. And that, Vital tells us, is how we have to be. Childlike in our excitement as we confront Leo's latest offerings.

When I joined the Emin, I was full of ideas about what I would meet. I had expected Leo to be a manipulative leader, leeching off followers who provided him with an income and satisfied his will to control others. At first that's what he appeared to be, too. He may be, for all I know. It's no longer important, because it doesn't begin to explain most of what I have seen. It takes a sort of genius to dream a religion. But it's no longer clear where the genius lies. Leo supplies the astonishingly intricate framework, but it seems as if the certainty delivered by the people here is as important. Is Leo himself the invention of his eager followers? Sometimes their faith must overwhelm him too. Like the time he stared at the mole in the jar, to see if he really could kill it, disturbed because some of them had told him he could.

As the appointed Apostle, Vital starts to deconstruct one of Leo's more recent texts: it is a meeting of the new seven-strong leadership, under Leo's guidance. Leo himself has written a characteristically cryptic description of the achievements of the first two days of the first Acropolis meeting. Vital reads aloud from Leo's bulletin. ' "The First Part: The first part induced a state of integrated wonderment," wrote Leo, "which mainly had to do with the smoothness of the inter-engagement – for at the end of the first day they were simply INTO IT up to the top of their heads, as distinct from the fulfilment of their notebooks. And this drives us to . . . The Second Part: It was then that the laying down of the early parts of the maze of progression began to be revealed, and this was taken up by the participants in a surprising give-way easement." '

Vital looks up and smiles: 'Now, you've got to admit that this is very strange language.'

'Yes,' people murmur.

'But you also know that – if you think of it – you somehow *know* what he's talking about.'

A buzz of approval.

'So this phrase, "Laying down a maze of progression . . ." Leo's laying down a maze of progression, so that if you put yourself at the centre, you're in the maze. Then you're likely to progress, aren't you?'

'Yes,' we say.

'. . . In order to get out of it.'

The congregation assents, 'Right.'

'Or in order to find out where you are in it.'

After about five hours of this I have had enough. I quietly get up and leave. The meeting will probably go on for several more hours, late into the evening. Lance follows me out, concerned at my departure. He leans into my car window: 'Take good care driving back to London,' he says. 'It's very powerful, what you've heard tonight. It can leave you shaken up.'

'Right,' I say and drive away. That's the last Emin meeting I attend: I leave the maze.

11

For weeks I still get messages on my ansaphone. 'Hello there. Message for William.' I recognise Lance's voice. 'There's going to be quite an amazing meeting going on on Sunday – um – and it would be great if you could get there. And it would be great to hear from you.'

'Hi. It's Constance. Can you call me today about a meeting.'

'I guess you're away at the moment, but you might want to know, regular meetings have moved to Tuesdays and Fridays, because there is a new Emin Jewels group meeting on Mondays and Thursdays. Hope you can make it.'

'Hello, William, this is Core. The Emin Jewels have been invited to a meeting of the Gemrod Endeavour at the Southern Lights Centre at 11.15 on Sunday morning. We haven't seen you for a while, William. Are you busy?'

Months after I've left the Emin, I call up Jeremy. He's busy again, producing an album for a new rap band, and that isn't leaving him time to go to the Emin. But he misses it a lot. 'Some of what they were doing was very real,' he tells me.

We talk. 'I could never work that out, if they're just going round in circles,' he says, 'or whether some of the things they're talking about just can't be put into written words.' Some things got him frustrated: the vagueness about money, for instance. He carried on paying £10 a week long after everyone else was paying £15, because despite the fact he's fairly well heeled, he didn't want to give more until someone explained what it was being used for. When he asked, he never got a decent answer. He doesn't put this down to malice, simply incompetence. 'They were so vague and unspecific about their goals,' he complains.

He's a searcher, a nouveau hippie, long hair and expensive clothes, keen to embrace the possibility of other worlds. I ask him why he didn't stick up for Jo when she made her stand. He answers that he was uneasy about that, but he felt he should accept what the Emin said as a whole, or not at all. 'It's like *The Silver Chair*,' he says. In the C. S. Lewis children's book a prince, bewitched by an evil queen by day, believed at night he turned into a raving monster, accusing the queen of treachery. To set himself free, he would have to believe all the apparently outlandish things he said in the hours of darkness, however strange and contrary they appeared. And in spite of anything negative, he says that some of the nights in those long meetings, he felt what he calls 'really powerful atmospheres'.

In December comes the Healing Arts Festival, another cranky hypermarket run by the British company New Life Promotions Ltd., the same people who laid on the Festival Of Mind, Body And Spirit. It's a chance to find yourself and get some Christmas shopping done at the same time. Beaming health enthusiasts sell Peking Royal Jelly. People hand you leaflets for strange, bobbly wooden massage devices that promise to cure anything from 'paralysis from stroke' to cancer and poor memory. A stall trumpets: 'Change your Life Forever with Anna Sawdon'. Anna Sawdon has decorated the stall with her own garish oil paintings of mystical symbols. She promises 'Cosmic Healing' for a trifling £15.

The aisles are packed for the four days of the festival. People bustle in the queue for Kirlian photography. It costs £15 for a photograph of your hands and a consultation. The picture shows an outline of your hands from which sprout tiny black lines, like iron filings stuck to a magnet. The black lines represent tiny amounts of electrical energy. That, they claim, is your aura.

Elsewhere in the hall is Kirlian photography's latest rival, Aura Photography. Dozens of snaps of happy customers are pinned up around the stall. Around their heads hang hazy greeny-yellow blobs, sometimes tinged with red or blue, artificially dubbed on to the photo by a system that measures the minute electrical field around one hand and translates them into colours. That's your aura too.

Upstairs in the lecture rooms, crowds pack talks by self-help gurus. You can attend lectures: 'Think Happy – Be Happy', or 'Initiation in the Sacred Hoop – Self Empowerment'. An American called Therese Godfrey is giving a talk called 'You Can Do It!'. In the programme, it promises that Therese will move us, make us laugh, and show us how we can truly do anything we want. Therese, it tells us, used to be an overweight, non-athletic smoker who learned that She Can Do It! She crossed the finishing line of the Kona Ironman World Championship Triathlon, which we're told is 'one of the world's toughest endurance events'.

I wander round in a daze. A nice Chinese woman hands me a free book called *The Key of Immediate Enlightenment* by the Supreme Master Ching Hai. The Supreme Master is actually a woman; a young fresh-faced Taiwanese guru who dresses in startling yellow robes and who preaches vegetarianism and yet another type of meditation. The woman tells me that if I sincerely recite the phrase 'Namo Ching Hai Wu Shang Shih', which acknowledges that Ching Hai is the Supreme Master, I will be saved.

'Professor Trance and the Energisers' hand me a leaflet called 'The Way of the Energisers'. It says, 'The Energisers reincarnate whenever collective religion becomes dogmatic and repressed by fear. They return in these times to reawaken our spirituality through our passion . . . We are rebels, creators, the re-birthers of spirituality and therefore the origin of and founders of all religions.' If I join them in Amsterdam they say they will teach me how to trance dance, and how to unlock my 'Serpent Energy' by something called Sexual Bioenergetics. I will also learn the 'Sexual Positions of Empowerment'. I can take a lot of drugs too, if I want: 'We value the use of natural hallucinogens or "teacher plants" for the purpose of dissolving ego and its tight cognitive structure . . . We are not fully using our human potential, nor are we in touch with "the potential reality" unless we have had a psychedelic experience.' So. The Energisers take hallucinogens, have sex, and imagine they're comic book super-heroes. It passes the time.

The Centre for Contemporary Shamanism have pinned up some photographs of their recent gatherings. One stands out a middle-aged man, naked except for a white waistband, kneels on the floor in front of a few offerings, caught half-way through some earnest ceremony. By his side a plump woman covered only from her waist downwards in a wrap, dances ecstatically and shamelessly, her huge bare breasts caught in mid swing.

Another picture, this time at the Scandinavian Yoga and Meditation Centre stand also catches my eye. In the photo, a smiling, pretty, blonde Nordic woman is pouring water into one nostril with what looks like a small ceramic teapot. The water streams out of her other nostril. As I'm trying to figure it out, a young bearded man behind the counter says, 'Would *you* like to try it?'

'What is it?' I ask.

'Nose cleaning,' he explains. He fills a little pot with warm water, adds a teaspoon full of salt and shows me how to poke the spout of the pot up my right nostril. Tilting my head, a steady stream of warm water starts, rather surprisingly, to trickle out of my other nostril. I pour for a minute or so, feeling the water pass through me, until the pot is empty. It is a peculiar sensation, though it doesn't leave me flushed with the feeling of inner cleanliness I suspect it is supposed to. Instead my nose dribbles damply, and the polite young man offers me a Kleenex. I wait for him to start trying to sell me a nose pot (£7), but he doesn't. Instead he hands me a leaflet that claims that another 75,000 people have also learned nose-cleaning from the Meditation Centre. He obviously thinks it's enough reward that I have learned the technique.

It's like a giant freak show, each stall presenting ever-stranger phantasmagoria. I watch a man lying on his side, with a burning candle poking out of his left ear. When I enquire, a stall-holder tells me that this is an ancient Hopi cure.

The biggest set up of all is always the National Federation of Spiritual Healers. They run a sort of psychic hospital. Dressed in sober white medical coats, men and women hover around their seated patients, pressing hands on heads, or on any part of the body that requires healing. Silently, frowning with the concentration, the doctors of the invisible paw the air around their sufferers in a strange, solemn dance. The ill sit there, equally earnest.

Meanwhile, up on a small stage, a robed Englishman with a Sikh head-dress and with a magnificent two-foot-long beard, expounds on the wonders of Kundalini Yoga. He is the perfect picture of the western image of an eastern wise man. Only his plummy, middle-class tones disrupt the picture. 'It is an attitude for your life,' the guru explains, sitting cross-legged in front of a microphone. 'We have forgotten our natural way of being and we need to unlearn, and relearn . . .'

Our teachers, our parents, our scientists, our TVs, our priests, our governments have misled us, and the fundamental wisdom of the ages has been distorted and perverted. Under so much here today, under the loud, smiling professions of love and purity, simmers a rage. I have been cheated. Everything I know is wrong.

I wander round, an outsider, dazed, amused, full of uncomprehending outsider's reactions, like: if the mundane world has become too much, too complex, too frightening, too hostile for these people to cope with, why are they dreaming up an even stranger, and more Byzantine one?

At the far end of the hall sits the stall for the Eminent Theatre Journey. The Emin. It is two months since I last attended a meeting. I recognise Mark and Opal running the stall. Will they be hostile or feel I have let the vision down by leaving? I approach and we shake hands, like old acquaintances embarrassed at not having seen each other for years.

'How are things?'

'Fine, yeah, great. Yeah,' Mark smiles awkwardly. 'You?'

I glance at a table, full of strange Emin props. A compass, a magnet, a picture of some flowers and a bell, and it brings back all the interminable rituals in the Welsh school on Willesden Lane. I ask Opal how it's going. She says, 'You're not coming to meetings any more?'

'No.'

She doesn't ask me why not. 'Some people stop coming,'

she shrugs, 'for . . . you know, whatever reasons.' She smiles. 'There aren't many of your group left now. I went on holiday and when I came back it seemed like everybody had gone.' Mandy, Jeremy, Jo and I have all left. Oliver left for college. Even Stone Bear doesn't go any more. Others stayed for a while, then drifted away.

I look around. There are cassettes and books on display. It's twice as big a stall as the last one. Maybe they're recruiting a lot of new members now. Seeing them here again makes me wonder if, for an enclosed, secretive, fragile organisation like the Emin, coming to a brash place like this, full of other groups who also claim to be the one true way, is like visiting hell. How can they sustain their ever-mutating creed in the face of all these other no less surprising certainties? How can they resist Anna Sawdon changing their lives, or Therese 'You Can Do It' Godfrey. Do they ever wonder about the Energisers who claim that they are the origin of all religions?

Opal looks exhausted. 'Yes I am really tired now,' she admits. 'It's been busy.'

I ask her if many people have shown interest.

'*Some* have,' she says, a little disappointed, but still smiling invincibly. 'Some are just interested in the tapes, some aren't really interested at all, but a few are . . . you know, genuinely interested.'

They are holding new Search For Truth courses for the 'genuinely interested'. For some, the whole process is starting all over again. I watch Mark enthusiastically questioning a young couple about whether they think there's more to life than just the world they can see in front of them. I can't hear their answer.

I shake hands and go, glad to get away. Opal wore an exhibitor badge on her jacket. It said that her name was Alice, something I had never known before.

Months later one of the Emin calls me up. In the London phone book there's a number listed as the 'Emin Network' and I've been leaving messages on an ansaphone for weeks, saying I was writing about them and needed to check some facts about the

Emin. Finally in late March a man called David calls me back. I don't recognise his voice.

The Emin, he tells me, simply don't exist. 'There isn't an organisation called the Emin, as such,' he insists. 'It's just a loose affiliation of people who once *used* to be in an organisation called the Emin Foundation which ceased to exist in the early eighties.' The Emin, he says, disbanded in about 1983 or 1984.

'So what about the Gemrod Petition and the Gemrod Endeavour?' I ask.

For a second, my caller sounds a little alarmed that I know about them, but answers that they are just small independent clubs who research into esoteric matters. They're no different from sports clubs, except their interests, he says, are a little deeper. Some people have tried to label them a cult, or a New Religious Movement, which is absurd. It's not a religion. 'We just carry out work of a philosophical nature.'

When I ask him what the connection is of these 'independent clubs' with the Florida headquarters, he replies, defiantly, 'Well, there *isn't* one. All the groups act totally independently. There is no particular connection with Florida.' At this point he becomes anxious to end the call. He does not want to answer questions over the phone, he says. If I want to note them down and send them to him, he will supply some written answers. 'You see, we've had trouble with journalists. A great deal of reporting has been, shall we say, sensationalist. We have never been taken seriously. They seem determined to paint us in the worst possible light,' he says. 'There is absolutely no harm in what we do.'

'No,' I agree. After all, they don't even exist.

'You seem to have done some research already. Can I ask where you got this information from?' he asks.

'Oh,' I say, 'an ex-member.'

THREE

The Age of Kali-yuga

1

Two homeless boys are lurking outside the temple in Soho Street, central London, a door next to Govinda's Vegetarian Restaurant. A young Krishna devotee asks them if they want to come in for a meal and listen to a bit of teaching from the *Bhagavad-gita*. The older boy, wrapped in a grey blanket, pulls his friend away. 'They're devil worshippers in there,' he shouts. 'That's what you are, fucking devil worshippers.'

The devotee, clad in saffron robes, is not much older than them, with a U-shaped ochre *tilaka* mark on his forehead, rising from the bridge of his nose to his forehead. The make up is made with clay from the River Ganges. It represents the foot of Krishna, pressed on his head.

In the downstairs window there is a series of models depicting our reincarnation. A baby, a boy, a young man, and so on, round to a crabbed ancient who dies, becomes a skeletal corpse and is reincarnated as a baby again. The light bulbs which once traced the circular path of life no longer function.

From up the stairs you can hear the sound of hand cymbals, *kartals*, and chanting.

The first time I hesitantly walk in off the street. 'OK to look round?' I ask the plump woman dressed in a pink sari. She looks up from fingering her beads behind a desk on the ground floor. 'Sure,' she answers, taken aback that I should even bother to ask. 'First floor. You should take your shoes off.'

I thank her. 'Hare Krishna,' she calls after me up the stairs. A pile of footwear is stacked outside the first-floor temple door. A notice warns you not to leave any valuables outside.

In the white temple room, His Divine Grace A. C. Bhaktivedanta Swami Prabhupada sits cross-legged under a painted wooden canopy, impassively watching the *kirtan*, a ceremony of dancing and praying, singing and chanting the names of God. He is a little shinier than he was in life, but other than that the statue, made of resin, is extraordinarily lifelike. In the mornings, a pair of spectacles is placed on his nose, so he can scan the copy of the *Srimad-Bhagavatam* propped up in front of him. In cold weather, his bald head is covered by a woollen cap. His mouth, as in life, is caught in a broad half-smile.

At the other end of the ornate temple room, behind an iron screen, stand the deities; statues of Krishna and his consort Radha, immaculately dressed in huge, elaborate purple robes, heavily sequinned and intricately embroidered. To their left stand the deities of the other incarnations of Krishna – including the huge, saucer-eyed Jagannatha, who to the uninitiated looks like a gonk on speed, but who is Krishna in an ecstatic incarnation. The room, painted a clean white, has stylised pictures of the blue flute-playing God, Krishna, around alcoves in the walls.

The devotees performing *kirtan* are chanting the names of God, banging Bengali *mridanga* drums, ecstatically swaying backwards and forwards before the deities, and spinning round in a circle on the marbled linoleum floor. Some men wear Indian-style *dhotis* and *kurta* shirts. The women are dressed in bright saris, bright cotton material wrapped around their heads. They sing, 'Jaya Prabhupada, Jaya Prabhupada!' All glories to Prabhupada.

The temple always smells of sweet incense. It lingers on my clothes for days afterwards. A garland hangs around Prabhupada's neck and flowers have been placed in vases around him. This wintry morning, someone has also thought to clothe Prabhupada, the latest in a line of thirty-two disciples that stretches back to Lord Krishna himself, in a grey woollen cardigan from Marks and Spencer's.

The son of a cloth merchant, Abhay Charan De was born in 1896 in Calcutta and studied Sanskrit, Philosophy, English and Economics at the local Christian Scottish Churches College. At around twenty-three his family arranged for him to marry an eleven-year-old girl, and when he'd found a job as a department manager with Bose laboratories, she moved in with him. But Abhay was drawn to a religious life within the ancient tradition of Vaishnava Hinduism, a devotional sect founded by the sixteenth-century monk Lord Chaitanya Mahaprabhu, who believed that by chanting the name of Krishna, the only true God, and by studying his works and devoting ourselves to his service, we could free ourselves from the cycle of birth and rebirth.

In his devotion, he left jobs, allowed businesses to fail, became unable to support his wife, and repeatedly tried to carry out vows to spread knowledge of Krishna. In 1953 he finally abandoned his wife to become a celibate holy man, after she had sold some of his books to raise money for food. After initiation, he adopted the Sanskrit name A. C. Bhaktivedanta Swami Prabhupada, and started wandering around India visiting and worshipping at Krishna temples.

It was in 1965 that he became filled with a missionary conviction to take Krishna Consciousness to the most spiritually dark place on earth. So it was on 17 September that year that the sixty-nine-year-old guru landed in America at Boston's Commonwealth Pier, with only a pair of *kartal* cymbals, a suitcase and seven dollars, horrified at the scale of his task.

He wrote a mournful prayer to his God: 'My dear Lord Krishna, You are so kind upon this useless soul, but I do not know why You have brought me here. Most of the population is covered by the material modes of ignorance and passion. Absorbed in material life they think themselves very happy and satisfied, and therefore they have no taste for the transcendental message of Vasudeva [Krishna]. I do not know how they will be able to understand it.'

Krishna's timing, however, appears to have been excellent. In 1966 he was strolling New York's grim Bowery district, when a group of middle-class college-educated hippies spotted the old man, dressed conspicuously in saffron and white pointed shoes. They approached him eagerly and were invited to attend a lecture on the *Bhagavad-gita* – part of the *Mahabharata* which consists of a dialogue between Lord Krishna and his disciple Arjuna. They were hippie searchers who had experimented with acid and peyote, read Plato and Lao Tzu, and dabbled in anything from Buddhism to astral travel. Now they had their own personal guru.

Within a few months the calm, authoritarian guru had managed to persuade these feckless, well-heeled drifters to take up a life which appears to have turned the liberalism of the times on its head. To become a devotee of Krishna one must practise strict sexual abstinence unless married. Alcohol, drugs, gambling, meat and fish are all forbidden. One must turn one's back on all forms of 'sense-gratification' and chant the names of Krishna daily.

In July 1966 the gentle but stern old man and a few devoted hippies formed ISKON, the International Society for Krishna Consciousness. Aided in its earliest days by the beat poet Allen Ginsberg, the movement mushroomed with extraordinary speed. Prabhupada's innocence and devotion attracted many. He told them, 'The word guru means heavy.' That they understood.

They, in turn, had to explain to him what LSD was. They told him how to attract followers with psychedelic posters to concerts and happenings. Prabhupada was shocked by the prevalence of sense-gratification. After they had stormed New York they moved to Haight Ashbury in San Francisco and the self-denying Calcuttan appeared on unlikely billings with Ginsberg, LSD guru Timothy Leary, Moby Grape and scatological rock group the Fugs, writers of such tunes as 'Group Grope'. Krishna, bare-footed, long-haired, playing the flute surrounded by girlfriends, one of the most ancient images of a deity, looked like a perfect hippie role model.

The gay Ginsberg was more a spiritual tourist than a devotee. He wasn't so keen on abandoning all sense-gratification. At one lecture in New York's Tompkin Square Prabhupada enjoined all his followers to act like 'innocent boys'. As the words passed the guru's lips, a lascivious guffaw suddenly burst from Ginsberg.

Krishna Consciousness first arrived in Britain in 1968. Growing up in Calcutta under British Rule, Prabhupada was always keen to return something to the land that had taught him Shakespeare, so he dispatched three married couples to London to seek influential followers amongst the youth movement, following his success conquering youth culture in New York and San Francisco.

In February of that year the Beatles had gone to India to see the Maharishi Mahesh Yogi, so he reasoned they would obviously be interested in what he had to offer. For days Prabhupada's missionaries waited outside the Beatles' Apple office in Saville Row, sending in offerings of holy food known as *prasadam* and trying to catch a glimpse of the Fab Four. They finally doorstepped George Harrison, who invited them to lunch and they told their plan to him; they would record the Hare Krishna mantra together. George Harrison agreed, though he proposed they cut down the mantra to only three and a half minutes, 'So they'd play it on the radio,' he explained pragmatically.

In August 1969 'Hare Krishna Mantra' by a group who named themselves the Radha Krishna Temple reached number 12 in the charts, and Krishna Consciousness burst upon Britain. A steady stream of hippies started to make their way to the brand new temple they had established in Soho Street. Prabhupada's own guru, Guru Maharaj had attempted a mission to convert the British back in 1933, but it had failed.

When Prabhupada arrived the next month to open the London temple in Soho Street, he was driven from Heathrow airport in John Lennon's white Rolls-Royce.

George Harrison later sold them his Hertfordshire estate at a reduced price, which they renamed Bhaktivedanta Manor, to the fury of stiff-upper-lipped locals who have been campaigning to have the temple closed down ever since.

Understandably, Prabhupada was proud of achieving what his own master had failed to do. Prabhupada wrote, 'The boys and girls in London are doing very nicely.'

On my first visit I gawp at everyone touching their foreheads on the lino as they enter or leave the temple room: such acts of devotional subservience are alien to us in the west. The next time I drop by, I decide to do the same, partly because it seems to be the respectful thing to do, partly to see what it feels like. I drop awkwardly to my knees, embarrassed, lowering my head to the cold floor, but when I look up, no one is staring at me as though I'd done anything bizarre.

After the first time it's easy. Sometimes I look up after prostrating myself and I do catch a startled look on someone's face – but that's always the face of a newcomer, invited in by the devotees who trawl up and down distributing Prabhupada's works on Oxford Street. Acts of self-abasement and servitude to Krishna, or to temple seniors, are part of daily life in the temple. For the westerner the fear of this submission becomes part of the attraction. It turns western liberality on its head.

I start turning up regularly, two or three times a week. At first nobody really takes much notice of me. They're used to people dropping in to sample the temple. I become a vaguely familiar face to devotees who greet me with a 'Hare Krishna!' Sometimes I arrive at 7am to join the disciples performing the morning *kirtan*, then share a breakfast of *prasadam* with them. By the time I get to the temple priests have carefully bathed and dressed the deities; the devotees who live in Soho Street have already been awake for three hours. Others like myself drift in and out during the long ceremony, where the men dance before the statues and the women dance behind the men. At around 8am each morning, an Asian postman comes in, lays flat on the floor, deposits a few coins in the offertory box in front of the deities, then goes home to bed. Other times I attend lunch-time and evening programmes to listen to readings from the *Bhagavad-gita* or the *Srimad-Bhagavatam*.

On the second floor there's a small shop selling incense, Krishna badges and some of the many translations and meditations Prabhupada wrote. One day an older devotee, in his forties, urges me to buy a copy of the guru's book *The Bhagavad-gita As It Is*, a tape of Prabhupada chanting, a set of *japa* chanting beads and the small orange bag which disciples keep them in. 'Who knows,' he says, 'you may be one of those rare souls who have already found your way on the spiritual path in previous lives.'

His name is Adikarta dasa. Lean, and with a slightly world-weary air, he is an Englishman who was initiated by Prabhupada before his death in 1977. He shows me how to chant, counting one bead each time I recite, 'Hare Krishna, Hare Krishna, Krishna Krishna, Hare Hare, Hare Rama, Hare Rama, Rama Rama, Hare Hare.'' Repetition of the names of God brings you closer to Godhead. The string contains 108 beads. Prabhupada decreed that devotees should complete sixteen rounds a day. It takes about two hours, non-stop.

'Look at this,' says Adikarta, holding up my hand. 'We're all blood and pus. We're rotting. Life on earth is just birth, death, old age and disease. All the time we do things to try to make us happy, but we're not happy. Happiness on earth is an illusion, *maya*. But if we remember we can leave our earthly bodies by chanting, and by learning devotion to Krishna.'

If you walk into the temple while several devotees are chanting, the noise is like a swarm of bees. Some pace the floor, back and forth, brows knitted in concentration; others sit cross-legged against the wall where figures of holy cows are depicted in bas-relief.

Adikarta asks me what I do for a living. I tell him I'm a pop-music journalist.

'Oh yeah?' he smiles. 'Do you know Nick Kent?' Nick Kent is a well-known music journalist who writes passionately about rock music; heroin-thin and clad in black, he hung out with Keith Richards and the Stones in the 70s and was briefly famous for being assaulted with a chain by Sid Vicious.

'I smacked him in the face once,' Adikarta says proudly. 'He was having this big argument with Chrissie Hynde one day, so I whacked him one. Knocked his tooth out.' He grins, 'Of course, that was before I found Krishna.'

An odd coda to Adikarta's story. When I speak to Nick Kent about the incident, he confirms the tale. It was the worst thing that ever happened to him. He remembers his girlfriend of the time, Chrissie Hynde, used to work in Sex Pistols' manager Malcolm MacLaren's King's Road clothes shop, Sex. So did a man whom Kent believes was having a nervous breakdown at the time. One day Kent had a serious row with Hynde, who he believed had been sleeping with other men, and Chrissie's fellow shop worker suddenly turned violent, attacking Kent and chipping one of his teeth. Two weeks later, remembers Kent, the man flipped and flung himself out of a high window, apparently in a suicide attempt. The only thing that saved his life was that he fell on to the roof of a parked car below. Now, here is the former Sex sales assistant, preaching sexual abstinence, telling me of the prurience of my flesh and instructing me how to chant the names of God.

It's a strange clash of cultures. The Soho Street temple sits between a yuppie wine bar, Taylors, and a gay rendezvous called The Edge, both places of intoxication and sense-gratification where overpaid media youths bray into mobile phones. The religion itself is an ancient one, and Prabhupada himself was the follower of an ancient tradition of teachers, but here in Soho advertising land, half a world away from Calcutta, the drama of worldly rejection seems almost flamboyant. The denial of the western values the devotees grew up with becomes a spiritual mission. In the Hare Krishnas, you learn Sanskrit, you deny Darwinian evolution, you prostrate your unworthy body on the floor, and instead of glorifying the body beautiful, you regard it as a bag of rotting meat. Women cover their bodies from head to toe to avoid arousing lust. Possessions are kept to a minimum. There is a TV upstairs, but solely for watching videos of Prabhupada's lectures.

One Sunday afternoon at the Soho Street temple some Asian tourists come in and stand to one side of the temple, watching the young sock-footed devotees playing drums and singing in Sanskrit. The white devotees shake their heads from side to side, bang their *mridangas* and dance with their palms raised in adulation. A young Asian girl videos them. I have a fantasy – probably inaccurate, but fun to indulge – about them showing it when they get back home: 'Look Auntie-ji, just *look* what they're doing these days in London.' As they leave, Kesava Bharati, the American president of the Soho temple calls after them, 'Come back any time.'

After 1pm, following a *kirtan*, the singing of devotional songs, a verse from the *Bhagavad-gita* is read. '*Yasya sarve samarambhah . . .*' reads a young man. 'One who is understood to be in full knowledge whose every endeavour is devoid of desire for sense-gratification,' the young disciple recites Prabhupada's translation. 'He is said by sages to be a worker for whom the reactions of work

have been burned up by the fire of perfect knowledge.' Prabhupada created a spiritual hothouse. Today's lean-faced lecturer has
been in ISKON for only three years.

In the early morning, when the *Srimad-Bhagavatam* is read, we
repeat each Sanskrit word aloud, and then together, the whole
verse. But the lunch-time session is a more casual affair, an
introduction for newcomers.

Next the young disciple reads the 'Purport', Prabhupada's
sermon on the verse; written in the elderly Calcutta man's old-
fashioned formal Anglo-Indian English. The fusty language gives
his writing its own holy dignity. 'Only a person in full knowledge
can understand the activities of a person in Krishna consciousness. Because a person in Krishna consciousness is devoid of all
kinds of sense-gratificatory propensities. Development of this
knowledge of eternal servitorship to the Lord is compared to fire.
Such a fire, once kindled, can burn up all kinds of reactions to
work.'

Today's lecturer, wearing a sweatshirt that says 'Chant Hare
Krishna' looks up and starts to improvise around Prabhupada's
theme. 'We should listen in a submissive way,' he tells us. 'I don't
mean we have to accept dogmatically, but we should enquire. We
should never stop enquiring, Prabhupada said.'

Some listeners, uncomfortable on inch-thin foam cushions,
shift stiff limbs on the floor. Others remain cross-legged. A few
homeless, who've come for the free food, slumber. Curtains have
been drawn to hide the deities. Unseen, a priest is performing his
ceremonies of obeisance; we can hear him ringing a muted bell
before them.

'Scientists in their ignorance say all this was created from a big
bang,' the devotee is saying, cross-legged on a pink cushion.
'Scientists can make water, but they can't make an ocean. They
can tell you every last substance that is in a leaf, but can a scientist
actually make a leaf? Of course not.'

He shakes his head. 'If a scientist talks about a molecule, "Come
into my laboratory and look down this microscope and I'll show
you it," we don't answer and say, "I don't have to come into your
laboratory and look at your microscope. You're just brainwashing

me." It's funny,' the young man smiles, 'we accept microscopes and place faith in them, but we don't place faith in people who talk about the scriptures which are thousands of years old.'

Krishna Consciousness is, in a way, a form of fundamentalism. Krishna, in all his forms, is not a metaphor, or a representation, but a real God; one of the cornerstones of faith of the sect that Prabhupada came from is that other 'impersonalist' forms of Hinduism that deny the tangibility of a real Krishna as the supreme Lord in all his many forms are absolutely rejected. The statues at the end of the room are not simply depictions of Krishna, they *are* Krishna. 'No other religion shows you exactly what Krishna looks like,' the devotees announce.

We are living in the Age of Kali-yuga, 'the age of quarrel and hypocrisy', a time of decline into darkness which lasts 432,000 years, which began only 5,000 years ago when Krishna appeared in India. If we reach Krishna consciousness, abandon our materialist illusions, we will leave our earthly form and start our journey to higher planets, all of which are named in the scriptures.

Despite Prabhupada's genial smile and gentle manner, he was unerringly strict about doctrine. When a rival 'impersonalist' Hindu guru visited Bhaktivedanta Manor and distributed leaflets contradicting his tradition's teachings, a furious Prabhupada ordered his followers to use them as plates to eat their food off.

The devotees are mostly in their twenties and thirties, though some, like the temple president, are older. It is a devout, ascetic life. The men sleep in bunks in a dormitory on the fifth floor, the women sleep in rooms on the floor below. They rise around 4am each morning and wash carefully. Cleanliness is vital in the temple. Their days are filled with ceremonial starting at 4.30 when they make the early-morning offering to Krishna, ringing bells and chanting before him.

It's easy to amble in and out of the temple. Despite the strictness of their own lives, the devotees are tolerant of people like myself wandering in occasionally off the streets. No one presses me to join in more fully, and most members are too caught up in their own services and devotions to spare energy to proselytise. I leave the temple after each visit, still bemused but impressed at their casual hospitality, returning to my sense-gratificatory ways.

My favourite time of day at the temple is the midday meal, when the ceremonial comes to a halt and all the devotees line up cross-legged on the floor, chattering, and the rich smell of Indian food drifts up from the restaurant kitchens below. A few homeless drift in for a free meal. Those who have returned from the morning's book distribution tell stories about the hard time they have had on the streets amongst the unbelievers. Visitors from other temples from around the world swap bits of news. 'I'm on my way to meet some devotees in eastern Europe,' one young man tells me. 'We're walking to Moscow with an ox and cart, taking Krishna Consciousness to the villages.'

'What do they make of you?' I ask. 'Oh, they're always very interested.'

'I bet,' I say imagining the bizarre sight these emissaries from the capitalist west, dressed in the costumes of eastern poverty, must make.

Another devotee tells me, proudly, 'Krishna Consciousness is the fastest growing religion in Russia.'

The Soho temple's *prasadam*, the holy food that has been offered to the deities, is delicious. Eating it, even in a state of ignorance helps free yourself from karma, and offering it to people is an act of service to Krishna, so anyone is welcome to join them at their midday meal. Disciples humbly dole out food from steel buckets: rice, *subji* – vegetables, *dal* and *halavah* – a delicious sweet made from grains, butter and raisins. They pay particular attention to serving the temple seniors.

'*Haribol!*' Devotees now greet me cheerily when I go into the temple. 'Chant Hare Krishna!' I have joined the ranks of laymen whose faces the robed and shaven devotees are used to seeing around the temple.

One day, I sit eating *prasadam* with my *Bhagavad-gita* open beside me. A disciple sitting next to me, a devout white Zimbabwean, leans over and says, 'You shouldn't really read holy books at mealtimes. If you think about it it's obvious. You might spill a great big blob of *prasadam* on it.'

I've already dropped *subji* on it, but he hasn't noticed. I close the book and put it on the floor. He carries on eating for a while, then leans over again.

'You shouldn't really put it on the floor. If you think about it . . .'

I place it on the shelf behind my head.

Later, when I'm asked to help serve *prasadam*, he says, 'No don't do that, you haven't washed your hands. And you shouldn't really hold the plate over the bucket. If you think about it . . .'

He used to be in a rock band, and came to London with dreams of making it in the music industry. He says he knows all about the lures of intoxication. Now he realises that rock music is just a form of sense-gratification. 'I used to dream of fame, but that is *maya*, illusion. Now I realise that all that is coarse. After a while it just didn't appeal to me.' Sometimes he delivers the lunch-time sessions, playing beautifully on a harmonium and singing Sanskrit prayers in a rich voice. He tells me, 'The best music, the only real music, is the music of the devotees. I have some tapes if you want to listen.'

After we've finished eating a young devotee wanders around with a small bowl for donations from visitors like myself. 'Whatever you give, Krishna will repay it a thousand times,' he beams. I drop £1.50 into the bowl.

One morning, after I've joined in the early *kirtan* and eaten a breakfast of rice and *subji* from my paper plate, I'm asked to perform a service of my own. On my knees, with a cloth and bucket, I slowly clean the tiles of the temple after morning *prasadam*. Another older devotee helps me. 'You should go to India,' he says. 'I'm saving to go and meet my spiritual master.'

In the Hare Krishna movement, everything Indian acquires a holiness. Many disciples not only adopt the clothes, but adopt a sort of odd body language too. Spurning the plastic spoons offered, they scoop up their *prasadam* with their fingers, and thank the servers with palms pressed together. Some even acquire twitchy pseudo-Indian neck movements.

I hang around the temple that day and help a couple of devotees shift furniture out of the library, where videotapes of Prabhup-ada's lectures are kept, so they can give the room a fresh lick of paint. On one wall hangs a plaster cast of Prabhupada's foot-prints, painted gold. At the lunch-time lecture, one of the women in a red sari sits behind the microphone and tells us in a northern England accent, that service and devotion to Krishna can make anything pure. 'Arjuna was a great warrior. He killed tens of thousands of men,' she says. 'But he suffered no bad reaction because of it because he was Krishna conscious.'

She tells us we must chant, and meditate on the greatness of Krishna. We don't have to come to the temple to do it. Krishna is anywhere. 'Sometimes it's not always easy to come to the temple. Some people might have parents who say you mustn't go there. It doesn't matter. Even those families who lock their children in their rooms and say, "They're a cult, they're trying to brainwash you!" and they put locks on the doors to stop you coming. But they can't stop you from thinking about Krishna.'

After lunch, upstairs in his office, Kesava Bharati, the temple president, is delivering a session known as Questions and Answers which newcomers are encouraged to go to. The guru tradition that Prabhupada came from requires leaders to be attentive to their servants, and servants to be ever inquisitive about Krishna.

I sit cross-legged on the floor opposite him. A young, round-faced girl in a hippie Donovan hat props herself up against a bookcase and says disappointedly, 'No stimulants?'

'No coffee, no tea, no alcohol,' smiles Kesava.

She says, 'I've heard that chocolate has caffeine in it.'

'Yes,' smiles Kesava. His low desk has a Motorola mobile phone on it and a laptop computer. Chapters from the new ISKON translation of the *Mahabharata* lie on a computer disk nearby.

'I have to give up chocolate?' she says, shocked.

'Yes. You do. It's not so hard.'

'Even *white* chocolate?'

Kesava is an American. He wears gold-rimmed glasses and his head is shaven. Grey hairs sprout in tufts from his ears. He laughs. 'Even white chocolate. Have you tried carob?'

The girl makes a face.

A small girl dressed in a sari and a pair of pink-framed spectacles comes in, prostrates herself before Kesava and joins us. She's Jenny, an American who first met devotees on holiday in Malaysia; she got stuck in London in transit to Israel, so she came to the temple to find somewhere to sleep and ended up staying two years.

'It's a small thing, giving up chocolate,' Kesava says. 'Once you've given it up you won't notice it. It's all part of becoming regulated.'

He unzips his specially bound *Bhagavad-gita* and announces, 'Chapter six, verse seventeen. *Yuktahara-viharasya, yukta-cestasya karmasu* –' He stops and looks up at Jenny. 'Have you learned this yet?' he asks sternly. She blushes and shakes her head. 'If you're not in, you're out,' he scolds.

He reads on: 'Extravagance in the matter of eating, sleeping, defending and mating – which are demands of the body – can block advancement in the practice of yoga.'

The disciple Jenny complains to him she has been finding it hard regulating extravagance in the matter of sleeping, 'But I feel tired all the time. Maybe I'm doing too much service?'

Kesava raises his eyebrows. 'If you're tired you must overcome it. You must concentrate on your service.'

Apart from the perpetual practice of book distribution, handing out Prabhupada's books in exchange for the donations that keep the temple running, women also spend hours sewing the exquisitely elaborate costumes that the deities are dressed in twice a day. After twenty-five years the temple now has 200 different sets of clothes for them.

'I just seem to always want to sleep more,' Jenny continues wearily.

'Well,' he concedes, 'we all need different amounts of sleep. Four hours, five hours, six, seven. We have to work out how much we need. Some people,' he says, incredulously, 'even need eight hours.'

Kesava draws the meeting to a close: 'I'd love to talk more, but I have sixteen rounds to chant.'

Jenny touches her forehead respectfully to the floor again and leaves.

I walk down the narrow stairs with the girl in the hippie hat. 'Ow,' she giggles and clutches the banister. 'I don't think I can do this. My knees are too fat for sitting cross-legged all the time. My legs have gone all funny.'

Considering he founded ISKON when he was seventy, Prabhupada achieved an astonishing amount in the twelve years before he died, galvanising a younger generation of spiritual devotees out of a rootless generation. He was undoubtedly the guru, the leader. One thing that he left in a mess, though, was the question of succession. He died leaving eleven successors, each in charge of geographic zones, but the nature of their role was less clear.

Introducing the oriental notion of the master–disciple relationship to the west had produced disciples, but no one was sure exactly what their new role of master meant. Some believed that they were there simply to deliver Prabhupada's message. Others believed that they were to assume Prabhupada's mantle as charismatic leaders.

Hansadutta Swami was a German guru, put in charge of the northwest US and parts of southeast Asia. After Prabhupada's death, he developed a taste for expensive sports cars and guns. 'Have the Krishnas turned violent?' screamed the press after repeated police raids for alleged arms violations. Hansadutta was relieved of his leadership by the movement's general council.

The story of Keith Ham is more extreme. He had been one of the very first band of converts who had stumbled on the aged guru wandering the streets of the Bowery. Prabhupada gave him the Sanskrit name Kirtananda Swami. Kirtananda became one of Prabhupada's favourites and became the guru leader of the West Virginian community of New Vrindaban, named after Krishna's birthplace. Prabhupada had dreamed of it being 'an ideal village where the residents will practise plain living and high thinking'. He proposed, 'they should keep cows and use the dung for fuel as in India, and use bulls to mill oil'. Several photographs of Kirtananda before his master's death show him, smiling, dressed in robes and open sandals, clutching his *japa* bag, often standing next to Prabhupada, his face radiating bright enthusiasm.

In 1986 two people who had been involved with power struggles at New Vrindaban were murdered. Following the discovery of one of their acid-dissolved bodies in a creekbed at the commune in 1987, Kirtananda was given a thirty-year prison sentence for racketeering, mail fraud and conspiracy to commit murder.

In London things went disastrously too. Here the leader was a Lebanese–American, James Immel, known as Jayatirtha, who had for years been a model disciple, living modestly. The responsibility of guru-dom seems to have been too much for him. Accused of drug abuse and of sleeping with female devotees, he was summoned before the general council in India and relieved of his post. Jayatirtha immediately phoned London and his disciples there boarded up the temple doors to prevent ISKON officials from entering the Soho Street building. A charismatic leader, he still retained a loyal following. Soon he was successfully out-manoeuvred by the governing body and became the first of Prabhupada's official successors voluntarily to leave the movement in 1982. The next leader, Bhagavan dasa, an American medical student, also ran up against the confusion of what his role should be. He, too, eventually left of his own volition in 1986 after criticism that he was too lordly in his approach. His attempt to take Prabhupada's mantle had included eating off a gold dish, drinking from a gold goblet, and supposedly keeping a BMW for his private use.

On 13 November 1987, a headless body was discovered in a shop called Knobs and Knockers in Regent's Park Road, London. The corpse was that of Jayatirtha. His murderer, John Tiernan, had been one of Jayatirtha's followers for years. He was discovered crying, with the severed head on his lap. He reportedly told the police, 'The head is off the beast.'

After his expulsion Jayatirtha had set up a small splinter group, which had travelled first to India, then Nepal, to England and California, with his followers, some of whom appear to have believed that he was a reincarnation of Jesus Christ. Tiernan followed him everywhere. Jayatirtha took LSD with one of his followers, Geraldine Saunders, a friend of Tiernan's, and became her common law husband, referring to her as 'Holy Mother'.

Later, when he began sleeping with another woman, Tiernan was devastated and began to see him as the beast predicted in the Book of Revelations. After the murder he said he felt 'euphoric', and told police, 'I did not want innocent children and men and women to be abused any longer. It is like the whole world has been lifted off my shoulders.'

The thirty-one-year-old Tiernan entered a plea of manslaughter due to diminished responsibility. He is still receiving treatment in a mental hospital.

Some disciples drift in and out of the temples, dipping in and out of the various differing regimes. One day an Irishman of around forty appears at one of the Question and Answer sessions. In the 70s he was a committed devotee, but has been footloose since then, going through occasional bouts of devotion, unsure of himself. 'What's your name?' asks the temple president.

The Irishman answers with his Sanskrit title which I can't make out. 'That's a beautiful name,' smiles Kesava. 'Where did you get it?' The Irishman smiles back and gives the name of one of the leaders who fell from grace in the discord after Prabhupada's death. Kesava pauses and nods. 'It was different then,' he answers. It sounds as if he is apologising to the Irishman. 'After Prabhupada left us we made errors. Sometimes we treated others like they were him. It was a mistake.'

After the disastrous interregnum, a new sense of proportion has returned to ISKON in recent years. A new national and international structure is slowly evolving to fill the place of the guru who left them. The excesses have been curbed.

Six months after I had sat with the American devotee Jenny during Questions and Answers when she had complained about the onerous nature of her service, she is sitting on the round pink cushion in the temple, addressing the lunch-time programme, teaching from the *Bhagavad-gita*, chapter 15, about the need for detachment and surrender to the Supreme Personality of Godhead. Her discontent seems to have evaporated. She says she has found her happiness in the service of Krishna.

She talks about the nectar of book distribution. In December, the London temple had a book marathon, a special push to give out as many books as they could. One of the favourite saffron-coloured sweatshirts that devotees wear is one that proclaims, 'World Revolution through Book Distribution'. That month they distributed 25,487 books and raised £103,912. Jenny describes how she stood in Oxford Street watching the Christmas shoppers, all busy desperately trying to placate their illusory need for sense-gratification, all miserable. When she approached some people for a donation they would yell at her and she'd smile back and say, '*Haribol!* Chant Hare Krishna.'

Afterwards I meet her in the library, where a young man is quietly mouthing Bengali and Sanskrit from textbooks, trying to learn the languages before he goes to India. I ask her if she really meant it when she said she felt blissful on Oxford Street. She smiles behind her pink-framed glasses and says, 'It's a completely different level of existence.'

Her mother, in America, is a Christian. Jenny is grateful for the Atlantic Ocean between them. She tells Jenny, 'Jesus is the only way.' She says, 'You're going to hell!'

2

One day a man who lives near me calls round. He's heard I'm writing about cults and says he was a member of a group known as the Brahma Kumaris for some years. Like ISKON, they are a sectarian Hindu group. 'Why do you want to talk about them?' I ask. The man thinks about this, then answers that one reason is that talking about it could be a sort of therapy. He left them ten years ago but he still thinks about them all the time. His life is in a mess.

Since leaving, he's never read anything about them and he thinks that it's time someone spoke out. But talking about them scares him. When he was a member he was told that the punishment for apostasy would be that he would cry tears of blood. He's not sure whether he believes that or not. 'What if I *am* defaming the truth?' he wonders. 'Then I am going to experience hellfire and damnation,' he says in his troubled Scots voice.

His name is John. He's in his early thirties and has bright blue eyes, pale rather feminine skin and long hair down to his waist, which he is forever pushing out of his face. He sits on my sofa and sips herbal tea and eats toast, unbuttered but with Marmite. He is a vegan. He was born into what he calls 'a pretty shitty family, a pretty seriously dysfunctional background'. He has few good words for his parents. His mother beat him, he says, when he started to go out with girls. 'They're not resolved people,' he says. 'A lifetime of psychotherapy and Oprah Winfrey shows. We have the material.' But his family background may account for his obsession with mysticism. His grandmother, and later his mother, used to go to a spiritualist church. He remembers standing outside the Hare Krishna temple in the hippie market at Greyfriars in Edinburgh, and wanting to go up and visit. His mother told him they gave you sweeties that made all your hair fall out.

Growing up, he caught the coat-tails of hippie-dom, reading *Oz* magazine and getting into motorbikes. At sixteen he had some sort of mental breakdown – which also formed the basis of his spiritual experience. It was, he says, 'a major freak out'. At first he wanted to kill himself because his family life was so awful. He broke down and cried, asking for help from whatever was out there. What happened next he describes in terms of feeling the sensation of light coming down from above, and of the eggshell breaking around him. He became hyperactive and his mind started racing for twenty hours a day. Everything appeared to be clear to him. To the alarm of his mother, his previously taciturn character appeared to have changed through 180 degrees. She sent him to see a therapist.

Obsessed by the spiritual, John started to search for the perfect faith that would answer his questions. He consumed huge numbers of guidebooks. At sixteen he read Arthur Waley's *Tao Te Ching*. He read textbooks of hippie millenarianism like *Survival into the 21st Century* and *Finding the Master*, which listed modern spiritual movements. He began carefully evaluating which one would be right for him.

After a spell at drama college, he began visiting various spiritual organisations. A fastidious man, he had to be absolutely sure he was joining the right one. He visited the new age community at Findhorn in Scotland, but was revolted by its middle-class values ('very New Age Club Med'). He tried ECKANKAR, a secret science of self-realisation invented by a Las Vegan. He experimented briefly with Scientology. He spent some happy days at the Hare Krishna temple in Soho Street, and at Bhaktivedanta Manor.

But he had already worked out what he thought he wanted from a religion, and he wasn't satisfied. It had to be free of charge, because he was suspicious of religions that you had to pay to join, it had to be non-evangelical, and it had to have an element of gentleness. It also had to be vegetarian. He was, he admits, looking for everything that was as far away as it could be from the Calvinism of his Edinburgh upbringing.

When he came across the Brahma Kumaris at a house in Tennyson Road, Kilburn, he was convinced that he had found the absolute and perfect religion. The Brahma Kumaris are, like ISKON, a recent development of an older Hindu tradition. They were started in 1937 by a diamond merchant called Dada Lekh Raj, who, at the age of sixty, believed he had become the channel for the god Shiva, the supreme soul. He gave up his business, changed his name to Prajapita Brahma, and started teaching a form of open-eye meditation and expounding his message from Shiva, until at the grand age of ninety-two he was killed in a plane crash.

What John especially liked about the Kumaris is that they are run by women. Women are in all the highest positions of spiritual authority in the movement. It wasn't, he admits now, exactly a coincidence that he had also chosen to go to a college in Yorkshire which had the highest female to male ratio he could find. However the Brahma Kumaris also practised total celibacy. He wonders now what part of his own psychology pushed him to embrace a cult that forbids men from even touching the sari-clad women to whom he admits he was often deeply attracted, and which elevates them to the status of untouchable leaders.

After meeting the London leader, a woman called Dadi Janki, John became a member of the sect. Meditation was hard at first, because it stirred up all the demons from his upbringing. But soon it became blissful. He describes his first months with the Brahma Kumaris as exactly like first love – with all the pain, and anxiety, and the feeling of needing always to be as close as possible to the object of his obsession.

His mother was distraught about him joining a cult. Anxious to placate her, the Kumari leadership insisted – against John's wishes – that he join a local household near his mother in Edinburgh, to deflect anti-cult groups' criticisms that the cult tore children away from their parents. His mother was not placated. John remembers her storming into the Kumari centre, refusing to remove her shoes, threatening to sue them, trying to fix him up with girls to break his celibacy. 'She made a real arse of herself,' he says. 'It was,' he believes, 'an incredible affront to my mother's ego. Because I was being taken away by another woman.'

He admits now that he probably did receive some pleasure from, as he puts it, 'stuffing it all in my parents' face, because I had such a fucking awful family experience. Not that I was deliberately doing it, but I was aware that this bunch of people were ten thousand times nicer than that bunch of people.'

As in ISKON, it was a life of self-discipline. John would rise in the Brahma Kumari household he lived in at 3.30am and have a cold shower. After that he would run to the centre, spend three-quarters of an hour meditating and return home to eat breakfast and prepare his workclothes. After another meditation there would be a lesson delivered by the local woman leader. Then he went to work for a full day on a government scheme. Back at the house in the evening he would wash again, change, eat and then meditate at the centre. In the evening he would teach meditation, or attend another lesson for two hours. After an hour's socialising he went to bed. He kept this up for a year, blissfully happy.

The first thing to crack was his sexual abstinence. He began masturbating, which made him feel spiritually drained and guilty. Members were encouraged to confess their sins in letters to the elders in India. He doesn't think anyone ever read them. He began to challenge the authority of the woman who led the group. He began to wonder what life would have been like if he had carried on working in the theatre.

He started on a period of self-doubt that has left him in mid-air ever since. 'I was unhappy,' he says. 'But I thought this could very well be God, because I was having all these amazing experiences, and their philosophy was pretty damn sensible. They were great people and very disciplined. So I thought I better stick in there and see what happens.'

I leave the room to make John another herbal tea. When I return he has woven his hair into a long plait.

Escaping Edinburgh John moved down to London and back into the community where he was originally happy. There the group was bigger and the atmosphere less intense. In India the Brahma Kumaris have become a huge organisation with consider-able influence, preaching peaceful global co-operation. They are highly regarded in the United Nations and have been affiliated as a Non-Governmental Organisation since 1980. The London group used to invite politicians and scientists to address their public meetings. Once John met Lord Carrington and was invited round for tea.

But the sect no longer fulfilled his need for a total religion. He discovered that many followers didn't follow the path with the same exacting discipline as he did. He began to turn against it. He began to see the saris and *kurtas* they wore and the spicy food they ate as a form of Hindu imperialism. Arguing with the upper hierarchy, he slipped from being one of the movement's shining stars to become one of the thorns in their side.

Worst of all, he began to believe that the members were being controlled by the hierarchy. 'In a sense it *was* just mind control,' he says. 'The philosophy ties up your mind. It sets you in a spin. It answers everything. As the ultimate Zen poem it locks you in and gets you to concentrate on this link with Shiva – so in one way it's not a bad deal, but I had to start questioning it.' It was, he admits, a form of self-indoctrination that was no longer adding up for him. The pressure of consensual behaviour was too much. 'I started to question the roadmaps, and that just wasn't in the picture of things.'

In 1984 he was involved running a wholefood shop, living away from the group, when the business collapsed and John found himself alone. He had a major mental breakdown. Life ground to a halt.

One of the main messages that Prajapita Brahma passed from Shiva was that we were at the end of the Age of Kali-yuga, the age of ignorance. In either 1986 or 1996, the world was going to end violently, probably in a nuclear war, to be rebuilt by the Brahma Kumaris who would start a new golden age. Despite questioning the sect, John was still unable to disengage himself from these teachings. For two years he wandered aimlessly around London, sleeping in the building vacated by the wholefood shop. He felt under immense stress. It was futile to do anything because the world was about to end. He remembers bursting into tears unexpectedly while queuing at the greengrocer's. He felt unable to communicate with anyone because no outsiders could understand the spiritual language he had learned with the Brahma Kumaris, and the Brahma Kumaris didn't want him either because he was a trouble-maker.

At the same time his apostasy troubled him. A Brahman who leaves the path is lower than the lowest of the low. He was haunted by the phrase that his Edinburgh leader had written to him in a letter the first time he had missed morning class, 'You will cry tears of blood.' 1986 came and went. The world didn't end.

John has been left in that strange never-never-land between cult and the outside world and he can't find a simple way out. He has only worked sporadically. 'I used to sweat at the thought of filling in a CV. How can I explain these things to people?' He finds occasional work as a driver for rich businessmen, both in Britain and in America. Other times he signs on.

He has had sexual relationships since leaving the Brahma Kumaris, but he feels that people find him strange because so much of his life is still tied up with something they do not understand. 'It's very, very, very difficult,' he says. 'Most of the time I'm in this nihilistic spiritual malaise. There is no God. What is worth doing?' He has tried therapy again, but he feels that even therapists recoil when they hear him talking about religion. He feels that they're always attempting to reduce his state of religious paralysis to a psychological problem they can understand. When they do occasionally try to encounter his belief, he finds them impossible to respect because he feels he has a much deeper understanding of a subject that they haven't even considered. 'A lot of the time,' he says, 'I'm seriously suicidal.'

He is still on a spiritual quest. The mundane world doesn't satisfy him. 'I've ridden a motorbike at 150 miles an hour, I've been in penthouses on Fifth Avenue, I've met the most powerful bankers in the world. I've even met Kylie Minogue in a nightclub. In terms of the world I've experienced it and it's not up to much. None of these things are worth aspiring to. Actually, that's not true. Kylie Minogue was worth aspiring to,' he laughs suddenly. 'I blew it completely. Went weak at the knees.'

He is trying to avoid meditation. It's still incredibly powerful for him, but it doesn't help his state of mind. It stops life dead in its tracks. 'I can't stop doing it,' he says. 'I'm like Ray Milland in *The Man with the X-Ray Eyes*.'

Those who leave cults enter a strange and impossible in-between world of belief and disbelief. Some pass through it easily. It's as if John has never emerged on the other side.

When I ask him if he blames anyone or anything he answers seriously: 'I want to know who this soul Shiva is, who spoke through Prajapita Brahma. Because if the world doesn't end in 1996, Shiva is basically a bullshitter.'

The anti-cult movement portrays cult members as zombie-like victims. In the cults I have joined that's obviously not the case. They are happy in their beliefs. But there are a few, like John for whom the process leads to derailment. His life is on permanent hold until 1996. What then? 'Basically, I have to wait for about three years,' he answers. 'If the world doesn't end in three years,' he laughs abruptly, 'I'm going in there with a shotgun. I'm getting my lawyers. Listen, I'm going to say, this is *serious*. You've got to come up with some answers.' He jokes about it. He plays with his plaited hair some more.

'I'm sort of gearing up for that. Until then I am literally dragging myself along . . . day by day.'

FOUR

Mars Sector 6

1

On 8 May 1954, something odd happened in Maida Vale. On that palely sunny spring day, a thirty-five-year-old man was finishing the washing up in his bedsit, carefully drying four plates, when a spaceman spoke to him. A crisp voice that seemed to come from inside his head boomed: 'Prepare yourself! You are to become the Voice of the Interplanetary Parliament.' Understandably startled, he dropped the plates on to the floor, where they broke.

George King, the son of a Shropshire schoolteacher, had become convinced from the age of fifteen that he was from a generation that would visit other planets. He had had a lifelong interest in both mysticism and science. Nevertheless, he was unsettled by the communication. He relates to his followers, who now reverently refer to the event as 'The Communication', how he didn't sleep a wink that night, and paced the floor of his small bachelor flat thinking about the momentous consequences of what had happened.

All his life George had inclined towards the mystical. He'd had a Church of England upbringing, singing in church choirs. But his mother was a psychic, and his grandmother had been quite a respected medium in her day. George grew up fascinated by eastern philosophy, diligently poring over the works of the imaginative Madame Blavatsky, founder of Theosophy and the great-granny of the spiritualist new age movement, whose peripatetic life as a medium at the turn of the century had spread a heavily re-written and romanticised version of oriental reincarnation beliefs around the western world. George King had been fascinated by her fantastical stories of a Great White Brotherhood who lived in the Himalayas, the secret immortal Masters she had dreamed up, pieced together from her own imagination and a grab-bag of oriental myth. But her writings were too complex and verbose and he believed there was something more yet to learn. The Communication confirmed it.

King had declared himself a pacifist during World War Two. Instead he served as a section leader in the fire service during the Blitz. He believes that his psychic powers helped him uncover survivors amongst the rubble. George had also practised yoga for many years, which gave him a mental stamina he now sees was part of the reason the space beings chose him.

Eight days after the Communication something equally startling took place. A portly figure, dressed in immaculate white, strode through his front door. Without opening it. George claims he recognised the apparition immediately as one of the great yogic masters who lived in the Himalayas. The Swami read his thoughts and announced, 'It is not for you to judge whether you are worthy to be chosen, my son,' and then proceeded to tell George that the world was in grave danger. Misguided atomic research and failing morals were imperilling life on Earth. As the new Aquarian age dawned, George was being called upon to help overcome the wrongs of materialistic science, and replace it with the holy occult sciences. To help him prepare to become the Voice of the Interplanetary Parliament, George would soon receive a letter from a school of yoga in London, inviting him to take a course in advanced Prana-yoga, a form of yoga in which the universal life force is controlled through breathing.

Having delivered his message, the rotund oriental left, passing once again through George's front door. In his own account of this supernatural event, George adds the melodramatic touch of dashing to the door to open it after the figure had disappeared, only to find that the corridor outside his flat was deserted.

Seemingly miraculously, the letter arrived. He attended the yoga classes, and having learned the necessary techniques, he began to receive communications from a 3,456-year-old Venusian known as the Master Aetherius. Thus it was that George King, sometime taxi driver, started his journey to become His Eminence Sir George King, OSP, Ph.D, Th.D, DD, Metropolitan Archbishop of the Aetherius Churches, Prince Grand Master of the

Mystical Order of St Peter, HRH Prince De George King De Santorini, and Founder President of the Aetherius Society, a religious movement that takes its religious imagery in equal measures from the redoubtable Madame Blavatsky and the more futuristic world of Dan Dare.

After thirty-five years as the Aetherius Society HQ, the shop at 757 Fulham Road has a slightly faded air about it. It is no longer the vanguard of the new age that it was in the 1950s. The walls are painted cream. On the ground level, there is a shop where you can buy copies of Sir George King's publications, oddly dated-looking books, with titles like *You Are Responsible!* which deliver King's warnings against the new invention, atomic power. Hanging on the wall are several carefully-painted signs: 'Operation Sunbeam. 432 phases performed'. 'Operation Condition – Condition Green'. It's a boyish, sci-fi world that has never grown up. Pictures of flying saucers displayed there are curiously similar to images in science-fiction magazines of the 50s – upside-down soup bowls with small port-holes for the aliens to peer out of.

A smart, middle-aged woman sits behind the desk smiling at me as I leaf through copies of the *Aetherius Society Newsletter*, full of news from members around the world. There are branches in Nigeria, Canada, America and New Zealand. When I buy a copy of the Aetherius Society journal *Cosmic Voice* ('Magnificent Celebration of our 33rd Birthday in America!', 'Outstanding Developments in Operation Power Light!', 'Latest Operation Sunbeam Phases'), she disappears into one of the back rooms to find some change.

'Have you seen one of these?' She hands me a leaflet: 'A Series of Self-Development Courses'. The courses include spiritual healing, mantra yoga, personal magnetism, kinesiology, pendulum dowsing and yoga breathing. 'Founded in 1955 by His Eminence Sir George King,' I read, 'the Aetherius Society is an organisation which teaches advanced metaphysics, and applies these principles in very practical ways for the benefit of the world as a whole.'

'I recommend the healing course,' she says. 'It's really frightfully good.'

*

The year after the Communication saw the Society launched on a wider world. George King embarked on a round of furious activity to promote his message. In January he started to book the Caxton Hall regularly for public meetings. In them he would descend into a trance and become 'overshadowed' by the Master Aetherius, or by one of the members of Madame Blavatsky's Great White Brotherhood, a gentleman named Saint Goo-Ling. Sometimes the communications came from a Martian bearing the rank Mars Sector 6. In a tremulous, deep voice, Sir George would relay these fantastical messages from outer space. On 4 June 1955, for instance, the Master Aetherius spoke through King. 'Good evening,' he boomed. 'It is with great pleasure that I can speak to you again.' He proceeded to instruct the listeners that they were to put water in a blue glass bottle and leave it in sunlight for fifteen minutes. The water, treated with added fruit juice, was to be drunk three times a day as a health-giving tonic. At the same meeting he announced that between 20,000 and 30,000 mother ships and 180,000 to 280,000 remote-controlled vessels had visited our planet to 'pour into your earth a great magnetic energy of which you are in urgent need'. At a later meeting he advised against sitting with your back to the engine whilst on train journeys. At another he announced that the Moon (or 'Luna' as he preferred to call it), was inhabited by disembodied creatures who lived in plastic 'bubbles' below the surface.

Mars Sector 6 is charged with the duty of looking after Earth. In his predictions for 1956 he warned of the danger of hurricanes but added that it was possibly going to be 'an excellent season for wool'.

Among the transcriptions of these early transmissions are wildly strange stories. Mars Sector 6 delivered a gripping account, to the astonished audience at Caxton Hall, of a great space battle which had taken place in 1954, unnoticed on Earth, but of huge importance to our survival. The Evil Fiends of Garouche, an intelligent species of fish, came to the solar system 'to annihilate all humanoid life on Earth by drawing away the atmosphere'. In the terrible confrontation, many Martians lost their lives. Three times, related the voice, George King came close to being killed in action around the Evil Fiends' satellite. Mars Sector 6, speaking through the hero's own lips, warmly praised Sir George's courage.

Mars Sector 6 had a very contemporary method of ending his transmissions. At the end of a message, Sir George, deep in trance, would bark, 'Martian relay . . . OUT!' before coming to.

The transmissions were painstakingly noted in the Aetherius Society's books and magazines. In them, the hero of the battle of the Evil Fiends of Garouche narrated his visits to Mars and Venus, and to the Satellite Number 3 which hovers invisibly round our planet, directing cosmic energies towards it. The tone of his writing is curiously Edwardian. In these fantastical, Swiftian adventures, King addresses us as 'dear readers'.

On 27 July 1958, at a meeting on Holdstone Down, King was overshadowed by the Master Jesus, who like Aetherius, also comes from Venus. Jesus delivered a modern-day address which the Aetherius Society hold as one of their most sacred documents, 'The Twelve Blessings'. Once a week they meditate to a reading of the blessings. About quarter of an hour before they are read the lights in the chapel are dimmed, and a green light is switched on. Incense is burned. Then the blessings are read: 'Blessed are they who work for peace . . . Blessed are the Planetary Ones . . .'

King's Aetherius Society struck a chord. The science of the Cold War 1950s had created miraculous and terrifying new weapons. People's suspicion of the new atomic power and the strange, unseen force of radiation was given voice in the Master Aetherius's warnings. An emissary from a far advanced civilisation, he warned of the grievous dangers of the science of atomic fission, which he implored us to abandon. King claimed to be the herald of a new science, a sacred science, which would restore the balance to a Dr-Strangelove-world gone mad.

The Voice of the Interplanetary Parliament embarked on a series of colourfully-named missions which were based on capturing spiritual energy beamed at planet Earth, storing it in batteries of his own design, and releasing the energy at times of terrestrial crisis. There was Operation Starlight, which involved King climbing mountains around the world to charge them with spiritual energy. Operation Bluewater took eighteen months and saw King in a speedboat off California, executing a series of marine manoeuvres and directing energy to 'offshore psychic centres' to prevent earthquakes and floods. The Operation Prayer Power he started in 1973 was his most democratic movement, and still continues today. It can involve anybody, not just initiates, and captures our prayer powers in King's impressive-looking storage units, covered in dials and wires. The prayer power is ready to be released during 'emergency' periods. Our hands are 'spiritual guns' radiating energy to be used in the fight for Terra.

King was also among the first to attach religious significance to the flying saucers that were suddenly being spotted everywhere. A collection of sci-fi oddballs collected around Sir George, lingering on his every communication. Their enthusiasm was boundless. One of them, the irrepressible Harold Mattam, eagerly dashed around Britain in the late 50s on UFO-spotting trips, recounting them in the cult's magazine *Cosmic Voice*.

Mattam's missions weren't always successful, but they were full of an Englishman's enthusiasm for UFO spotting as an amateur pastime. When the Master Aetherius announced that UFOs would be visible above Whitstable in Kent on 7 and 8 May 1956, Mattam raced to the highest land in the area, climbing the biggest hill he could find.

He writes, 'Some way up I was strongly impressed to visit an inn, although not particularly wanting a drink. The landlord was the only person around and after he had served me, I asked him: "Do you know that flying saucers will be operating in Whitstable today?" The landlord, Mattam noted, looked flummoxed by this statement. 'He stopped his work, regarding me in a startled manner, and then gave a feeble grin.' Mattam doggedly tried to win him over, across the bar, probably consuming several more drinks in the process. 'I spent an hour with him and his wife and I feel sure that they are now firm believers.' That night Mattam, armed with his camera, waited patiently for the UFOs to arrive.

Sadly he admits he failed to see any, but records optimistically, 'I received a strong impression that space craft were in the area.'

George King, now a fragile elderly man, lives in a Los Angeles bungalow with his wife, whom he has grandly dubbed the Lady

Monique King, Bishop of the American Division. There is an Aetherius Centre there too, on the same block as King's home – just south of Sunset Boulevard. Both are small, old buildings, painted in shocking pink. Sir George has his own transmissions room in the bungalow to receive communications from space.

Though he's absent from the Fulham Road centre, his presence is everywhere. Photographs show him as an impressive-looking figure, even in his seventies. He has a large, square head, thick eyebrows and noticeably large ears. Older photos show him dressed in a scientist's white coat, in front of panels of old-fashioned knobs and dials, Prayer Energy Batteries of his own design.

King is an avid collector of titles, sobriquets and qualifications. The walls are covered in certificates, and photographs of him receiving certificates. In gown and mortar-board, he accepts a Doctorship of Divinity from Van Neuys University. The title of Archbishop was bestowed by a small schismatic organisation, the Liberal Catholic Church. King is also Lord of the Manor of Allington, having bought the title in 1991. A formal document in the Aetherius chapel in the basement certifies his Lordship and displays the Manor's coat of arms.

His knighthood was bestowed on him by the Byzantine Royal House. There are those who cast doubt on the currency of King's many titles. When I call the College of Arms to ask who exactly the Byzantine Royal House are, a sniffy gentleman called Tim tells me he believes they are one of the many minor families who claim an obscure royal descent and distribute titles to friends and bene-factors. 'We don't set a great deal of store in such titles,' he says with regal hauteur. Tim himself carries the College's sobriquet Rouge Dragon Pursuivant. When I tell Tim the man I'm calling about is George King, his tone darkens. 'Oh yes, we know all about *him*.' The Rouge Dragon Pursuivant may be of the opinion that such knighthoods debase the very notion of titles, but it's good enough for Sir George to have it entered on to his passport.

At the bottom of the stairs there is another framed certificate that declares Sir George to be a freeman of the City of London. Near it is a dusty reply written by a secretary to Prime Minister Margaret Thatcher. It thanks him on her behalf for his own letter of congratulations upon her joining him as one of those who have been given the freedom of the City. King's political sympathies lean rightwards. One document announces that Sir George is a 'member of the Republican Presidential Task Force', and congratulates him for his 'ceaseless generosity and unfailing dedication'. Another welcomes Sir George to the Republican Presidential Legion of Merit and praises him for his 'patriotism, commitment and integrity'.

The building at 757 Fulham Road is also home to the College of Spiritual Science. I choose a one-day-course in Psychic Development here, given by two Aetherius Society members, Tony and Marie. Ten of us turn up to learn the secrets of their sacred science. It's a cranky audience, all of whom save myself are firmly convinced about the existence of a psychic world waiting to be discovered. There's a West Indian man who announces, 'The name is Blissett,' and who frequently sees ghosts; a young Indian man who says that once, while working on a roof, he became aware of a strongly perfumed smell around him which he believes was a spirit of some sort; and a prim middle-aged lady who announces herself as a healer.

'Science is just catching up,' Tony tells us. 'We're only catching up with things that have been known about in the east for centuries.' Science, he says, is just on the verge of proving that the soul exists. He has proof. Scientists, we are told, measured weight loss in 'I think it was about 250' terminal patients and at the moment of death, their bodies miraculously became very slightly lighter. The soul actually *weighs* something. 'The occultists have known about this for centuries.'

We're told about pendulum dowsing, visualisation exercises, Kundalini yoga and our spiritual guides, all the corners of the new science which the conventional scientists ignore. Towards the end of our day a woman, who dresses in black because she says that is her astrological colour, interrupts while we are on the topic of guardian angels. '*I* have a guiding spirit,' she announces abruptly to us. 'I cannot do without him.' She is dark haired, in her mid-thirties, with a sad face and a southern European accent, possibly Greek. 'I am a single mother,' she informs us. 'A lot of people have let me down. He is there for me and has *never* let me down,' she says fiercely. She wants desperately to tell us all about this man. 'When I struggle, when there is no solution to a problem, he is there for me. I love him. He's a really good person. I want to know about him. What should I do to let him know I want to know more?'

'When the time is right,' answers Tony in measured tones, 'he will tell you.'

'When?' she beseeches.

'In time.'

'I need his strength,' she insists. 'I just want him to be there and stay there.'

'I wouldn't worry too much who it is . . .' says Tony.

'But when they're your friend, you want to know the background, don't you?'

The playfulness of the day, all pendulums and crystals, suddenly becomes serious and melancholy. It's as if she is pressing Tony to somehow magically make the secret friend who saves her from her loneliness more real. 'I live my life with him now,' she is saying.

'Excellent,' says Tony, calmly. 'But I wouldn't rely on him too much because, after all, you do live in a physical world.'

But the possibly Greek woman is defiant, unstoppable. She wants to tell us about her passion for the invisible friend who saves her from loneliness. 'Sometimes, when my children are asleep, I just sit down and talk to him and know that he is listening. I'm his friend. If I had a bad day I will tell him. If I cooked a meal and my family appreciate it, I know a genuine person is listening to me.'

Slightly anxiously, Tony nudges the topic round to thought transmission.

On a Sunday morning I attend the Aetherius Society Divine Service. Men in dark jackets mill around inside the shop's front door. Many wear ties displaying the Aetherius symbol, the Sanskrit mantric word 'Om' followed by a triangle. Forewarned that dress code is formal, I have donned my suit.

'Hello?' A woman approaches me. 'Is this your first time?'

She beckons a young man. 'Show the gentleman downstairs.'

Downstairs, the small room where I was taught about psychic development has become a chapel. Rows of chairs face a gold crucifix encrusted with coloured glass; to its left is a lectern bearing the Aetherius symbol, to its right is a small altar. The young man instructs me to bow once before the cross and then again to the altar before taking my seat.

Many in the forty-strong congregation are wearing what look like academic robes, coloured green or beige. They denote the level of Temple Degree the members have reached by passing various exams in Aetherian doctrine set by Sir George. The service is a series of recited mantras and prayers. In beautifully synchronised unison the congregation chant, 'Om Mane Padme Om,' over and over for several minutes to charge the air with spiritual energy, palms raised to transmit the energy to the world. The words resonate in the small, airless room. Each week, tape recordings of the more important communications received by Sir George are played.

Today the lights are dimmed and the air conditioner is switched off so we can hear the Eighth Blessing of Master Jesus. 'Blessed,' a voice hisses through the loudspeaker, 'is the Solar Logos, for upon this you and I depend for that vital energy which doth take us through valuable experience.' He talks close to the microphone, enunciating each word with slow gravity. You can hear the spittle in his throat. 'Even I stand back in awe, when I this pronouncement do make, for indeed here stands a sacred jewel in the heart of God . . . itself . . .'

The blessing was delivered to Sir George on 14 September 1958. You can hear the noise of old cars passing in the background on this carefully-recorded transmission from space.

'Thrice blessed is this mighty Logos . . . Seven times blessed is each one of its children . . .' The congregation sit, eyes closed, palms carefully placed upwards on their thighs. 'Seven times blessed is each one of its nine thousand dimensions . . . Seven times blessed is each one of its nine million, four hundred and fifty-six thousand, nine hundred . . . and twenty-one cloaks . . . Eight times eight times eight times eight times eight times blessed is the body of this . . . and twice blessed in that . . . by that . . . as that . . . is the soul of this.' The strange, mathematical catechism booms loudly around the room. 'And once blessed in the heart of God, is the spirit of this . . . Thus endeth the Eighth Blessing.'

Later, Richard Lawrence, ordained as a Bishop in the Aetherius Society, and one of their highest-ranked members stands at the lectern, dressed in elaborate embroidered ecclesiastical robes and a square red cardinal's hat that is topped off with a red pom-pom. He delivers news of Sir George, calling him 'our Master'. Things have not been going well. The recent Los Angeles earthquake badly cracked the foundations of George King and Lady Monique's small pink Hollywood home. The repairs are going to be extremely expensive. It would appear that even the success of Operation Bluewater to protect the western seaboard from earthquakes has not been able to protect the Master. 'I know you are generous people,' says Bishop Lawrence, shining with love and concern for his Master. 'I know at this vital time you will rise to the challenge.'

The Aetherius Society soldier on, year after year, knowing that many of us sceptics find George King's stories of space ships and prayer batteries incredible. Maybe they secretly thrive off our scepticism. They acknowledge that they are a cult, but point out that the word wasn't pejorative until the anti-cult movement arrived in the 70s. Meanwhile anti-cultists like Ian Haworth regard the group as a harmless eccentricity. They believe that the world of cults can be divided between a classification of 'destructive' and 'harmless' cults. 'Destructive' cults are those which the anti-cult movement believes use 'mind control'. But as far as Haworth is concerned, the open guilelessness with which the Aetherius Society promote their message is harmless. It is regarded as innocuous.

Although the Aetherius Society has members in Ghana, Nigeria, New Zealand, America and elsewhere, the membership remains small. I suspect too, they probably prefer it that way.

Richard Lawrence is a business-like, smartly dressed, sensible-looking man. He loves his work in the Aetherius Society. I phone him and tell him I'm writing a book about movements like his and he agrees, slightly warily, to talk to me. He invites me to meet him in a small carpeted room at the back of the Fulham HQ. Photographs of the Master stare down at us from the walls.

Sir George, he says, was ridiculed and mocked for being a herald of the New Age of Aquarius long before such things were fashionable. The Aetherius Society still carry that cross.

'Some people find our beliefs so bizarre that they don't even consider them. That's the big problem.' They don't care enough to find out the truth.

He tells a story about a man who came to a yogi asking for the truth. The yogi told him to stick his head in a bucket of water until he almost drowned. When he came out of the water the yogi asked him, 'What did you want most when you were in the bucket?' The man answered, 'Air.' The yogi said, 'Well, when you can say truth, instead of air, then I'll teach you.'

Lawrence despairs of the scientists who turn their backs on what the society has to offer. 'I've lectured to academics and presented them with evidence, because we do *have* evidence, *objective* evidence. I don't think we'd be here after forty years if we didn't. And the best reaction you can hope for is nil. If they don't say much, they're not arguing with you, you've made headway. But it doesn't make them keen to join the Aetherius Society and help humanity.'

Richard Lawrence was confirmed by the Archbishop of Canterbury and had wanted to be a priest at fourteen, but Christian theology never satisfied him. 'We're accused of eccentricity,' he says, sadly. 'They say a man lived for thirty-three years in one part of the world and that he is the Son of God. That's bizarre. Much more bizarre than saying he came from Venus.'

Richard found the truth when he was at university in Hull, studying music. One day he went to a lecture by a member of the Aetherius Society and tried their meditation, visualising white light with his palms raised, and sending out his love to the world. Back in the hall of residence afterwards he couldn't stop the feeling that energy was rushing through him. The sensation was overwhelming, and worrying, so he got up at three in the morning to go and find the lecturer, walking four miles to find him and tell him, 'Now look what you've done.'

If he needed further proof, it arrived while he was still at university. As a student on limited funds he once had to choose between buying gym shoes or purchasing tapes of Aetherius Society lectures. He chose the tapes. Shortly afterwards, however, he spotted a UFO one day, in a field. It was cigar shaped, and no sooner had he seen it than the UFO disappeared behind a tree. Hurrying to search the place where it had vanished, he found instead a brand new pair of size nine gym shoes. 'That to me,' says Dr Lawrence, 'was a great sign. One of our teachings is that what you sacrifice will be laid at your feet.'

At the front door of the shop as I leave, Richard Lawrence tells me the pop star Holly Johnson used to come here for healing after he was diagnosed as HIV positive. And that one of their biggest supporters was Dave Davies of the Kinks. If you look at the back of his 1983 album 'Chosen People' you will find in the sleeve notes: 'I dedicate this recording, its songs and its feeling to the work of Sir George King, Ph.D, DD, whose great compassion, love and inspiration is a constant guide and help to us all.'

At seventy-five, Sir George still battles to save the world and usher in a Golden Age. He never tires of using the powers he was given forty years ago to channel healing energy around the world. He is currently working on the closing stages of Operation Power Light. For Phase 15, he has driven in his 26-foot mobile home to Pismo Beach, California. It may be due to a flight of whimsy or the vanity of title that makes Sir George choose to stay at a motel called Knight's Rest, but he conducted Phase 5 of the operation from here too, back in March 1993. Actually, he was planning to move on the day before, but he was ill in the night, and was not sure if he was feeling well enough to drive on.

At exactly 11.30am Pacific Time, he starts to channel healing energy from one of his specially charged mountains, Ben Hope in Scotland, and spread it around the world. To most people he would look like an elderly man, once impressively large, now shrunken and slightly frail, dressed in a Pismo Beach baseball cap, sitting in an aluminium garden chair placed on the motel lawn in the shade of a tree, overlooking the blue Pacific Ocean. They would not recognise the task he was performing in co-operation with the unseen Masters from Gotha.

Indeed, half-way through the operation, the motel's new maintenance man, recognising neither the Primary Terrestrial Mental Channel nor the task he is performing, starts to mow the lawn he's sitting on, forcing a disgruntled Sir George to move back inside the cream and blue Lazy Daze motorhome he has christened the Lady. Half-way through the operation he has lunch. Sometimes he takes a little sherry before he eats.

When it is exactly 1.30pm on his Swiss Heuer stopwatch, the operation is complete. He switches on his Sony hand-held tape-recorder and dictates the following message to his followers: 'Well, that is it everybody! Two hours. This was the big one! Phase 15 of Operation Power Light for the benefit of all life on Earth – healing and upliftment . . . and I think the people on Terra need it! It is over and done with and now I am going to sign off. I have had a very nice lunch, by the way, and now I am going to sign off and go and have a little rest. That is it from me, Primary Terrestrial Mental Channel. The time now is 1.35pm PDT and Phase 15 of Operation Power Light is finished . . .'

2

Like the former *Grandstand* presenter and Green Party spokes-person, David Icke, who announced to journalists gathered at Gatwick Airport in spring 1991, that he was the Son of Godhead, Benjamin Creme is another media favourite. Mr Creme, an elderly soft spoken Scottish painter of strange abstracts, geometrical shapes with titles like 'Rising Kundalini' became famous for his proclamation that Christ was alive and well, and living amongst the Asian community in Brick Lane in London's East End. At a cost of roughly £100,000, Creme placed adverts in seven-teen newspapers around the world. They appeared in April 1982 announcing: 'The world has had *enough* . . . of hunger, injustice, war. In answer to our call for help, as World Teacher for all humanity, THE CHRIST IS NOW HERE.' The Third World War was cancelled. The presence of the Christ, or Lord Maitreya, on earth guaranteed that. Even more thrillingly, it promised that within two months he would speak to humanity through a world-wide television and radio broadcast.

The broadcast never came. But Creme remains unruffled. It will come soon. He has never attracted the outright ridicule with which David Icke was pilloried ('Is Icke bonkers?' mocked the *Sun*. 'What do you think? Phone 0898 400690'), but like Icke and George King, he claims to be a psychic channel through whom higher forces communicate. And like both of them, he has become a guru figure to hundreds who buy his books and turn up regularly to his meetings.

He is seventy-one now, but he still flies around the world to address crowds, heralding the dawning of the new age that the Lord Maitreya will bring. At the height of his fame he claimed to have about 150,000 subscribers to his magazine, *Share International*. These days audiences are smaller. The Maitreya is still coming, he insists. The cynicism of the media has simply made the task more difficult. Those who believe him point to the list of predictions that the Maitreya has made through him.

'Nelson Mandela will be released,' Creme predicted in September 1988. Mandela was released in February 1990. 'Terry Waite and his fellow hostages will be released,' he declared in April 1990, four months before the hostages were freed. 'A Democrat will become the next President of America,' he said in January 1991. Clinton took over the White House in June 1992.

Other predictions that proved not quite so accurate are omitted from the list. Like the mid-80s communication forecasting that Prince Charles was about to ascend to the throne.

Today, in a cream suit, he addresses another hundred people at the Friends House in Euston Road: mostly middle-class, middle-aged and troubled at the iniquities of the world economy, attracted by the mystical compassion of Creme's message.

He too is an inheritor of the wild visionary tradition of Madame Blavatsky. Her fellow Theosophist Alice Bailey, whose writings influenced Creme deeply, claimed she was a channel for one of Blavatsky's secret Brothers Dwaj Kuhl from his secret home in the Himalayas. For thirty years she was his amanuensis. All of the world teachers – Jesus, Buddha, Krishna, Imam Mahdi – were preparing the way for the emergence of the leader of the Masters, the Christ, the Maitreya. As Bailey created her own fantasy from Blavatsky, Creme spins a new theme from the writings of Bailey.

On 8 July 1977, Creme announces at each meeting, the Maitreya descended fully grown into Pakistan. Eleven days later he boarded a British Airways jet and flew to London. He now lives in the capital on a Visitor's Permit which he has renewed several times. For fourteen years he lived among the Asian community in London's Brick Lane, 'as an ordinary man'. Though Creme has frequently said he will show himself to members of the press, he has yet to do so. Last year he moved to live among the Asian community in south-west London to escape what Creme describes as media harassment.

On tables at the back piles of newspapers, books and magazines are laid out. *Share International*, the monthly magazine, deals with topics like world poverty, which troubles Creme and his followers deeply, alongside Creme's own spiritual outpourings. The list of contributors for the latest issue includes various academics, the former president of Tanzania, Julius Nyrere, and an extra-planetary referred to as 'The Master ——' who doesn't wish his name to be revealed. His articles are dictated telepathically through Benjamin Creme.

At the start of his meetings, Creme is 'overshadowed' by one of the Cosmic Masters, just as George King claims to be. He sits at the front of the audience, hand raised, transmitting energy to the members of his congregation one by one. Within a few seconds of beginning his 'overshadowing', his fair Scots face, under his white septuagenarian's hair, turns an alarming shade of red as the higher powers flow through him. All the blood rushes to his head.

Afterwards he repeats his message calmly, undaunted by the length of time it has taken to prepare the world for the Maitreya, in his quiet Scottish voice. The address is almost exactly the same each time, save for the latest announcements of claimed sightings of the Christ around the world.

'We are entering a new cosmic cycle,' he says, matter-of-factly. A transformation of consciousness, the Age of Aquarius.' Cosmic energies are transforming every department of life. Old economies will disappear. Old institutions will be left high and dry.

The new age becomes, once again, a bizarrely poetic metaphor to encompass unfathomable global change. Our world is unstable, collapsing. Weather patterns are changing. Millions are starving. Commercialisation has become the world religion. 'Market forces are the forces of *evil*,' says Maitreya through his earthly channel. His believers agree.

But the Age of Aquarius which Maitreya will help us usher in will save us from the destructive individualism of the past. The Maitreya is a simple, gentle God of brotherhood and sharing. But first we must endure further chaos. Creme calmly predicts a stockmarket crash starting in Japan which will destroy the world economy, readying the world for a new age economy. 'It will happen some time this year, in 1994,' he says. 'It is a bubble that will eventually burst. They cannot continue. They have no more value for humanity than casinos. They have no place in a society based on sharing and justice.' His message is one of spiritual anti-capitalism.

The Maitreya's global broadcast is still on the agenda. However, the cynicism of the networks means that he has scaled down his ambitions. Instead of demanding all the channels to yield to him, Creme says he now will accept one sincere channel. The other networks will be so impressed, they will pick up the programme. He has, Creme announces, been offered the chance to broadcast on a small station in San Antonio, Texas. It's not the global broadcast originally wanted, but in the face of indifference it will have to do. Creme says he will time his broadcast for maximum attention.

Afterwards, a young man in a blue jacket, with greased black hair, suggests enthusiastically that the Maitreya should time his broadcast to coincide with the World Cup. ' 'Cause then the whole world's satellite TV will be directed towards America.'

Creme smiles thinly at us as if to say, 'there's always one nutcase in the crowd'. He says, dryly, 'I'm sure the Maitreya is well aware of that and he doesn't need you or I to tell him what the best time is.' And the audience laughs. What a silly suggestion.

3

The new age has thrown up another style of guru too, the therapy guru. The Human Potential movement first began to appear in America in the early 70s, with a Californian known as Werner Erhard at the helm. Born Jack Rosenberg, he is the inventor of Erhard Seminars Training, better known as *est* or more recently the Forum. A car dealer and encyclopaedia salesman, he had what he called an 'enlightenment experience' in 1963, which led him to immerse himself in the teachings of the Zen philosophers and Ron L. Hubbard. By 1971 Erhard claimed he had achieved 'permanent enlightenment' and started to give courses and seminars. In 1974 six and a half thousand white middle-class seekers gathered at San Francisco's Civic Auditorium to hear the thirty-nine-year-old talk on 'Making Relationships Work'.

Erhard told his students that they should think of themselves as the cause of events, rather than the victims of them. We are responsible for what happens to us. Taking his own creed to vertiginous absurdities, Erhard once famously said that the Vietnamese who were burned to death by napalm created it themselves, and the Jews were responsible for Auschwitz. 'You're the god in your universe. You caused it. You pretended not to cause it so you could play in it.'

est became notorious for fund-raising activities like the World Hunger Project soliciting donations for a campaign to end world hunger by 1997. Those who bothered to ask discovered that the money wasn't actually *going* to Africa, or Bangladesh, but into further consciousness-raising exercises. One horrified donor was chided by an *est* representative, 'You're hung up on logic and all that kind of bullshit. To understand the Hunger Project you've got to forget everyday logic.' To enrol in the absurd project you had to embrace a series of commitments that began: 'I am willing to be responsible for making the end of starvation an idea whose time has come . . .'

Early *est* seminars were gruelling affairs, according to those who decried it as a mind-bending cult. You were allowed three toilet breaks during the day, and one meal break. Apart from that you were supposed to sit in a chair unless told otherwise. You were told you were a machine, and that all your beliefs and strategies were meaningless. By day two the floors of hotel ballrooms were full of writhing bodies crying hysterically over the traumatic life events they were reliving. By night they would be told to sit on the floor and imagine they were terrified of the persons around them. Shrieks would fill the rooms, until they were told the healing truth: that if they were afraid of people, then others too, would be afraid of them.

est seminars came to Britain in 1977. Soon afterwards came Insight, a similar Human Potential organisation which was the brain-child of a new age guru John-Roger Hinkins. Hinkins was originally just christened Roger in 1934 by Mormon parents in Rains, Utah. He claims to have undergone a profound spiritual experience during an operation to remove a kidney stone; the stone was excised and John the Baptist entered his body instead. From that point, he believed he had become the vessel of what he called the Mystical Traveller Consciousness, a spiritual entity which only becomes incarnated once every 25,000 years. In deference to the disciple who had entered his body, he renamed himself John-Roger, or J-R. J-R has an addiction to acronyms. Following his spiritual rebirth, he founded what he called the 'Church of the Movement of Spiritual Inner Awareness' better known as MSIA, pronounced 'Messiah'. He is also the creator of the Prana Theological Seminary and College of Philosophy in Los Angeles, where Prana equals Purple Rose Ashram of the New Age.

J-R lost his job at a California high school soon after the school head walked into a darkened classroom to find the embodiment of the Mystical Traveller Consciousness trying to hypnotise his pupils, but his career as a guru was already in the making. He was running classes called 'Soul Awareness Discourses' and writing best-selling self-help books with titles such as *You Can't Afford the Luxury of a Negative Thought*. In 1978 – as part of his campaign to 'do battle for the soul' – he launched Insight, a keep fit course for the psyche which mixes meditation, mysticism, discipline and self-help ideologies. Bruce Gyngell, for a while Mrs Thatcher's favourite businessman and head of TV-am, is an Insight trainee, along with quite a few others. By 1985 an estimated 50,000 people had 'graduated' through Insight seminars. Gyngell is the recipient of J-R's very own Annual Integrity Award. To several ex-MSIA members, it seems that J-R's own integrity has not been of the highest calibre. It's another of the many strange battles between ex-cult members and their gurus; cult and anti-cult. In the 80s some of them accused J-R of attempting to coerce them to have sex with him. He replied by announcing that his accusers had been influenced by a powerful negative force called the Red Monk.

You can pick up leaflets for Insight seminars at health food cafés, alternative bookshops. The seminars are scheduled at weekends or in the evening, on the assumption that the middle-class professionals that attend are too busy to make other times. A weekend will set you back only about £350, though you are welcome to give more if you wish. On the leaflet Arianna Stassinopoulos Huffington trumpets about how her Insight seminar changed her life: 'I was at last living from my being rather than my head. And I knew that this surge of new life was only the beginning . . .'

A third group who helped you find self-realisation through seminars were known as Exegesis, a 'self-religion' founded by an *est* graduate Robert D'Aubigny, who changed his last name from the more prosaic Fuller which he inherited from his father, a Sussex meat salesman. Back in the early 80s his organisation charged a little over £200 for a five-day course.

In my first year at university the first relationship I had was with a woman called Sarah, dark haired, slightly vulnerable, intense and devoted to Van Morrison records. We didn't have a great deal in common. One awful day I went for a long walk on the beach with her and told her awkwardly that I didn't really want a relationship. The fact was that I didn't want a relationship with her.

In those days, a steady stream of students were travelling up from my university to London and spending their weekends doing Exegesis courses. Sarah followed them and became one of the 7,000 people who took part in their seminars.

Mike Oldfield, the musician who had become famous at nineteen for 'Tubular Bells' which went on to sell somewhere approaching twenty million copies, was one of those who had attended the sessions. Years later, when I was interviewing him for an American magazine, he described to me the total change in his personality that this form of therapy helped bring about. Oldfield had been cripplingly shy. His upbringing had been traumatic. 'My mother,' he said quietly, 'was . . . er, she spent most of her life as I knew her in mental institutions. She was addicted to barbiturates.' He had witnessed her being driven away in an ambulance. He believes that what he endured drove him into extreme introversion. For years as a musician he had been incapable of performing in public. In the seminar he 're-emerged' from the womb screaming like a new born baby. 'I realised afterwards that I must have not liked being born at all,' he said. After Exegesis, he became wildly, almost manically self-confident and posed naked for photographs in *Melody Maker*.

Sarah's change of character was less dramatic thankfully, but still noticeable. She came back, bright and bursting with energy. At a party she came up to me and listed all my shortcomings. There was little hope. She declaimed, 'The trouble with *you* is that you're emotionally constipated.'

After college she remained involved with Exegesis. I only saw her once after that a couple of years later. I bumped into her in the crowd at the 100 Club in Oxford Street where she was dancing to a band called Big Sound Authority, a white soul band who enjoyed a fleeting success when they picked up a few fans from the recently split Jam. The Big Sound Authority's minor hit was a song called 'This House (is Where your Love Stands)', a relentlessly positive power soul anthem. The group had attended Exegesis seminars too.

Sarah, dancing at the concert was unquestionably happy: infinitely happier at least than she had been at university. Exegesis had closed down, she told me. Instead they had set up a tele-sales company, which she was involved with. Now they were beaming their positive attitudes down phone lines.

Exegesis was closed down in 1984 following the death of a schizophrenic man called Ashley Doubtfire who had attended an Exegesis seminar. Instead, attention was switched to the tele-sales business, a company called Programmes Ltd which had grown out of Exegesis in 1981.

Programmes Ltd offered their tele-sales skills to companies wanting to sell products, as well as management staff-training seminars. Their catchy founding slogan ran, 'The business of transformation and the transformation of business.' Well-trained graduates worked as telephone sales operatives, a job for which they were often hugely over-qualified, for rates far below those they could earn elsewhere simply to stay within the environment of Exegesis that had transformed their lives as surely as they were going to transform business.

A 1983 BBC documentary 'The Second Oldest Profession' captured the true nature of the business of transformation and the transformation of business. The morning sessions began with group chanting. Success was celebrated and failure shunned. One scene summed up their route to success:

Phoner (being questioned about his lack of success): Between three and four I had a lot of problems with engaged signals.

Team leader: Your comment about the engaged tones, I don't want to hear it. If someone comes to you and says 'I've got a lot of engaged tones', would you say to them, 'Ah, never mind,' or say 'Take a look at your energy and the amount of intention you're putting out'?

Other phoners: The energy . . . the intention.

Team leader: You know the dynamics of getting through and you know how to get orders. It's simply putting out energy and being consistent with your intentions. You fell asleep for an hour. It's about energy and consistency, isn't it?

Phoners: Yes!

Team leader: Then get it!

By putting out energy, Sarah and her friends made the telephones ring. They believed in magic. And in a curious way it worked. Programmes Ltd has become one of Europe's biggest telephone marketing companies. It also specialises in management training for companies like British Telecom, the Clydesdale Bank and British Midland.

FIVE

The Pinstripe Guru

1

Tottenham Court Road Station; Central Line eastbound platform. Unsurprisingly the dot matrix indicator says there is a six-minute wait for the next train, so passengers read the adverts on the wall opposite. Among all the posters promoting health-giving mineral water and holidays are three that offer various other paths to heaven.

The first is a grainy black and white photo of an empty wheelchair. Underneath the picture is a scornful line of newsprint that reads "There is no evidence for miraculous healing" – *Independent on Sunday'*. Below that: '*You* decide. A boy deaf since birth . . . a young man with a 19-year history of asthma . . . Maurice Cerullo. Earl's Court August 15–22. 3.00pm. Admission free.' It's an ad for a summer visit by yet another of the charismatic healers who, from Billy Graham through to Reinhard Bonnke and onwards, appear from time to time to recapture our wayward souls.

The second recommends something Maurice Cerullo would regard as one of the devil's works that he has come to save us from. 'Change. As individuals our lives are subject to change and uncertainty and we spend a great deal of effort trying to control them . . .' It promises an answer to the stresses of modern-day living, inviting you to attend the School of Meditation in Holland Park, a school originally set up to teach the Transcendental Meditation method of the twinkling-eyed Maharishi Mahesh Yogi, briefly beloved of the Beatles.

In contrast, the third poster doesn't appear to be advertising anything spiritual. The large ad for the School of Economic Science, which has been pasted up more or less between the two looks a far more sober and sensible proposition: 'Economics: A Fresh Approach to a Vital Subject,' it trumpets. It is obviously intended for more serious, intellectual minds.

'This course starts from the basic principles which govern all economic activity. "My interest never flagged," said one student. It takes the universal natural laws and shows how they apply today. "If the laws are understood they can be seen everywhere." It explains their relevance to the modern economy . . . The course also looks at the role of government in economic affairs. "An enjoyable course – well conducted by knowledgeable lecturers . . ." It covers taxation, distribution of wealth, the factors of production, but all from first principles. If you'd like to enrol . . .'

Those who've studied economics already might wonder briefly about exactly what those 'natural laws' are, but to most people, it looks like a fairly straightforward course in basic economic theory. The course costs £45 for ten lessons. The address is 90, Queen's Gate. At Warren Street, there is another billboard for the School of Economic Science which offers another set of classes, this time in philosophy. 'Philosophy,' it proclaims. '12 Practical Discussions. This course in practical philosophy draws from many of the worlds of teaching – both East and West – and presents a coherent approach to life and its purpose . . . £54.'

The London headquarters of the School of Economic Science is a beautiful pair of white regency buildings in South Kensington. On the pillared porch, a neat middle-aged man says, 'Yes, that's right. Come in. It's just about to start.' It's just after 7pm and I'm late. In a rear office, a row of smartly-dressed men in well-pressed suits sit at desks and take your course fees. One takes my cheque for £54 (I chose philosophy) and hands me a neatly-written receipt. He's doing a survey on how people heard of this course. 'I saw the advert in the tube,' I tell him when he asks. For around forty years now, the school has been successfully advertising its philosophy and economics courses on the London Underground.

Evening-class students are used to dusty classrooms and genial first-night confusion. This place, in contrast, is run with neat efficiency. Nor is there any of the laid-back hippie chaos of the Festival Of Mind, Body And Spirit here. I am ushered upstairs to a large first-floor room with french windows, chandeliers and fine plaster mouldings, where there are chairs arranged in rows facing a podium, on which sits a small table adorned with a small jug of water and a dainty vase of flowers. To its right stands a large old-fashioned blackboard on an easel. I notice, while we're waiting for our philosophy teacher to arrive, that there is a hole worn in the middle of it, but don't think anything of it. The floorboards are bare, slightly uneven. There is a school-like smell of chalk and cleaning fluid.

Lesson one is billed on a handout: 'Philosophy: the love of wisdom. The need for self-knowledge. A practical exercise in the refinement of observation.' We can choose any one of six different teachers. Because they know we're all busy London careerists, we can attend the course any night of the week between 7pm and 9.30, or on Saturday mornings. It's very convenient.

Tuesday's teacher, Miss Crammond, a small tweedy woman, sweeps into the room, smiles and asks us, 'What is philosophy?' in the sing-song voice of a children's TV presenter. She is grey haired, has a receding chin and smiles invincibly at us. It's our first day, and we're all shy, and we shuffle in our seats and look at the floor, so she answers brightly for us: 'Philosophy is the search for wisdom.' We nod sagely.

She declaims a quote from Plato's *Republic* that pooh-poohs fair-weather philosophers unable to cope with the rigours of the subject: 'When they come within sight of the great difficulties of the subject, they take themselves off.' We're not going to be like that. We're going to take this course seriously and make better people of ourselves.

Miss Crammond peers through glasses, reading from prepared notes. It is impossible not to think of Joyce Grenfell when you hear her fluty, old-school BBC English and see her elderly but happy face, ever-smiling in the face of our philosophical ignorance. Her technique is to ask questions, and then try in her well-meaning manner to nudge us round to the right answers. What the right answers are, though, soon becomes a source of bemusement to some of her students.

Her next quote is not from Wittgenstein or Descartes, but from the Gospel according to St Thomas: ' "Whoever knows the all but fails to know himself, lacks everything." That's a very interesting thing to say, isn't it?' she beams at us. 'Is it possible for a man to be wise without knowing himself first?' she enquires.

Like any first-night evening class audience, we are unsure of ourselves, and though we shake our heads, we remain mute: 'What do you think is stopping us from knowing ourselves?' she asks.

Finally someone attempts a long and rambling answer. It's all about the programming we receive in life. He blames it on having to do O levels. 'It's because of our education,' he says, uncertainly.

Miss Crammond's eyes sparkle. She has just scored a bullseye, and so early in the class too. 'You're right!' she sings out. 'We *are* burdened by . . . education, quote unquote.' She draws inverted commas in the air. 'So, how are we to know ourselves?'

There are about sixty of us this first night. One man pipes up and asks hesitantly, 'Is it really possible to know ourselves? I mean, know ourselves *completely*?'

Miss C. nods. 'It is possible,' she asserts with unshakeable confidence.

The man looks puzzled and opens his mouth, perhaps to ask, how she can know this philosophically, but he closes it again without speaking.

The philosophy teacher pours herself a glass of water and peers at her script again. 'Let's continue. What do you think is important if we are to know ourselves?' she demands.

Pause. 'Objectivity?' a voice suggests.

'Certainly,' answers Miss Crammond benignly, but this is not the answer she is looking for.

Another voice: 'Freedom from prejudice?'

'Yes,' answers Miss Crammond, still looking dissatisfied. No one has supplied her with the right answer, so she supplies it herself. 'What about *people of like mind*?' she asks. 'Isn't that important?'

A few would-be philosophers are beginning to sense that something is not as it should be. 'Surely not if they've all got blinkered views?' someone asks.

Miss C. cups her hand round her ear and giggles. 'I'm sorry. Would you mind repeating that? I'm a bit deaf.'

The sceptic hollers, 'Blinkered minds,' across the classroom.

'Oh. Yes. That's a good question.' She ignores it. Instead she reads another sentence from her notes. 'To move forward in philosophy is to move forward in company because it is mutual love.'

After a confusing hour, we break for tea, served in teacup and saucer in the basement, by equally tweedy-looking ladies in cardigans and long skirts. They look so archetypally English, that none of the students seem to spot their uniformity of dress. Long skirts are in fashion. No one really notices the absence of visible calves.

In the second half there is still no sign of Adorno or Kant. Instead we get one quote from the Sanskrit Vedic scriptures and a nugget of Zen philosophy. 'Nan-in, a Japanese master during the Meiji era, received a university professor who came to enquire about Zen,' reads Miss Crammond. 'Nan-in served tea. He poured his visitor's cup full, and then kept on pouring. The professor watched the overflow until he could no longer restrain himself. "It is overfull. No more will go in." "Like this cup," Nan-in said, "you are full of your own opinions and speculations. How can I show you Zen unless you first empty your cup?"'

Many students laugh. What a silly professor. 'How much of what the professor heard would be his own learning, his own concepts?' Miss C. enquires of us.

A blonde woman, who is captivated by Miss Crammond's address answers: 'All of it?'

'Yes,' smiles Miss Crammond. The lesson we are learning tonight is that we have to throw everything we know about away in order to grasp the true meaning of philosophy. Our pedestrian expectations of what this course was going to be are an impediment to our self-knowledge.

What happens next is stranger. From her dais, Miss Crammond announces that the school has developed an exercise which can help us on our path to self-knowledge. This is the 'practical exercise in refinement of knowledge' promised by the course notes. To the astonishment of many, who have brought folders and notebooks as if preparing for an exam, she proceeds to lead her sixty-strong class in a meditation. At Miss Crammond's orders we sit up straight in our chairs and place our feet firmly on the ground. 'Feel the weight of the body on the chair,' she intones. 'Feel the weight of the feet on the floor.' Pause. I can hear someone giggling quietly, embarrassed. 'Feel the pressure of the clothes on the skin . . . the play of air on the face and hands.' Pause. 'Feel the sense of taste in your mouth . . . and smell the air as you breathe in,' she tells us. 'Let form and colour be perceived through the eyes. Refrain from judging what you see, just let it be perceived . . .' Outside the french windows, a London plane tree sways in the breeze. 'Let sounds be received in the listening, as they rise out of silence and return there again.' Taxi brakes squeal outside.

In the first week, the exercise stops there. But this meditation is to become a central part of our activity as students. By our second lesson we have been told to practise it twice a day. Gradually as the weeks progress, it will be extended into more metaphysical realms. 'Let our hearing go out beyond the furthest sound, to the stillness beyond.' We are told to listen to the silence beyond the silence. 'Now,' this nicely-spoken old woman will conclude, 'without reducing this large field of awareness, simply rest in the awareness of your existence . . . without limit.' In the stillness of our separation with the every day we will discover our true selves. At root, the School of Economic Studies teaches the Hindu doctrine that our personalities are an illusion. What we imagine to be our characters, are merely an illusion created by our corrupting contact with the world. Joy and pain are an illusion. Illness is an illusion. They are what the school calls *ahankara*, self-identification. Through a life of discipline we must lose our individuality and re-join the Absolute self.

But on our first day, the full mystical content of our course has still to be spelled out. After a few seconds of silence, Miss Crammond asks, 'There. What did you get from that? What did you observe?'

The eager young blonde woman gushes, 'It was very relaxing.'

Several appear to have found the exercise silly. 'What were we *meant* to observe?' one middle-aged woman asks sniffily.

The blonde woman argues back on Miss Crammond's behalf. 'I found it relaxing.'

'Yes,' glows Miss Crammond.

Afterwards, as we pour out on to the busy road outside, a couple of young women clutch each other and burst into wild laughter, running away down the street. They won't be coming again. Several are more confused, trying to work out exactly what this course in philosophy consists of. I overhear one red-haired Australian turn to his companion, and ask in puzzled tones, 'This isn't a *religious* place is it? Only it didn't make itself out to be in the advert . . .'

2

In the whole colourfully eccentric splatter of cults, there has never been one as genteel, stiff-upper-lipped and absurdly British as the School of Economic Science. In many ways, it's quite the strangest cult I join. Despite the beaming vision presented by Miss Crammond, it has also been accused of being one of the most authoritarian. At 90 Queen's Gate, the pale upper-middle-classes disappear into a life of servitude to a bizarre physical, intellectual and – most importantly – aesthetic regime originally dreamed up by a now elderly Scottish barrister called Leonardo Da Vinci MacLaren, who wears crumpled pinstripe suits, has an overbearing affection for Mozart and fine wine, and who smokes like a chimney.

'This isn't a religious place, is it?' The School of Economic Science wasn't originally intended as a religious place at all, and still denies that it teaches religion of any sort. They prefer to call what they teach a philosophy. And they see themselves as an academy of higher thought, on the lines of Socrates' model, or the Academies of the Renaissance.

The original school was established by Leon's father, Andrew MacLaren, a self-made Glaswegian who clawed himself out of poverty to become a fervent disciple of tax reform, believing that land, not income should be the source of government revenue. In 1914 he joined the Independent Labour Party and later became an MP. His staunch but eccentric views finally led him to resign from the party in 1943 in disgust at its descent into what he called the 'welfare-state mentality'. Instead he threw his energies into setting up what would now be called a 'think tank', the School of Economic Science, an informal group of his friends and colleagues who got together to discuss MacLaren's tax reform ideas.

It was Andrew's son Leon who transformed the school into one of Britain's few home-grown cults. In many ways Leon resembled his father. He learned his passion for Mozart from him, and still embraces his economic theories. Having studied law, he too joined the Labour Party and tried to become a Labour member of parliament, standing against Winston Churchill for the seat of Epping in the 1939 pre-war election. History, of course, records Churchill's victory. Like his father too, he switched his allegiance to the Liberal Party.

But the difference between father and son lay in the fervour with which Leon began to embrace the mystical ideas of the Greek–Armenian mystic, carpet-dealer, gold prospector, type-writer mechanic, dancing master, guru and some say con-man George Ivanovitch Gurdjieff and his Russian pupil Peter Ouspensky.

Amongst the ranks of more genial new age school-ma'ams and masters Gurdjieff is the sadistic PE teacher. In pre-revolutionary Moscow, Gurdjieff established himself as a mystical guru who taught that the practice of self-discipline, cold baths, breathing exercises, chanting and choreographed movements could bring the self into close contact with the higher cosmic order. His philosophy had a self-denying, fatalistic edge which suited the morbid modernism of the times. He began to develop his ideas publicly in the years leading up to the First World War. It was a strange version of the Hindu philosophy that we are separated from true self by the distractions of the world. Men, he taught, were merely blind machines who operated under external influences, like the ant-like workers in *Metropolis*. Only by performing his exercises, known as the System, could they hope to gain the discipline needed to escape their mechanistic state. 'When a machine knows itself,' he wrote, 'it is then no longer a machine.'

The exercises included subservience to a master. You had to remove the illusory outer shell of personality to get through to the true self beneath. More than five hours' sleep a night was an impediment to self-knowledge. Austerity was embraced. In its extreme form, as occasionally advocated by Gurdjieff, it boiled down to the philosophy that if you carried out any task you were ordered to, however unpleasant, you could reach the enlightened state required to eventually break out of your machine mould. The middle classes, more used to servants chopping wood and cleaning for them, performed these tasks for the Master.

After escaping the revolution, Ouspensky arrived in London in 1921, followed by Gurdjieff a year later, where they attracted a fashionable following of millionaires, peers and intellectuals. T. S. Eliot and Katherine Mansfield were among those who turned up to Gurdjieff's lectures and meditation sessions. Katherine Mansfield followed Gurdjieff to France where, ill with TB, she attempted to follow his prescriptions for a cure that would these days be called 'holistic' and which involved, once again, duty and service. In a retreat his followers had established at Fontainebleau, which he called the Institute for the Harmonious Development of Mankind, she followed Gurdjieff's System, scrubbed carrots at midnight, ate a basic diet and slept on a bed above the cattle in the cowshed because Gurdjieff believed their odour was beneficial to health. She died a matter of weeks after her arrival.

Gurdjieff's doctrine of self-denial must have struck a chord, though, with MacLaren's impoverished Scottish family background. He first encountered Gurdjieff's mysticism through a group called the Society for the Study of Normal Psychology, originally founded by Ouspensky and led by a Harley Street paediatrician, Dr Francis Roles, which he joined and soon began to dominate by the force of his own personality. By 1947 Leon was firmly in charge of his father's School of Economic Science and the school was leaving the solid shores of social science for a more metaphysical, disciplinarian course set by Gurdjieff's teachings. Andrew MacLaren, who had established the school in the first place, was not so enthusiastic. Some ex-members relate how he tried to barge in to one of the meetings his son was holding in Church House, Westminster, to denounce his son's creation but was apparently barred by members of the school.

*

One of those who became caught up in the school in the 50s and 60s describes Leon MacLaren as a man who habitually wore a black coat and pinstripe trousers, a white shirt and a black bow tie. He remembers his clothes were always expensive but crumpled, ash-strewn and over-worn. Other disciples mimicked this mode of dress.

Despite his demands for a regulated life in his followers he was a heavy smoker and fond of good wine. Under his coat he developed a noticeable paunch. He spoke in a low, quiet, authoritative voice that commanded attention. His cigarette smoking was an act of theatre in itself. 'Just think what can be done with that space of silence between inhaling and exhaling,' says one disillusioned ex-member, Giles, who originally joined in the 50s after reading an advert for a course in philosophy very similar to the one I read and who was awed by MacLaren. 'Oh, it was a theatre trick that he used to the greatest possible effect, and of course there were others who were affected by his appearance and his technique. I remember one chap in particular who made a thing of drawing in and slowly exhaling. It was obvious he was copying MacLaren.'

By the early 60s MacLaren's tube station adverts attracted a following of up to 3,000 pupils. In the courses they attended, Giles, and the 'tutors', whose shoes Miss Crammond now so cheerily fills, taught MacLaren's own blend of Christianity and Gurdjieffian discipline.

Leon MacLaren systematised the Gurdjieffian System and mixed it with his own religious, political and economic ideas. It was, as it is now, an extremely gradual induction. You started studying the philosophy or economics courses, which gradually took a more and more mystical direction. Those unsuitable or unattracted were gradually weeded out. Only in your third year did you become subject to the discipline, and begin to find all your hours filled with performing menial tasks for the school: cleaning, carpentry, decorating the premises, as well as hours attending study groups. Most students took to the tasks with relish, pleased to further the school's ideas. When you had assimilated enough of the creed, you became a tutor in your turn; but it was a pyramidal structure with MacLaren at the apex.

The ghost of Gurdjieff ruled. 'We were deliberately put on to activities to cross-grain our temperament,' Giles recalls. 'I was put on to the one thing that I detested more than anything else – carpentry – which was probably why I was put on to it. How they knew that, I don't know. I was given a job of measuring quite an expensive piece of timber which was designed to support the main weight of a skylight we were building and I cut it short by two inches. It was typical. The whole thing was a complete waste and I felt very guilty about that. Oh I did. The look I got from the tutor in charge of that particular group was withering.'

Giles became a tutor too, and joined the process of laying out MacLaren's system for other followers. His entire life became bound up with the philosophy. He became eager, even desperate, to persuade students to join MacLaren's curious enterprise. 'If I lost a student, I could feel very bad about that. Oh yes. I could lose sleep over that.'

MacLaren's dealings with his followers often displayed an authoritarian streak which may have attracted him to Gurdjieff's dictum, 'For a man to wake up, become conscious, a big stick is necessary.' As with so many gurus, we can only speculate as to the inner workings of Leon MacLaren's mind. He doesn't do press. But the cult which he created was one that was – and still is to a lesser extent – built around a deeply, almost pathologically sexually repressive atmosphere. Encouraged by MacLaren, disciples came to believe that sex was a highly perilous area: sexual activity was equated with a lack of self-discipline.

Giles remembers one class where a man innocently mentioned just touching a woman student while dancing. MacLaren exploded, 'You will not do that!' he shouted. 'It was the most incredibly sexless environment,' remembers Giles sadly. 'People didn't hug each other. It was driven out of us.' When discussing sex, MacLaren seemed to lose his dominating froideur. Another ex-member recalls MacLaren lose his temper one day when a woman asked why the school demanded that they behave so obediently. 'All women do is lie around dreaming of how to seduce a man,' he yelled. Giles still shakes his head in incredulity at how he and his colleagues found themselves living a monastic lifestyle at a time when the sexual revolution was just gearing up.

By the time Giles cracked up he was one of those close to the centre. He blames his time in the cult for two relationships which never got off the ground. The first was with somebody who was outside the school, so Giles dropped it. The second never really started. He was invited to a dinner party with the second woman, but it clashed with one of his tutor groups. He rang MacLaren and asked what he should do. There was a pause before MacLaren answered, 'Well, you must do what is most important to you.'

'Of course,' says Giles bitterly, 'I picked up the phone and another relationship bit the dust. I didn't really have any more after that. A lovely piece of blackmail.'

Giles suffered a complete mental breakdown, during which he says he came very close to suicide. He went to visit MacLaren in his chambers. Still loyal to the ideals of the cult, he arranged with MacLaren to leave it gradually, so as to make as little fuss as possible. Though he accepts much of the esoteric teachings of the school, he is deeply bitter about the way MacLaren appeared to be able to control him and his colleagues: 'He dominated in the way that Hitler dominated Nazism and Stalin dominated Communism.'

3

The Maharishi Mahesh Yogi, the lascivious guru later derided by the Beatles as 'Sexy Sadie' arrived in London in 1960 hoping to acquire British followers, looking especially for converts among the more influential classes. The only thing that tempered the Maharishi's grandiose ambitions was his total innocence. In his scented rooms in Prince Albert Road, near Regent's Park, he would issue orders to his followers. 'Go and see the Queen and ask permission to build meditation cells at Buckingham Palace. We could have them underground, under the gardens. She will be very pleased with the idea.' 'Go to 10 Downing Street and ask for an interview with the Prime Minister.' One day he asked, 'What is the biggest hall in London?' 'The Albert Hall, Maharishi.' 'Call them up. Tell them we will take it for a world congress soon.'

Curiously the last request was granted by Leonardo Da Vinci MacLaren. MacLaren wanted to go further, to a purer version of the faith, to the source of oriental mysticism. Introduced to the Maharishi by Dr Francis Roles, MacLaren became obsessed by his approach to meditation, and set up the 1961 World Congress at the Royal Albert Hall. It was attended by 3,000, nearly all members of the School of Economic Science.

The meeting was a comical affair. Before the Maharishi appeared, the disciplined audience sat bolt upright and listened to a performance of – inevitably – a Mozart violin sonata. In the School of Economic Science, MacLaren's Old Testament new age cult has elevated Mozart's position to one of Godhead. MacLaren believes that after Mozart music plummeted downhill. He follows the Gurdjieffian notion that there is a 'fine' art that reflects pure consciousness and 'coarse' art that corrupts; uninitiated simpletons might suggest that fine art is what they like, coarse art is everything else.

After the Mozart, the smiling, daffodil-waving figure of the Maharishi wandered on-stage, to deliver one of his woolly lectures on the benefits of his method of transcendental meditation. About half-way through the meeting, the abrupt metaphysical about-turn the school appeared to be taking, launching from a world of strict obedience into the genially peaceful meditation practices of the Maharishi, became too much for one of the members. She stood up and began shouting abuse at the shocked Indian, before being frog-marched out of the hall.

The Maharishi's influence remains. In their second year, students are invited to become Initiates, to take part in Transcendental Meditation. They are asked to bring a piece of white linen for purity, flowers for beauty and fruit for the inner self. And a material offering of money. The recommended sum is one week's salary, offered in a sealed envelope. They then begin a form of transcendental meditation based on chanting a mantra.

But links between the Maharishi and MacLaren were short lived. Maybe they were both too ambitious for each other. Some feel the Maharishi pulled out because he disapproved of

MacLaren's authoritarianism. MacLaren's friend Francis Roles's next find had been yet another guru, the Indian religious leader known as the Shankaracharya of the North, who taught in the same tradition as the guru who had instructed the Maharishi. MacLaren, obsessed with the idea of finding the source of all philosophy, promptly disappeared to India.

Even today, students follow in MacLaren's footsteps and make the pilgrimage to see the elderly Shankaracharya, who gives audiences seated under a canopy, and delivers his teachings to them through a translator. One tutor tells me, 'He comes out with these *marvellous* ideas.'

Back in London, enthused by what he had seen, MacLaren instituted the next phase of his authoritarian ministry. The thaw was over. A new regime of holy servitude began – part Gurdjief-fian discipline, part oriental mysticism, part Christian mysticism, part social snobbery based on MacLaren's conviction that the only true art is high art. He created a panoply of semi-divine figures which included Shakespeare, Mozart, Da Vinci and the Romantic poets, all of whom are revered alongside Newton, Plato and oriental philosophers.

The cult's lifestyle revolves around a notion known as the Measure. We are all asleep and have to wake up to the Absolute, to the higher world. The Measure forms the basis for disciplining and regulating our lives, to wake us from our slumber. After a few years in the school, members are encouraged to meditate twice a day, at sunrise and sunset, even during the long summer days when sunrise is at 4 am. They are encouraged to study Sanskrit, or calligraphy, or any of the other subjects in vogue. They are asked to perform tasks, like scrubbing floors, cleaning or redecorating classrooms and preparing food. At two week-long residential courses a year, plus a couple of weekends, they are invited to perform about three hours of manual labour a day 'to bring about simple efficiency and happiness', and then, at further group study meetings, they discuss what they've learned while at their labours. They are also advised to eat a vegetarian diet of fresh food.

In the years following MacLaren's discovery of the Shankaracharya, his sexual discipline seemed to have become even stricter. At the week-long retreats, men and women were separated. Women were enjoined to wear only long skirts. Hair was to be worn in a bun. 'Sexually it was an absolute switch off,' remembers one man. 'Which is, of course, exactly what was intended.'

Week two, term one. We philosophy students are still a long way from being told of the existence of the Measure, but ever more quotes from the Vedas and the *Bhagavad-gita* are starting to appear.

Miss Crammond greets us again cheerily and asks if we have practised the Exercise, the mild form of meditation we practised in the first lesson, feeling the weight of our body and the play of air on our faces. A stiff, middle-aged man complains, 'I'm not very good at it. I had a very religious upbringing and it seems to feel like a religious ritual to me,' he says apologetically.

Miss Crammond raises her eyebrows, horrified. 'We're not trying to *brainwash* you!' she answers. 'We're just trying to connect you to yourself.'

Over the weeks Miss Crammond drip feeds us the school's beliefs: that the only way to knowledge of the absolute truth is to first re-connect with the reality of the self. A keen young Spanish woman who attends the class has already studied some philosophy and is becoming puzzled by the apparent lack of intellectual rigour in the pronouncements Miss Crammond reads from her pre-prepared sheets. She puts up her hand. 'Excuse me. But how can a subjective idealist know that reality exists?'

Miss Crammond looks puzzled. She cups her hand round her ear. 'I'm a bit deaf, I'm afraid. Can you repeat the question?'

The Spaniard repeats her question.

Miss C., rarely thrown off balance, looks positively alarmed. 'Can you repeat the question?' she begs.

By the end of the first term we no longer ask questions about subjective idealism. By the second term the classes have dwindled in size, to only eight or nine. Apart from regular practice of the Exercise, our lessons have become a succession of diagrams drawn by Miss Crammond on the blackboard. She picks up a giant wooden compass and draws a circle on the blackboard. This, she explains, is the circle of life. Death leads to birth, birth leads round to death. In the middle of the circle is the hole, worn through over the years, by the compass drawing endless circles on the board. She draws lines from the circle to the centre. This is us, she says, re-connecting in rare moments with the Absolute.

On other days she draws concentric circles, marked 'Body', 'Mind' and 'Consciousness'. Miss Crammond is too short to write the word 'Consciousness' outside the biggest circle which contains the others, so one of us has to help her. We discuss the relationships between them. Gradually, numbers are whittled down to those who are still interested in the idea of the higher consciousness.

'The mind,' Miss Crammond reads, 'extends beyond the body in time and space.' She looks up, peering through her gold-rimmed spectacles. 'Well, what do any of you have to say about that?' Pause. 'What does that say about the mind?'

One of the genteel disciples asks if she is 'talking about psychic powers?'.

'Well, yes,' answers Miss Crammond. 'But it's more than that. You see the mind can know something that's happening hundreds of miles away.' She tells a story about how she once had a terrible feeling that something bad had happened to a friend's baby, so she phoned up and learned the baby had died. 'That was an example of the mind stretching thousands of miles to learn something that was happening very far away . . . I'm sure we all have examples of that?'

The true mysticism of the followers drips through. Once one has reached true enlightenment, true self-knowledge, one is capable of magic, because we are all one self, and we can therefore know anything.

A terribly prim woman in a black skirt and gold twinset is nodding, wide eyed. She looks ecstatic with recognition. 'I have a daughter who lives in America who works with horses,' she tells us in clipped home-county tones. 'One night I woke up with this really *awful* idea that something *dreadful* had happened to her. I just couldn't get it *out* of my head. So I phoned up the farm in America where she worked and said, "Is Phillipa all right?" They said, "Of *course*. Why shouldn't she be? We just saw her go out riding half an hour ago." But then a little while later I got a phone call from Pip in hospital,' she says, still amazed. She explains what happened in earthy detail. 'A stallion had tried to mount the mare she was on, you see, and she had fallen and broken her collarbone. But I *knew*.'

'Absolutely,' agrees the marvellous Miss Crammond, practically singing from the joy of it all. 'That is the heart of a mother going out to a daughter. A heart can know what's happening to a loved one hundreds of miles away.'

Cults, we are told by those in the anti-cult movement, practise a form of subtle brainwashing. It is obviously far too subtle to have an effect on the dozens upon dozens who have already abandoned the course by this time. I too appear to be immune to it; a year of lessons delivered by Miss Crammond and her colleagues has left me unmoved.

The few who are left by this stage in the course, are simply those who want to believe. I witness nothing that could be called thought reform, or brainwashing. The yearning dedication of those who stay, turning up week after week in their quest for the big answer to life, is somehow ignored by those in the anti-cult movement who try to tell us that behind the fluty-voiced Miss Crammond lurks a malicious agent of mind-control.

In 1984 two journalists from the *Evening Standard*, Peter Hounham and Andrew Hogg, published a stinging exposé of the publicity-shy School of Economic Science in a book called *Secret Cult*. They traced the network of properties owned by the cult. As well as the huge Oxfordshire mansion, Waterperry, where MacLaren now lives, the school also owns a gigantic mansion called Sarum Chase in Hampstead, Preston Brinscall Hall in Manchester, the two houses in Queen's Gate, and numerous smaller buildings around the country. The properties are worth millions, and have been amassed through donations. One of the gifts, curiously, was Necker Island, one of the Virgin Islands, which was later bought by Richard Branson to become his hideaway.

To the authors of *Secret Cult* it looked as though they had uncovered an international conspiracy. There were branches in

Ireland, Holland, Belgium, Malta, Australia, New Zealand, America and Canada. Most damning, the book accused the school of deliberately infiltrating our corridors of power. Several lawyers were members. Roger Pincham, chairman of the Liberal party, was a member too. He brazenly admitted it (stunning other Liberals at the time when Pincham's claim that the school had taught him how to levitate himself was published). Other followers had stood as Liberal party candidates. The evil nature of the cult was there for everyone to see.

The book is a perfect demonstration of how, if you start looking for a malignant cult, that is exactly what you will find. It assumed that members had taken positions as wealthy lawyers, churchmen and politicians because they were in the cult; it didn't reach the more obvious conclusion that they were in the cult simply because they shared the elitist upper-middle-class professional values that the school espoused.

Besides, if they were really trying to infiltrate the corridors of power, why on earth had they chosen the Liberal party?

Half-way through each lesson we go for a tea break downstairs. Sandwiches are served, prepared by the women in long dresses who hover in the kitchens.

On one wall in the tea room there is a large painting, fifteen feet by four, of a huge oak tree, rooted firmly in the soil. In its branches roost several birds. From all directions, birds flock towards it. The school takes particular pride in its artistic achievements. It's beautifully executed, figurative, but above all, allegorical. Abstract art, just like modern music, is not encouraged.

I ask a man who has been in the school for years why they always display prints by artists like Botticelli, and yet nothing from the twentieth century except their own careful paintings. He replies, sniffily, 'The artists selected by us are the ones that reflect the pure consciousness more *greatly*.'

In the painting in the tea room, many species of birds are painstakingly and accurately depicted. The uplifting message of the painting is emphasised by the motto underneath: 'My son! All things fly to the self as birds fly to the trees for rest.' In the allegory, the oak tree is a particularly solid, traditionally English representation of the Absolute self in which all souls find their rest.

The only worrying thing about the painting is that many of the birds flocking towards it are of the web-footed variety: mallards, egrets and gulls. Not having claws, they are going to have a great deal of trouble perching in an oak tree. Each time I look at this painting I decide the painter has subconsciously represented one of the truths of the School of Economic Science. It is a school of quiet snobberies. There are many people they don't actually *want* to roost in their tree.

At one end of the tea room there is a bookstall selling texts by or about the school's approved figures: Kahlil Gibran, Mozart, Gurdjieff, Ouspensky and Shakespeare. There is also a set of volumes by a little-known Renaissance philosopher called Marsilio Ficino, who translated the works of Plato from Greek, and whom the school have 'rediscovered' and placed on a pedestal. The school reveres the ideas of Plato who believed that God could be uncovered through discovering natural laws, and who preached that freedom could be achieved through a strongly-ordered society led by philosopher rulers.

The work of translating Ficino's letters has been painstakingly carried out by a group within the school known as the Renaissance Group. No translators or editors are credited. In the quiet name of service, the copyright belongs to the school.

The school dreams genteel dreams of being the vanguard of a new, cultured, refined, disciplined Renaissance. If there is a millenarianism in their beliefs, it lies here. The world has gone to pot. TV has dimmed our brains. Populism has rotted the mighty British culture. Lack of respect for authority is undermining the nation. An undercurrent of Royalism bubbles underneath their longing for an ordered world. They long for a safely certain ancient world where Mozart will be played for ever. But philosophy can restore the balance which has been lost.

One Sunday morning I go to an improving lecture at the Queen's Gate address on 'Philosophy and Being English', by a middle-aged historian introduced as Miss Linda Proud. She decries the debased educators of today who spurn study of the Bard. Peering over the lectern in her tortoiseshell-rimmed glasses she announces, 'Language requires constant work to keep what *purity* it might have. Newspapers are written by people who have not studied language. They may have done a degree at university, but today we have a situation where we're reading the language written in a state of ignorance, as it were, where it is not being nurtured by people of a certain position.'

We people of a certain position smile, conceitedly. The genteel, refined members of the cult of the School of Economic Science are not so much infiltrating the corridors of power, but retreating into timorous, obedient certainties to escape from a modern world that has already overwhelmed them.

'What we're lacking today is people with a sense of *language*,' Miss Proud ploughs on smugly. She looks to Prince Charles as an upholder of the new philosophy, she says. We need leaders, not democracy. 'Politicians today, I think by the very nature of democratic society, are not allowing themselves to speak the truth. So we will only develop a culture of truthful speaking when a sufficient body of people, such as the people in this room,' she smiles, 'take it upon themselves to speak the truth at all times.'

Faces in the room light up with self-satisfaction. The audience clap with polite enthusiasm as the Sunday bells from a nearby Kensington church fill the air.

The school also runs its own independent school for children of the vanguard, St James. The houses at 90 Queen's Gate also provide the premises for the junior school. The rooms we are taught in double up as their classrooms. Sometimes their work is pinned to the wall. One week I notice they have been working on collage pictures of the countryside. The pictures are oddly uniform. All seem to have the same shaped horses, the same shaped birds, the same shaped cows grazing on their same shaped hills.

Around 600 pupils go to St James – a girls' school, a boys' school and a junior school. The teaching ethic shares much with the School of Economic Science. Nearly all the staff attend courses at the School themselves. Exam results are average to good. Discipline is old-fashioned; they still retain corporal punishment. 'There are two key factors in education,' a spokesperson tells me. 'The love of the teachers and the discipline of the teachers. One without the other is an imbalance.'

Pupils must offer the vegetarian food that is served to their neighbours before eating. Reading is taught by the traditional method of 'sounding out' individual letters. Unless parents object, meditation is taught from the age of ten. Parents are asked to ensure that children do not listen to corrupting pop music or watch too much TV.

The more unusual items on the curriculum include teaching about the Upanishads and Socrates; Sanskrit and Greek are taught too. Not surprisingly, pupils learn a great deal of music by Mozart. And as for drama? 'Lots of Shakespeare,' notes the *Daily Telegraph Schools Guide* approvingly.

The spokesperson tells me, enthusiastically: 'I think some of the things we're doing will be highly attractive to the wider world, when they see the results.'

Back in Miss Crammond's classes, numbers slowly continue to dwindle as we are asked to accept ever more complex eastern classifications of the world. We learn the three gunas – the states of – *sattwa* (harmony), *rajas* (activity), and *tamas* (inertia); we learn that the body is made of earth, air, fire and water; that a particle of earth is made of one half earth, one eighth fire, one eighth air, one eighth water and one eighth space; and that these same elements form, in the body, a hierarchy of blood, bone, fat and, as Miss Crammond delicately puts it, 'the finest refinement of elements, the . . . ah, generative fluids'.

We are born with a balance of elements. Illness happens when our balance of elements is disturbed, she says. A young man in a grey suit interrupts to ask a question; a few weeks previously his wife gave birth to a baby that is seriously underweight. He's worried about it. Can the balance be restored?

Miss Crammond, concerned, replies, 'Presumably that's something to do with a desire in the foetus itself . . .'

A usually cheery Belfast woman is shocked, 'What do you mean, *desire*? I wanted to be six foot tall and that didn't work.'

Miss Crammond giggles and answers simply, 'Desire dictates form.'

The woman suddenly becomes worried by the implications of this. 'Hold on. What if a child is born deformed?'

'It's desire,' answers Miss Crammond. 'They say you get the body you deserve.'

The woman is becoming more and more agitated. 'Who says? Who *says* a baby gets the body it deserves?'

'The sages. The wise men.'

In the tea break, the woman from Belfast remains unplacated. Her husband has been worried by some of the stuff she has been talking about since she joined the courses. He has told her: 'Be careful what you're getting into.' In the break she talks to Miss Crammond about it: 'I really do find it really, really difficult to slot into my own belief that any child would actually *desire* to be born ill.'

The ever-smiling Miss Crammond clutches her teacup and saucer and answers: 'It's not a desire to be born ill. It's a desire not to obey the laws of the universe.'

Confused, the woman tells me she's thinking that perhaps she's not going to sign up for the next term's course.

At the end of our last lesson of the winter term, Miss Crammond treats us to a bit of music. 'I'm not going to tell you what it is, I just want you to listen.' Out of her small tape recorder come the strains of the *Elvira Madigan* slow movement from Mozart's C major piano concerto. She closes her eyes, blissfully, to the halting piano. When she opens them, she says excitedly: 'Well, I'm *dying* to know what you think.'

Before we file out, she says, 'I think I've probably given you more than enough to think about for the vacation. I hope I shall see you at the Christmas party.'

We have already been handed a large white copperplate printed card, inviting us to the school's Christmas concert.

*

The Pinstripe Guru

After I've stopped going to lessons, I call up the school's publicity officer, to check a few facts about the school. He is wary, tired of people trying to knock the school. It turns out he is David Boddy, for twenty-one years a member of the school, a former press adviser to Margaret Thatcher and one-time director of public relations for the Conservative party. I ask him about all the women in long skirts. He answers, charily: 'In classes, the ladies are encouraged to dress with honour and dignity. Which, yes, generally means that their bodies are covered with long skirts. In general, there are enough temptations of the flesh around today.'

The last time I see the magnificent Miss Crammond is at the Christmas concert, dressed as always in a long skirt, hiding the temptations of her flesh. It is held at Sarum Chase, a beautiful and immense 1930s mock Tudor mansion high on the hill above Hampstead which the school bought in 1971. Men in dinner jackets throng around the staircase, sipping mulled wine. Inside, some of my keener fellow students have chosen to recite Dylan Thomas's 'A Child's Christmas in Wales' and one-time Gurdjieff follower T. S. Eliot's 'Journey of the Magi'. Giggling children from the junior school perform a sugary scene 'Dulce Domum' from *The Wind in the Willows*. The choir sings a verse anthem by Orlando Gibbons. Then we all stand for 'Good King Wenceslas' and 'Hark the Herald Angels Sing'. All the vulgar modernity of the world is held at bay. First-year students, dressed in conspicuously informal jeans, look ill at ease and out of place. This wasn't what they expected in a Christmas party. Awkward besuited men bellow the lines earnestly from song sheets. At times like this you can see the school was always just as much Leon MacLaren's own bizarre charm school for gentlefolk as it was a cult. Behind the choir, looking oddly out of place, is a portrait of Shankaracharya, draped in saffron robes, white bearded, with a red mark on his forehead. In another room, suitably placed overlooking the vat of mulled wine, is a photograph of their other guru, Leonardo Da Vinci MacLaren, lying on a hillside in his baggy black suit, under a shock of black hair. He appears to be smirking. And who can blame him?

As I leave, I feel like a posh schoolboy at an earnest, well-meaning, stolid, self-satisfied public school, going home to pater and mater after the end-of-term concert. I take the glorious Miss Crammond's arm as we descend the large oak staircase.

'Wasn't it lovely?' she smiles. 'See you next term, I hope?'

SIX

Day-Glo Jesus

1

The young moustached man in the Jesus Revolution T-shirt stands behind the table, hammer in hand. On it sits a tape deck. Lifting the hammer, he bawls, 'Worldly music!' and brings it crashing down on the machine, sending it jumping into the air.

He picks up a hated squash racket and cracks it in two over his knee. 'All sorts of stupid sports!' A cheer goes up from the crowd as he junks the remains in a galvanised iron bin.

'Beer!' The hammer comes down again, this time crushing a can.

'Nasty videos!' And again. Whack. Applause.

'We're purging the church, right? How much of this applies to *you*? Come on, be real.'

He consigns an *Argos* catalogue to the garbage. Next some holiday brochures, 'Family holidays?' the man sneers. 'Go to Turkey. California looks *nice*.' The crowd hoots.

Next, a wad of credit cards. 'Keep yourself free from the love of money!' A cigarette gets crumpled into the bin. A pair of sunglasses is crushed as the destroying hammer of God takes its revenge on behalf of the rejects and the misfits.

'Ostentatious jewellery? Hundreds of pounds that could have been spent for the Lord!'

Finally he holds up a black shirt bearing the name 'Guns 'N' Roses' and shreds it. 'Demonic T-shirts!' People blow whistles and cheer. Someone's letting off a hooter. He throws the remains in the bin and proudly holds up another shirt, just like the one he's wearing. 'Jesus Revolution.' Photo flashes light up the stage.

*

'Celebrate Jesus and Catch Fire,' blasts the leaflet. 'Wembley Praise-Day 1993! Hallelujah! In the UK there is the ongoing Spirit of a Jesus people's movement, a Jesus Revolution. God adopts the homeless generation. The Wembley stage will be crowded with ex-homeless people testifying to the saving power of Jesus. Come and take part!'

Outside, the tarmac at Wembley is crowded with shiny new Transit vans, painted loudly with the slogan, 'Love Power and Sacrifice'. They are the troop transporters of the Jesus Army, the militant wing of the Jesus Fellowship: the 'Rambo cult'.

Hundreds in the crowd wear the Jesus Army combat jacket: a large, military camouflage jacket with bright-red epaulettes, covered in red and green badges which proclaim: 'Jesus Army – We fight for YOU!' This is one of the fastest-growing religious sects in the UK. Over 2,200 are now fully covenanted members. Many have given up their homes, friends and families to live communally, donating every penny they earn to a central purse. Along with the West Indian Pentecostal churches and the Greek Orthodox church, the Jesus Army is one of the only sections of the Christian church growing in Britain. Noel Stanton, the man behind this mighty movement, has boasted of 200,000 people around the country who turn up to Fellowship rallies. Every year new members join.

People stand on stage and witness: 'My name is Geraldine. I was drinking, doing drugs. I was involved in the occult. An' gay relationships. I was just a mess really. And then I met Jesus in the Jesus Army Marquee . . .' And everybody claps and whistles.

'Rise, you downtrodden,' the congregation sing, palms raised heavenwards.

In the centre of the stage stands a small, surprisingly un-prepossessing man in neatly-pressed trousers. He is in his late sixties and combs long wavy hair across the balding dome of his head. Amongst all the burly youths, whooping around the stage dressed in T-shirts that blare 'England for Jesus' he looks out of place, a little like an elderly father, come to collect his kids from a party. But when Noel Stanton wanders to the mike, raises his arms and whispers, 'Bless you!' the crowd quietens, to hear what he is going to say.

Today he relates a vision that came to one of the Jesus Fellowship in a dream. He talks in a quiet, intense whisper. An angel dug up the foundations of the Wembley Conference Centre and replaced the building with the Church of Jesus, filling the foundations with the water of baptism. And the crowd, alive in the age of miracles, starts to cheer again.

'I need My church, says the Lord, and I who am the Creator, I now build My church,' intones Noel, brimming with the inspiration of the Holy Spirit. 'And you belong to My church. And so I come to you, says the Lord, as One who owns you, who has purchased you, and who has . . . brought you out of an old slave rulership. Into My blessed rulership.' This is the Jesus Fellowship, the church Noel founded. He believes that they form the righteous church, living the life ordained by the Apostles. 'And you are part of My body, you are part of My bride. You are precious to Me. You are beautiful in My sight. And I love you. And I am with you. And I make you . . . more and more splendid.'

2

Two weeks after the Wembley Praise Day, an empty 1970s school building just off the A43 in Northampton is hosting another big festival. This time it's a men-only event, Men Alive for Jesus. 'Join over 600 other men for a lively day of friendship, power and vision! Men find your calling in Jesus Christ!' There are a series of seminars to attend: 'Spiritual Fatherhood in Action'; 'Moving Forward – No Backsliding'; 'Male Leadership and Serving Authority'. Pausing at a stall selling Jesus Army paraphernalia, I buy a plastic badge that says: 'When you meet, give the greet. Say JESUS! No shame, say his name.' It costs 30p.

Eighty men are crammed into a small school classroom. I am squeezed next to a young black Irishman, whose face I recognise straight away from one of the many testimonies of the saved in the *Jesus Army Streetpaper*. Under this man's picture the caption read:

145

'Found God healing the hurts of the past.' According to the article that accompanied it, he had been put into care as an infant and had suffered sexual and racial abuse while in care. He spent four years in borstal and was committed to a special hospital. At sixteen, after a suicide attempt, he met the Jesus Army in Leicester Square. 'I was crying out for God.' Now he's found Him.

Before the meeting starts the whole room starts to pray. An invisible switch is thrown. I have never heard anyone speaking in tongues before: eyes closed, brows knitted, the Irishman next to me starts to talk in a long, low unstoppable alien babble. Others in the room are speaking in strange, unrecognisable never-before-uttered languages too. It is the language of God. Those who are in the spirit believe they can interpret messages from this holy jabber. God is broadcasting through His followers. Some simply passionately repeat the name 'Jesus!'.

The title of this meeting is 'The Men God is Looking for'. A balding, bespectacled man in a green Jesus Revolution sweatshirt stands up to testify. 'I used to be a *feminised* man. I was always close to my mother and sought the company of women over men. But Fellowship has helped me develop my manlier character, the character I need to serve Jesus.' The room claps and whoops.

Another man rises to tell us about his marriage. He used to think of his wife as an equal, a partner. He wasn't the leader in his household. Then they joined the Fellowship and moved into one of their houses. 'We moved into Zion,' he says, the houses of God, the communities of the Jesus Fellowship. In Zion everything changed. It was painful. He learned that, as a man, he had to take the leading role. Their marriage was no longer the equal exchange society had told them it was. It has been difficult for them to accept, and they've rowed. Their relationship has gone through the most difficult time he can ever remember. They've cried more than they can ever remember crying. Finally, he says, it's starting to work . . .

The Irishman near me stands up. 'I've led a sinful life. I spent a lot of time in prison. I had a lot of relationships, know what I mean? But now I'm in the Jesus Fellowship, I've had the call to celibacy. I've been a probationary celibate for one year now.' To cheers and applause, he adds, 'It's given me a strength I've never had before.'

Noel Stanton's army tell their stories of new manhood, healing the hurts of the past, one by one.

Outside the corridors are alive with men, arms thrown round each other. A man with a fuzzy pen and ink tattoo that says 'MUFC' on his neck, is caught in an embrace with a man wearing a Jesus Army combat jacket. His eyes are closed and tears are pouring down his face.

The other cults I have visited have gathered most recruits from the middle class, the well to do, the people who were already assured of a comfortable life but were still dissatisfied with it. The Jesus Army conforms to an older, more comprehensible model of millenarianism, fuelled by the margins. Though the people who started the Fellowship were often the sons and daughters of genteel, church-going households, these are the people they have found.

Some lie on the floor limp. Eyes shut, friends with faces red from ruptured blood-vessels huddle around them, praying. It's a moving sight, all these hard-as-nails men people would cross the road to avoid, quietly clasping each other.

I fight my way through the bustle to another seminar: 'Pioneering in the New Age of Jesus Christ'. An elderly vicarish gentleman sits down next to me and asks, 'Are you staying for the meeting tonight? I'll stay for part of it,' he confesses with a guilty smirk, 'but I'm afraid I get tired very easily. It's the music. I wish they wouldn't play it so loud.'

A neat young Welshman who introduces himself as Paul lays his crutches on the table and starts to talk about backsliding. Backsliding is the flipside of the born again coin. Behind there is always the glassy, oily slope to Hell. All it takes to start teetering is to do the sort of ordinary, sinful things that most people do, like go to the pub, watch TV, smoke a cigarette, look too hungrily at a member of the opposite sex, or worse, the same sex.

With his well-groomed dark hair and small moustache, Paul looks like a young sales rep. Only when he moves do you remember he has artificial legs.

Leaning against the edge of a table, he testifies: 'I was an alcoholic,' his Welsh accent stressing every consonant in the word. At about thirteen or fourteen he started taking drugs, getting arrested for robbery. He was in and out of institutions and then in and out of prison. One day he laid himself down on a railway track and let a train crush his legs. The Jesus Army has scores of members who regularly testify to the misery of their lives before they were saved for Jesus. Paul is one of their star turns. He gave up drink when he joined the church and moved into New Creation Farm, one of the Jesus Fellowship's many properties in Britain, and one where many new members are taken to work, to give them a chance to rebuild their lives. But one day he was tempted by Satan and he went into town and got royally drunk, then passed out blind on his bed.

'I had a dream,' says Paul, to his audience perched on school tables and chairs, squeezed standing into any spare space of floor. 'I was in a lift, going down. It seemed to be going down a long, long way. When the lift stopped and the doors opened I stepped out and there, a couple of feet away, was this big black man, with a huge great afro and this big glittery suit.' Everybody laughs. 'You know, with huge great lapels. And he turns to me and he says, "Congratulations. Welcome." And he held out his arms. I turned on my heels to make it back to the lift, but the doors closed on me. I woke up in a cold sweat. My bed was drenched. And I sat up in bed,' Paul closes his eyes and shakes his head fervently. 'Thank you Jesus, for saving me from Hell!' The room starts clapping.

'*Thank you* Jesus for giving me another chance . . .'

A massive man in an army jacket rises: 'I have the word of God,' he announces. 'Someone in this room is suffering from some sort of pain in the neck area. And someone else has flu. If you need healing, make yourself known.' Several hands rise in the air to lay claim to the flu. The man passes around the room, laying on hands and anointing with oil from a small bottle.

The next one to stand is Rufus, a long-haired, hyperactive man with a grin permanently on his face. Rufus was one of Noel's earliest converts. 'I haven't prepared anything,' he shrugs, and starts giggling. The giggling is infectious. Others in the room start laughing too. Next to Paul's sombre Welsh warnings of sin, Rufus's testimony is giddy and light-headed, about how they mustn't act in holy ways. Rufus is trying to make a point, but he gradually loses his thread. Instead, as he talks, a spirit of weird hilarity starts to take over the room. To my alarm, everyone seems to be starting to laugh for no reason. Even the elderly gentleman next to me. Uncomfortable and conspicuously straight-faced, I watch the gathering cast their inhibitions aside and bellow like moon-addled madmen.

A man in his fifties, with a beard, stands up, opens his mouth wide to show uneven, black gappy teeth, and bellows with laughter. 'I would just like to say . . . HAHAHAHAHAHA!'

Noel is ministering in the school's big hall. His theme, too, is manhood. 'If you look at other churches, the men have left them, have abandoned them. In most churches, they are losing members. If you look at the congregations, there is a majority of women. But the early church was built on apostles. We need apostles today. We need *men*,' he raises his quavering, mild voice, 'with a fresh anointing of the Holy Spirit. We need men to be warriors for Jesus. We need men to be leaders.'

They sing a hymn: '*God is calling men to lead this nation/To lay aside all things of compromise/God is calling men of new creation/God is calling men who are alive.*' The words are flashed up on stage by a pair of overhead projectors.

The holy laughter that overtook the seminar is rippling around some of the congregation too. Some are on the floor, in paroxysms, while others gabble in tongues in a fulfilment of the Acts of the Apostles. ('They spoke in new tongues. They appeared intoxicated.' Acts 2:13–15.) Tears are dripping down tattooed faces.

At times during my year of joining cults it has felt like the world is going mad. Sensible, secular, half-hearted C of E Britain is becoming a nation of crackpot escapists and evangelical firebrands. But I have been keeping strange company. There have, after all, always been cults. Rapid social change always throws up new millenarian movements that turn the world upside-down.

This infection of holy hilarity is a strangely medieval scene of ecstasy to encounter in the dull modernity of twentieth-century Northampton. It's like a new outbreak of the fourteenth century's St Vitus Dance, which spread through Germany, Holland and Belgium, seizing the poorest members of society, and throwing them into trances and fits of laughter and dancing. Then it was interpreted as being caused by demons. When a similar epidemic hit Italy in the fifteenth century it was thought to be caused by the bites of tarantulas. Here, it is not the work of demons or spiders, but clearly the work of the Holy Spirit.

Some are clasped round each other, holding hands on heads, passing the healing force of the Holy Spirit through them. Demons are being expelled. The devil is losing.

Miracles soon become everyday affairs. Some children, bored at the back of the arena, are filling in a dinosaur colouring book.

3

Soon afterwards I call a number in the Jesus Fellowship magazine *Jesus Lifestyle*. 'Jesus Fellowship congregations and house groups meet in much of Great Britain. Join the blaze. Call the number nearest you.'

A man called Tom answers. He says the Jesus Army will come to my house and pray with me, if I want.

Or I can come to one of their meetings. Uncomfortable at the prospect of them coming on to my territory, I take the tube to North Acton on a Saturday night, and, as instructed, call them again from the station and wait by the Esso petrol station. After five minutes, Tom and another man, Charlie, pick me up. Tom, a large thirty-three-year-old black man with a friendly face shakes my hand and says, 'Bless you,' and thanks me for coming. 'I wasn't sure if you would, but I was praying for it.' Charlie is more taciturn: he has long dark hair and greets me nervily. Tom quizzes me about what brought me here and I give vague answers. He's a little nervous and a little shy, trying hard to make me feel at home. 'Good to see you, brother.'

'Do a lot of people just call out of the blue?'

'Oh yes. Some do. Doesn't matter how God sends them to us.'

The Jesus Army own two houses in London. Actually these are four houses knocked into two; large redbrick four-storey Victorian family houses, which rise up behind very ordinary-looking privet hedges and leggy rose bushes, just like all the other houses in Emmanuel Road, W3. Tom shows me them, proud of the Divine coincidence. 'Emmanuel Road!' grins Tom. 'Praise the Lord!'

He shows me round. Numbers 1 and 3, now joined by a corridor, are known as the Battlecentre, the HQ of London operations. Number 1 is the sisters' house. Number 3 is the brothers', though there are families living on the first floors of both. Up the road two more houses have been knocked together and renamed Spreading Flame.

Everyone is welcoming, obviously used to new faces. Before the 7pm meeting a round, matronly woman called Joan dressed in a long grey frock makes me a cup of tea and I sit in the living room, where a couple of young kids strum guitars. It is a conspicuously basic room, heated by a 1960s gas fire. An odd selection of frayed second-hand sofas and chairs are arranged around the walls. The patterned wallpaper is old, untouched since the house was taken over, and the walls are bare except for three mottoes. The first, roughly carved in wood, and crudely varnished reads: 'Jesus our King to thee we bow enlisted under thy command.' An old framed Victorian tapestry salvaged from some old church hall announces, 'They testified that Christ was risen and they were all of one heart and soul.' The third, a Jesus Army banner, says, 'Fighting evil with the love of Jesus.' A woman in her late teens or early twenties with long hair and gold-rimmed glasses wanders in. On her basketball boot, written in blue biro, are the words, 'Jesus is Lord.'

It's the Saturday before Christmas, but there are no decorations or cards. The Jesus Fellowship doesn't celebrate either Christmas or Easter. There is no TV in the house either. It's a bad influence.

151

'The TV is my shepherd,' the Fellowship announces archly. 'It maketh me sit down and do nothing for His name's sake.'

I am not sure what to expect, but the meeting turns out to be a simple affair, at the start anyway: guitars are strummed, Jesus Army songs, chosen from a mass of songsheets, are sung, and Tom, bouncing alongside me, bellows the chorus '*Zion is our home*' as loud as anyone in the room. What I'm not prepared for is the way the thirty people crammed into the living room manage to re-create the same wild peak of intensity I had seen before in Northampton. I should have become used to this ability to make the ordinary world evaporate by now, but it still comes as a shock. The quiet room, which people had wandered in and out of with slightly bored Saturday night looks on their faces ten minutes before has gone. Between songs, big Tom, standing next to me, speaks in tongues: 'Masur a basur. Aramash-te, armamar, karama lash-ante . . .' The words that emerge from these devoted mouths are all vaguely similar; mock middle-Eastern, full of rolling consonants and wide vowels.

An older member, leading tonight's chaotic, unstructured meeting says, 'Let us turn to our neighbours and pray with them!' Tom grasps my arm tentatively. 'Dear Lord,' he says, 'come down and lighten this man's soul. Take away his pain.' I am infected by a sense of mild panic, feeling eyes in the room are on me, full of expectation. Unlike the other faiths I have passed through like a tourist, which allow a slow conversion, born-again Christianity begs for a flash of instant revelation. There is a rush of sudden intensity; it's like being on a fairground ride that unexpectedly spins you off into the air. 'Open his heart.' Tom's big arms enfold me, full of hope and holy love. 'He is thirsty for you.' I have only met the people in this room what seems like a few minutes ago. Eyes shut, I can hear Tom's quiet voice above the general mumble of the rest of the room. 'He is a sinful man but he wants to come home to the warmth and the generosity of your spirit. Give him a sign, tonight. Oh Jesus, thank you. Armar-masur aray harama . . .' The room is full of people speaking in tongues. 'Give him strength, Jesus.' A young girl in spectacles next to me is chanting to herself in a small, quiet voice, over and over, 'Jesus, Jesus, Jesus, Jesus . . .' Uncomfortable, I open my eyes and stare at the plaster moulding on the ceiling, which someone, trying to enliven the drabness of the old room, has picked out against the white in a startling blue.

The music starts again. People rattle tambourines. Others bang bongos. Everyone is bursting with joy for Jesus, stamping around the living-room floor. At moments the meeting takes on the looseness of a hippie jam session, the girl playing three chords on the guitar and people making up their own little songs. 'Oh Lord cover me with your love.' I find it absurdly easy to raise my voice and bellow unrestrainedly along with them. When everyone else is throwing away their inhibitions, it is simpler to follow the flow. Standing still and remaining conspicuously silent seems impossible. But there is also something wildly and comically liberating about shouting at the top of one's voice, in this ordinary living room in the small, dark Acton street. It's easy to get carried along in this maelstrom. I realise that the heightened tension of the moment is making me grin and gape like an idiot. A few catch me smiling and smile back encouragingly. Being joyfully welcomed like the returned prodigal makes me feel a guilty impostor, someone fraudulently impersonating a long-lost son.

When we are asked to pray together again, Tom clasps me more confidently. 'I know you are meant for this life. Admit your sin and cast it before God. He is merciful. You see, that's the miracle. However much you have sinned, and that's the point, we all have, you must recognise them and cast them before Jesus. He will wash you clean.' Unlike many of the other doctrines I have encountered, there is a resounding familiarity about this language. As a child I sat through hundreds of dusty Church of England services. It imparts a comforting, nostalgic sense of meaningfulness to his words. But, simultaneously, the message is also horrifyingly bare. Tom tells me, 'You must abandon all your past hopes and find new ones in Jesus.' He wants me here and now to commit myself to a life in the Jesus Fellowship.

It is like standing on the edge of a cliff, knowing how easy it would be to jump. It is not that I am genuinely tempted to join the new Zion, it is simply that the same sense of awesome, vertiginous possibility is there. At this moment I could leap. Tom is presenting me with the rare possibility most of us never consider; right now, in just a few moments, I could abandon my job, my former life, all my friends, my possessions, my frustrated ambitions, my over-draft, my mortgage, everything, and disappear into this new fervent evangelical monasticism. Their reassuring world is ready to wrap itself around me. There is a thrill to being presented with the chance to tear everything you know into little shreds.

Even when people in the room seem to be locked intensely in their own prayers, I feel the pressure of their anticipation, their hope that I will take some massive leap to join them. They want new souls for Jesus with a desperate hunger. When the elder smiles and says, 'If anyone has the word of God tonight, I want them to speak out now,' a young Irish boy pipes out at me, 'I have a word.' He looks across the circle of the room at me and says, 'I know that you are seeking something, and I know sometimes it's hard, and it's a difficult journey, but whatever is hurting in you, whatever pains, whatever doubts you have, they can be taken away . . .' he tails off. 'Um, that's all.'

The sheer tension in the room bursts, and everyone breaks into laughter, a little embarrassed.

After the meeting, we drink tea, and make small talk, as if nothing unexpected had taken place. 'Are you working?' Conversation is odd and stilted. 'Yes,' I improvise, 'I work for magazines – um, as a sub-editor.' I realise shamefully that I am lying heavily, half to create a protective fiction around myself, half to try and make myself sound like someone who might plausibly turn up out of the blue at a Jesus Fellowship house. But I needn't worry. They are so confident in their faith, they expect people like me to see the light of their truth and simply arrive on their doorstep as I have tonight.

Tom, large and smiling, is trying his best to make friends with me. It's a bit like a first date. Smiling brothers and sisters drift through the room, saying 'Bless you!' to one and all. Unruly children are scolded for running in and out of the living room. 'More tea?' people ask me.

In the living room, Tom asks me to stay overnight at the Battlecentre. 'There are always beds here.' He wants me to dive blind into the communal life and abandon my old existence right away. 'I have to go,' I tell him, unsettled by the ferocity of their desire to save me from my sinful ways.

Tom's life has turned upside-down since he joined the Jesus Army. Before he was never sure what he wanted to do. Now he's half-way through a course in welding. He's just completed a Jesus Fellowship qualification, known as YUPPIES: Young Upwardly-mobile Prophetic Preacher. And he's started another course as a Leader in Training, driving up to Northampton to be lectured to by Noel Stanton. There's an article about Tom in the *Jesus Army Streetpaper*. In it, it says Tom was 'blown away by the love of Jesus'. He grew up in children's homes and never knew his own father. When he became a father himself, he never felt he was able to fulfil a father's role properly. Now he says, 'God has given me a real father's heart towards others.'

The next day I feel like I'm jet lagged. My head aches. In the evening I go to a drinks party and chat to a woman I know vaguely.

She works as an administrator for a theatre company, but surprisingly it turns out she was a member of the House Church movement for nine years, a home-based born-again charismatic movement that became a great source of inspiration for Noel Stanton in the early days back in the 60s and 70s. Everything I tell her about from last night, she recognises. My account disturbs her. She said for all of those nine years she hid the guilt that stemmed from the feeling she could never believe strongly enough. It used to affect her badly. She felt that there must be something lacking in her, not to be able to believe as strongly as all her church friends did. She wanted to go to university, but her church told her that she should stay with them. In the end, encouraged by her parents, she went anyway.

She tells me sadly and bitterly, how one of the members of her church committed suicide a few years ago. She believes that it was the same guilt, the same inability to match the fervour of belief of those around him that led him to do it. Even now, years later, she still feels guilty for leaving. I ask her if she still believes. 'Yes,' she answers, taking a cigarette off me, with a glass of wine in one hand. 'I do. But power corrupts.' She believes there was something very wrong with it all.

In return, she asks, 'When you were singing, holding up your hands, did you feel something?'

I admit I did, though to me it was more the force of other people's emotion that affected me than anything spiritual.

'Anyone would,' she nods. 'That's why *anyone* could end up doing what I did.'

Next morning, I get a phone call from Tom. 'I'm just calling to, well, see how you are,' he says shyly. 'We're all thinking about you here, you know,' he says. 'And we're praying. It's been a real blessing to us, you coming here, and finding the Lord.' There's a pause. 'I'm a bit . . . ah, nervous, you know, talking. But.' He giggles. 'And Wednesday, is it all right if we come to your house?' Nervously I succeed in putting him off this idea, inventing the excuse that my landlady (imaginary) does not tolerate visitors.

I can't help thinking how like a shy lover Tom sounds, calling for a date, to make sure it wasn't just a one night stand.

Two weeks after my first visit, the Battlecentre gets another phone call. A young Liverpudlian is calling from a phone booth in Victoria station, sounding desperate. His name is Jeff. He too comes to the Battlecentre, where he tells them about how screwed up things are getting. His life is a mess. He says he's an alcoholic, though he looks shockingly young, in his early twenties at the oldest. Things have been pushing him over the edge recently. His best mate got killed by a speeding car right in front of his eyes the other day. He was in Birmingham not so long ago too getting mixed up with some crack dealers. One day one of them held a knife to Jeff's throat and said he was going to kill him. Jeff believed it.

He's wanted by the police in connection with a couple of thefts, and for failing to respond to a magistrate's court order. At the Battlecentre, they pray with him. They offer him a bed. Jeff accepts. In No. 3 Emmanuel Road, London W3, Jeff finds Jesus and is born again.

4

Noel Stanton had tried a few careers before he became a Baptist pastor with a burning desire to build his church of manliness, a church that would help the downtrodden and the outcast. Born in 1926 on a farm in Bedfordshire, he worked for a bank before he was conscripted into the Royal Navy, where he became a committed Christian. After the war he worked as an accounts clerk and later became a director of a greetings card company. But he spent his free time preaching at village crusades for the National Young Life Campaign until in 1957 he was given the pastorship of a small Baptist church with about eighty members in the village of Bugbrooke, Northamptonshire.

He was a quiet, shy man, obsessed with a hunger to inspire a religious revival. After ten years he had made depressingly little progress and began to search for a miraculous answer, studying the Acts of the Apostles for clues of how the early church had grown. He believed he had found his answer in Acts 1:5 which relates that the disciples were 'baptised with the Holy Spirit'. Later, these same disciples spoke in tongues. The answer lay in being filled with the Holy Spirit. He had heard of it happening to others, and desperately wanted the baptism to happen to him. Then, in 1969, praying alone in the manse of the Bugbrooke chapel he finally achieved a state of ecstasy which he believes was the presence of the Holy Spirit within him. 'It was so intoxicating, so exhilarating, and so intense that I felt I was just not going to live any more!' he said. For hours Noel babbled in tongues. He says, 'It was a tremendous experience of life and fullness from which I didn't come down for a long time – and was the changing point in my life.'

In the following years his ministry began to change. He encouraged others to speak in tongues and to accept baptism as a renunciation of their past. To the disgust of some of the original congregation, guitars and tambourines replaced the organ. From the beginning Noel's ambition was to attract large numbers of young people. He set up something called TTMTT – an acronym for the sweet-toothed title Teens and Twenties Music and Testimony Time. People started to have visions. The first hint of the Jesus Army uniforms to come, arrived when the Bugbrooke chapel started organising a Jesus Lives! Crusade, to travel around the local villages. Followers all wore T-shirts that shouted 'Jesus is Lord. Happy New Life in Jesus.'

In 1972 they saved a house full of dope-smoking acid-dropping hippies, led by a long-haired acid pedlar called Rufus, just as Noel was coming to the conclusion, upon further reading of Acts 2, that a church required communal living.

Rufus was the smiling, long-haired, hyperactive Jesus freak I'd seen at Men Alive for Jesus. He'd been a child actor with the RSC and had appeared as the young Rostov in the BBC's 'War and Peace'. In the 60s his acting career had taken a slide as he'd become a dope-taking hippie. He met the Jesus Fellowship in a café in Northampton while stopping off there to visit his wife, Jessie. He became friendly with Noel, but remained cynical. But when Jess had a baby he began working on a building site to support her. His conversion came not long after the death of his father. Dressed in a greatcoat belted with string, Rufus turned up at one of Noel's meetings with Jess, the baby and their two dogs. At the next meeting he attended, Rufus fell on the floor, weeping, converted.

Rufus's house, where they shared food and belongings in the hippie tradition, provided a model for the future. It was the first of many occasions when Noel has looked to youth culture to provide ways of recruiting. Let's form a commune. Drop out and tune in to Jesus. They began to encourage members to pledge money to the 'Love Community Fund'.

Daily Mail, 16 Sept 1973: 'More than 200 people in a village of 800 have dramatically dedicated their lives to Jesus. Nowhere else in Britain has experienced such a concentrated surge of religious fervour. So many want to be part of the Bugbrooke Miracle that some travel for miles almost every day to attend prayer sessions.'

'God Came to Bugbrooke', 1974 Thames Television documentary:
Local resident A: All that clapping hands and stamping feet – it's not my idea of religion.
Local resident B: It's the kissing I object to.

Local resident C: *I* think kissing is a germ carrier.

In 1974, they bid £67,000 at an auction for Bugbrooke Hall, the old yellow-brick rectory with thirteen acres of parkland, though they didn't have any money for the mortgage and could only afford the deposit. Some members sold their houses and moved into smaller ones to provide the cash. Others donated jewellery to the fund. They renamed it the Jesus Mansion, or New Creation Hall; several members moved in to live communally and create a new 'discipleship centre'.

They believed they were the New Israel, a new community. Next year they took one of the most radical steps, declaring that all earnings could from now on be kept in common. Most began pooling their income. It had acquired a momentum of its own. 'Dare we set ourselves against the current of the world?' Noel Stanton challenged his wonderstruck followers, dressed in an orange kaftan. 'Dare we be a holy people?'

Fired by the unlikely mixture of 60s hippie ideology and Salvationist blood and fire, they bought a farm with the communal purse and set to work on the land. They renamed it New Creation Farm. This was the new creation. A new Eden.

Other steps were less bucolic and less liberal: the Jesus Fellowship began to build a new sexual puritanism. Men were urged to seek the fellowship of other men. Women were housed separately and discouraged from wearing trousers. In the mid-70s ex-hippie women adopted deliberately dowdy clothes. Jeans were cut up and re-sewn into ankle-length denim skirts. Make up began to disappear. One male member wrote in glutinous prose of those early days: 'Men took up their leadership and husbands brought a godly authority to their families. The sisters were beautiful in their loving support and made way for the men to find their strength and potential.'

Sex is full of Satanic temptation. In a community full of young people, desire is regarded as a suspect device that could go off at any second. Brothers and sisters are urged to avoid danger zones – like lingering alone in the company of a member of the opposite sex. Unmarried members are encouraged to spend time with their own gender. If not celibate, it is the men who take the lead in forming relationships. Pairings are carefully watched over. It's an icy ritual, something out of an Austen novel, but without the coy larks. According to the Jesus Fellowship guidelines, if a man falls in love with a woman member, he must go to his elder and tell him. If the woman is agreeable, the elder will then publicise the fact, so that any other man who might want to marry the same woman may make his desires known. Marriage is 'marriage for Jesus'. It's celebrated by large joyous ceremonies presided over by Noel. Sexual intercourse is for procreation and, though not totally banned, contraception remains discouraged. Married couples are expected to sleep in separate beds.

The Jesus Fellowship publish Flame Leaflet No. 10 as guidance to how they believe women should act: 'Women and the Church'. 'So? are women inferior? No! God's not into first and second class status. He's into equality! . . . So, how does God's order work? "The head of every man is Christ, and the head of every woman is man" (1 Corinthians 11:30). When women try to lead men in the church, things go wrong! . . . So, what about dress and fashion? We avoid short hair cuts and wearing trousers! Better to spend time in prayer, or serving, than in front of the mirror making up our faces! So, come on women – let's go for it! Godly femininity!'

But there were setbacks. Ex-members began to attack the cult for its excesses. Peter Eveleigh left the Fellowship in around 1986 and for a while became one of its most biting critics. In a leaflet, designed to look exactly like a Jesus Fellowship publication, he attacked Stanton personally, warning people to stay away from the Fellowship. It was headlined 'Rev N. Stanton's Kingdom. The Truth About Bugbrooke's Communities'. One section was head-lined 'Sexual Relations Restricted'. His account of Bugbrooke portrayed it as a place where members were bullied by the straitjacket morality to remain celibate: 'Marriage is taught as being inferior to celibacy and is referred to as a "lower way". For those who have been allowed to marry there is considerable restraint upon their domestic life. Sexual relationships within marriage are considered to be so potentially unhealthy that the "official" policy of the Community is for couples, from the earliest days of wedlock, to sleep apart in single beds. Contraception is "officially" prohibited.

'The women have no significant choice in the selection of a partner except the right to say no to an unwanted courtship, though it has not been unknown for a "sister" to be put under pressure to marry against her desire in the church's interest. For men it is often a long and humiliating process, often drawn out over several years, before their desire to enter into a courtship will be approved by the Community leadership. Many requests are turned down.

'Engaged couples who join the Community are expected to separate and in common with "all" other men and women are not allowed to display or talk of affection for one another without the critical approval of the Eldership. Only men over twenty-five may expect to be allowed to marry.

'Family life is not what the Community would have the outside world believe. Children within the Community are virtually prohibited from forming close friendships with children outside the Fellowship. They are kept away from any social activities at school, such as extra-curricular sport and drama. They are indoctrinated from the tenderest years and live under the expectation that if, by the age of eighteen, they have not accepted the Community's lifestyle, they will have to leave their homes and parents. One baptised seventeen-year-old, who had been brought up in the Community, expressed a fear of leaving. "I cannot leave because I'm afraid of what would happen if I died in the process." She later added, "I know that if I left, my family and friends would turn against me."

There were worse disasters. New Creation Farm had been plagued by a series of mysterious deaths that were cannon fodder for enemies who wanted to prove that the Fellowship was out of control.

On Friday 3 December 1976 David Gavin Hooper went missing. He was a quiet twenty-four-year-old articled clerk with a firm of Surrey solicitors, who had met the Jesus Fellowship the previous January, and who was so taken by the life he moved into a community house. At first he had enjoyed himself, but after a while, disillusionment began to set in. The last time his parents had visited him at Bugbrooke, they had thought he looked ill.

His absence was noted on Saturday at the Community lunch by his house leader, who sent someone to look for him. As the day wore into evening, twenty-four hours after he had disappeared, search parties were finally organised, combing the area by torchlight in sub-zero temperatures. It wasn't until a week later that a local villager, out walking his dog, came upon David's body in scrubland. He was naked to the waist. By his side, neatly folded, were his shirt, socks, vest, and his Bible. The coroner recorded a verdict of accidental death by hypothermia. The lonely death of David Gavin Hooper has never been fully explained, though it is obvious his mental state was precarious at the time. One member, who shared a room with him, confessed, 'No one really knew him.'

The local Church of England Rector of Bugbrooke at the time of David's death complained that he often had refugees and rejects appear on his doorstep. Some were escaping the discipline, like the women who said they had been told they were no longer allowed to practise contraception. Others simply wanted to leave, but having handed their income over to the common purse, didn't know how. Some were waifs and strays picked up on the streets of London by the Jesus Fellowship whom he believed felt lost once they reached rural Northamptonshire. Deep down, he thought, they believed the Fellowship was the only way to God.

Steven Orchard was nineteen. He had taken what the Jesus Fellowship called a 'virtue name', changing his name to Steve Faithful. Ruddy-faced and popular, he worked on the New Creation Farm. His father, Lionel, had joined four years before. Some say that Steve had been talking about leaving the sect, but others in the Jesus Fellowship say he was devoted to Noel. On Sunday 27 February 1978 he had sat in the chapel at Bugbrooke listening to Noel delivering a text from the Gospel according to James: 'What is your life? You are a mist that appears for a little while and then vanishes.'

The following day he finished mending his wellington boots and disappeared. That night, when he hadn't returned, a search was mounted. Early the next morning, members of Noel's flock spotted a body on the railway track that lay between the New Creation farmland and the canal. From the red hair they knew it was Steve's. The Jesus Fellowship maintain that Steve would never have committed suicide. They say that around 11pm, two trains passed at the point where Steve was trying to cross the line to walk on the canal. The coroner's inquest found that head injuries indicated that Steve had deliberately placed his head on the railway track.

That October, following the death of another young member, Mohammed Majid, at the farm, the *Sunday Mirror* ran the front page headline: 'Jesus Cult Deaths Probe'. It was one of a mounting number of anti-Jesus Fellowship stories that had begun appearing over recent years. Maybe Majid's death was the sort of thing that could happen when any group of town boys are let loose on a farm. Despite being warned against the dangers, Majid had gone swimming in the farm's water tank. But to some his death seemed to fit a pattern. 'Today the *Sunday Mirror* reveals the ugly reality behind the public face of a sinister religious cult.' The article claimed that five people linked to the cult had died in circumstances requiring inquests. Blame for deaths inside cults is routinely used as a stick by those who believe they are evil, though there is no real psychiatric evidence to suggest that most people inside such organisations are any less stable than they are outside them. Doubtless individuals' fragile states of mind are sometimes overlooked in the fervour, and in some cases people's latent illnesses can be triggered off by events in the group. But whatever the reasons behind the three deaths, the backlash against Noel's dream was gathering strength.

In 1986, following the Jesus Fellowship's expulsion from the Evangelical Alliance, they were also expelled from the Baptist Union. Among the reasons given were: 'The embarrassment of adverse publicity.'

When any cult rubs up against a hostile outer world, attitudes become hardened and bridges are burned. Attacks only serve to confirm everything that people believed in the first place. By 1986 the Jesus Fellowship were pouring out their own songs and hymns. In response to press reports and public meetings that were beginning to organise opposition to the church, one senior member wrote a hymn that began, 'Brethren we stand and here defy/The world and all its darkest power.' Satan was at work, trying to undermine the Jesus Fellowship.

The lines of battle were drawn up. The Fellowship defiantly quoted the New International Version of the Bible, Acts 24:14: 'I admit that I worship the God of our fathers as a follower of the Way, which they call a sect.'

Then on 18 April 1987 Stanton unveiled his most militant plan yet to combat creeping secularism. He launched the Jesus Army. The Fellowship has a fondness for acronyms. Originally it was named JAWBONE after the jawbone of the ass that Samson used to slay a thousand men: the Jesus Army War Battle Operations Network. Stanton announced that the brothers should wear army combat jackets because of their 'manly image', while the sisters should wear green skirts. Banners were made, displaying the colours of army green, alongside red for the blood of Jesus, and white for purity. A double-decker bus was bought. There was a sense that nothing could stop them now.

They wrote a ringing open letter to the Prime Minister.

> *Dear Mrs Thatcher,*
>
> *We urge you to call the nation back to faith in God. Christians are praying for a revival that will change society. The members of the church have become a Jesus Army to fight the evils in society and bring the gospel to the victims of vice. We pray that God will give you wisdom, compassion and strength for your responsibilities.*
>
> *Yours respectfully,*
> *The Jesus Fellowship.*

5

On New Year's Day 1994 I board a Jesus Army coach and travel up to Northampton with the cheese and pickle sandwiches I've made from ingredients laid out by the matronly Joan in the Battlecentre kitchen. Gary Wilmot has taken the day off from performing in 'Robin Hood and the Babes in the Wood' (featuring the Waterfall Rapids Spectacular) at the ugly redbrick Derngate Theatre, and the Jesus Army pack the circle and the stalls instead.

On stage, hair flopping off his balding pate, the sixty-seven-year-old Noel Stanton fires the crowd, reminds us of the proximity of Satan, berates us for tiring. But then, because it is the start of a new year, he sets targets for 1994, and reviews the achievements of the old. This year the church will seek 600 new converts. Last year 450 new members joined. Deafening cheer. They dedicate the latest household, the first on Tyneside, and the Jesus Army's seventy-second. They name it Flowing Waters. Like the Battlecentre, all the Jesus households have ringing Bible-time names like Bright Flame, Conquering Name, Crown of Life or Living Stones. Back in the Battlecentre there's a map of Britain with pins marking each household. There are eighteen other pins, orange and blue, which mark target towns where the Jesus Army are planning to 'plant' new households.

Six new married couples are asked up on stage. Some are old and grey, others are young and covered in badges and mottoes. They stand there, hand in hand, smiling shyly out at us.

And then Noel asks all the celibates and probationary celibates to join him on stage, and the aisles stream with single men and women. The true scale of Stanton's achievement becomes apparent.

It takes almost ten minutes for them all to cram on stage. There are hundreds, old and young. Men clasp each other. Women embrace and cheer. This is Noel's proudest moment, turning away the demon of promiscuity from the twentieth century. There stands Charlie, who met me at the station on my first day, looking shyly down from the stage; nearby big Tom beams down at us. He is a probationary celibate going through the one year trial period before he pledges himself to lifelong abstinence. More than 250 members have committed themselves to the celibacy that the Jesus Army urges on its members as the highest moral calling, higher even than marriage.

Gillian is one of the last celibates I recognise to make it on to the stage. Her progress is slow because a friend has to carry an oxygen cylinder for her. She has cropped black hair and black trousers which also mark her out as different from the usual Jesus Army women wandering around in their uniform of hippie ankle-length brown Indian cotton skirts and shoulder-length hair. A teenage runaway, Gillian got involved in drugs. Later she discovered she was a lesbian. In 1991 she caught pneumonia, then developed hepatitis. A year later, after further illnesses, she finally gave in to her doctor's advice and had an HIV test. She discovered she had AIDS. After several overdoses, she found the Jesus Army. Now she has renounced drugs and what she calls 'bad relationships'. She stands on stage proudly with all the others, clapping and cheering.

Celibates wear a silver ring to denote their calling, triumphant in renunciation.

'More and more young people are disillusioned with a sex-mad society and are seeking to live a pure and holy life for Jesus,' proclaims the *Streetpaper*. 'Staying single for the sake of the kingdom of God is part of the Jesus Revolution that is taking hold of this nation. A radical remedy for a desperate church.'

There's even a special celibates' song: 'Jesus I am resolved now/ To live for You alone/Called to this life of freedom/Embracing the narrow road . . .' Followers of the narrow road get a special magazine too: 'Make sure you read *Celibate Cutting Edge*, the inspirational bulletin of celibacy.'

Seven or eight members are led on stage to accept the Covenant, to become fully covenanted members of the Jesus Army. A leader delivers a little outline of their lives before finding Jesus, as ever stressing the waywardness of the convert, the rejection from which they are saved. 'Jake was homeless for four years, and addicted before he came to see us . . .' Each member pledges to keep the seven part covenant of faith, brotherhood, commitment, community, suffering, discipline and oneness with the words: 'Before God I do so make covenant in Jesus' name!' Big cheer for each covenant.

And then the strangest thing I have seen so far happens. Noel Stanton, vessel of the Holy Spirit, lays his hand on each new member's forehead, and I watch them pass out cold at his feet there on stage.

I look around. No one apart from me finds this out of the ordinary. It happens each time. 'You'll get used to it!' someone shouts at me when they see the look on my face. You see? Miracles happen.

This weird, ecstatic, trance-like state first appeared as part of the public covenanting of members in 1988 when newly covenanted members began falling into a trance at Stanton's feet. Now it happens to everyone who accepts the discipline. I had always imagined I lived in a damp-spirited country, whose cold-blooded inhabitants were immune to this sort of unbridled religious ecstasy. Now I am dumbstruck by the force of this belief.

One small fair-haired young woman takes much longer to succumb, and Noel stands there patiently pressing his hand against her forehead. She sways backwards and forwards, willing the miracle to happen to her, until she suddenly collapses like a shot horse. She falls forward unexpectedly and almost cracks on to the stage in front of her, Noel and another catching her at the last minute.

With his small sheepish smile, Noel turns to the crowd and says, 'Sometimes they do that. Fall the wrong way.'

Off the stage, big Tom smiles and says, 'I've got a present for you.' He hands me a copy of the book *Fire in our Hearts*, a triumphant history of the Jesus Army. In the front, in green pen, he's carefully inscribed three biblical quotes. Two are from the Gospel According to John. The third is from the Acts of the Apostles 4 – one of the Jesus Army's key inspirational pieces: 'They had all things in common . . . and they distributed to each as anyone had need.' He's written: 'Bless you William. May you know the joy of brotherhood and love for the church of Jesus Christ, our Lord and Saviour.' Two pages later, he's added another dedication: 'God loves you William. Jesus is a faithful and true friend. Jesus is your strength. May Jesus embrace you with his love, guide you with his light and set you free with his truth.' It would be cynical to say he is just doing his duty; duty and love have become inseparable. I am embarrassed by the shy sincerity with which he presents the gift. He has signed, 'Love in Jesus, Tom'.

Elsewhere in the theatre I meet another young brother, Danny, nineteen, whom I've met a few times over the last few weeks. Every time I meet him he smiles like we're old friends who haven't seen each other for a decade, and pumps my arm until it is almost yanked out of its socket. 'Good to see you, bro!'

Danny used to be a young hippie with shoulder-length hair. Last summer he gatecrashed the Glastonbury Festival, sneaking in under the wire fence that surrounded the site. The Jesus Army were there in force, in the Jesus field the Army take over each year. The day he broke in, Danny spotted a large wooden cross in the middle of the site, and felt drawn to it. The next day, he felt empty and meaningless. So he walked back up to the cross and began chatting to the Jesus Army followers.

The power of Danny's conversion was extraordinary. He was baptised, wearing a T-shirt that read 'The Modern Jesus Army', in a filthy paddling pool that some hippie had set up at the festival, under a notice that read: 'Go in peace, but when you do, don't fucking piss in my pool.' He says he experienced a moment of perfect stillness as his head fell under that dirty water.

At college in Cheltenham, he studies art. Unlike a lot of converts he is no drug addict, or criminal. He comes from a well-spoken middle-class background. But just as the Jesus Army saves the criminals from their past, it also saves Danny from his. This is a world where you require sins to repent as a condition of entrance. One day, I watch as one of the house seniors puts his arm around Danny and says, 'We saved Danny from middle-class-ness,' and Danny smiles penitently.

He grins and bounces off the walls like anyone's stereotype of a born-again brother. He is drenched in ecstasy. 'Wow. Bless you bruv'.' It's a real state. Every day I see him he's smiling, shaking people's hands with that wrenching grip of his. His happiness is unbounded. It makes me anxious whenever I'm around him. There are one or two of the younger members like this, in a permanent state of holy glee.

Danny visits the Battlecentre as much as he can, taking time away from college. He tells me he's thinking of jacking in his course. 'I like it there, but I feel like . . . it's a . . . I don't know . . . distraction. I feel so much *happier* when I'm here.'

The afternoon at the Derngate Theatre is taken up with a performance of *Jesus Live!* It's an amateur rock musical that loosely follows the structure of the Bible, starting with Genesis and the Creation using songs, slides and films. For the pre-lapsarian world the curtain draws back to show the Waterfall Rapids Spectacular that Robin and his Merry Men will be carousing around on stage tomorrow night. At the sight of this panto prop, appropriated for Jesus, the crowd stamp, whoop and cheer far more wildly than they can ever have done for Gary Wilmot. Scented smoke pours off the stage; 'It's supposed to be strawberry,' someone yells at me.

The stage fills with the Jesus Army, acting the role: downtrodden, abused, addicts and prostitutes. God's world is polluted by Satan's sin. They carry banners proclaiming the struggle against the lusts of the world. One reads: 'Rebels Against SIN'. Another 'Help AIDS victims'. A third: 'Remember your [sic] unforgiven'.

A thousand red day-glo crosses and yellow day-glo flags are distributed to everyone in the crowd. The flags have all been individually prayed over. Under fluorescent lights, 1,000 people wave their flags, then their crosses shouting, 'Yes! Jesus! Hoooeee! Praise the Lord!' People are yelping, bawling, singing, crying, shouting, jumping up and down, swaying to the music. Day-glo banners, let down from the ceiling, proclaim, 'The Church of Jesus Christ'. Day-glo Jesus comes to Northampton.

But the true climax of the show is just about to begin. Up on stage, the baptisms start. Hundreds flock towards the stage. Tom and I join the throng and he prays for me again, passionately, hopefully. 'Jesus wants you to be baptised today!' he tells me, and anoints my forehead with oil. Around me, bodies are tumbling in holy trances, filled with the power of the spirit. It's a feverish atmosphere. Outside, it's a quiet Saturday in Northampton, people nursing dull hangovers from New Year's Eve the night before. Inside the big stage is full of prostrate bodies, pole-axed by belief, so convinced of their proximity to Jesus, and people bending over them.

I step round the praying bodies to watch the baptisms. A portable baptistery made of a blue rubberised tarpaulin and an octagon of plywood, ten foot across and three feet deep, has been set up on stage. Fervent, smiling new converts wait for total immersion. Steve 'Capes' (I assume shortened from the virtue name Capable), the leader of the Battlecentre Household is there, plunging them under, fully clothed, to wash away the sins of the past, and to welcome them to a new life. People stand around with towels.

Each time another head goes under, a gigantic cheer goes up. The band are playing a close approximation of rave music. Wherever youth culture goes, the Jesus Army will follow it in its own bright-eyed born-again way. If the kids are searching for something, they reason, they will follow wherever their search leads. Rave culture, they believe, is simply a fumbling search for Jesus. It is the Army's duty to capture techno for Jesus. People wave their hands in front of their faces, spin round in trances. This is a new ecstasy. 'We're rebels for Jesus,' they shout. An Asian boy goes round with a giant foam-rubber crucifix, whacking smiling people on the head. 'Jesus loves you,' he shouts, walloping them with the cross.

One young woman lining up to be pushed backwards into the water can only be about twenty. 'We baptise you into the death of Jesus,' says Steve. When she's yanked back out of the water she appears to have fallen into some sort of trance. Her legs won't hold her and she almost collapses back in. When she's recovered her strength she stands by the side of the pool, dripping in her black dress. Other women, the same age, surround her and throw a towel around her as she cries, laughs and jumps up and down with excitement all at the same time. Their loving arms enfold her. She looks wild with happiness.

In the twentieth century, this sort of boiling hysteria in a crowd so utterly convinced of the rightness of what they are doing brings goosebumps to the back of the neck of anyone not caught up in it. I wander round in a nervy daze. Tom desperately, achingly wants me to accept baptism, but I tell him I don't want to. However repugnant I'm finding the extremes of their self-righteous ideology, I'm starting to feel deeply guilty for stringing along Tom's shiny, loving faith. He believes I'll come round in time.

At the next Jesus Live! Jeff, the young Liverpudlian alcoholic gets himself baptised too. He tells me, 'I'm alive with Jesus' love!'

While we are inside the Derngate Theatre, someone unknown smashes two windows in one of the Jesus Army's fifty-two-seater coaches, which had been parked in a lane outside the town. Later some members blame rowdy locals. Others suggest it might even have been resentful ex-members.

It's not an isolated incident. There have been attacks on some of the households by ex-members and opponents. Because of the risk of such attacks, some households are never left unoccupied; they leave someone behind on 'vigilance'.

Recently a thief broke into the Battlecentre, but didn't take anything. It amuses me to imagine a puzzled burglar wandering round the huge house looking for the television. Or the stereo. Or the video.

6

The power the more brutal imagery of Christianity appears to have over some people never fails to unnerve me. One Sunday I skip the Jesus Army meeting and visit another church, Power Praise and Deliverance Ministries International, and watch Pastor Jennifer Brown of New Jersey, thirty-something, bright-red power suit, black tights and black high heels, shouting through the microphone: 'The end-time is closer than you know.'

'Alleluia,' people bellow.

'I said the end-time is almost here. Say amen.' *Amen*. 'Say amen. And the church is sleeping. Say amen.'

'Amen. Jesus,' people assent. She repeats 'Say amen' so frequently the words become elided: 'Saymen'.

Her accent is West-Indian American, her extemporary oratory is unstoppable, and her subject matter nightmarish. 'And many of us here are asleep too. Satan wants us to slumber. I look among you with my spirit eye and I see many of you asleep.' She glowers at us past the mike. 'Say it: Satan wants us comatised.'

Palms raised heavenwards, her flock concurs: 'Satan wants us comatised.'

'Say it again.'

I watch a row of young girls sitting in a line of chairs, hair bunched into pigtails; one, around ten years old, big eyed in Sunday best, is terrorstruck as Pastor Jennifer approaches.

On a Sunday, the Power Praise and Deliverance Ministry are at work in Tottenham, in a hall thick with sweet air freshener. Two cans have been used before today's meeting in an effort to dampen the smell of nicotine and alcohol left by those who used the hall the night before.

In our loud, born-again congregation, mine is one of only two white faces in amongst about a hundred West Indian Londoners, all saved a few months previously by Pastor Jennifer and her husband, Dr Rev Vaughn Brown, of the Power Praise and Deliverance Ministry. They had placed a huge advertisement in my local paper headed, 'The foetus of deception in the church must die.' Under it is a picture of a human foetus on to which has been pasted a snake's head. The text says: 'Every day you lack prayer you get one step closer to hell. The devil gets bigger and bigger before your eyes.'

Pastor Jennifer has been leading the meeting today because Dr Rev Vaughn has been collecting their son from hospital. He was involved in a car crash early this morning. Or as Pastor Jennifer puts it: 'Satan tried to stop him. He was coming to collect us to take us to this meeting. Can you see how Satan is desperate to stop us? The car is a write-off.' Half-way through the service Dr Rev Vaughn and his son, neck encased in a pink hospital brace, arrive and wave to us. We give thanks. We clap and cheer because Satan has been cheated.

It is a long meeting, stretching from morning through to the evening. When Jennifer tells us to grasp our neighbours' hands and pray for them, every one of us does so. My neighbour throws her arms around me and shouts: 'Save him Jesus. Show him a light. Show him a sign,' but you can hardly hear her above the loud supplications of others. For hours the people in the congregation throw themselves on to their knees, or shake their hands in the air, or bawl out impromptu prayers with millenarian fervour, or are tongue-lashed by the unstinting Pastor Jennifer. Only occasionally does she soften and promise us our reward in the arms of Jesus. And then the band sing sweet, close harmony soul about our coming redemption.

The praying, the shouting and the singing are non-stop, exhausting and draining. The five-piece soul band and the pastor are attended by ushers who serve them with orange squash and iced water, but the congregation gets no break. After five busy hours of abasement, people are bawling, crying, shaking, convulsing on the floor. I peer out of half closed eyes and see faces filled with terror and ecstasy. Pastor Jennifer raises the pitch, then lowers it again to a whisper.

She kicks off her high heels and wanders around the crowd with her microphone like a manic talk show host. 'Don't let Satan pee on you,' she cries as we crowd around the altar. 'You're weak, I *know* you are. Satan is creeping up on you, like a serpent.' Behind me, a woman, possessed by the Holy Spirit, barks like a dog for fifteen minutes non-stop. In front of me, a huge man swings his arms wildly, thumping me repeatedly in the chest. There is no room for me to stand back and avoid his elbows.

Dr Rev Vaughn Brown now stands beside his wife, short, immaculately jerri-curled hair, smart suit and electric blue tie, as they start the collection. 'All those who have £20 come before us now.' Eight people rise and walk towards her. There, two smartly-dressed men hold out gold waste-paper bins for the offerings, smiling broadly. 'No,' Jennifer shakes her head. 'That is not enough. I want more of you to come up with your £20.' More people trickle up and more again. Then Jennifer summons the people with £10, before we, the rest of the congregation are led up to the platform covered in artificial flowers. She and her husband are the archetypal charismatic couple, with rich singing voices, Elmer Gantry theology and an authority based on their audience's fear. We are all weak. The devil is strong. The end-time is near. If we all stand together maybe we can make it. Five pounds is a minimum donation.

At Pastor Jennifer's cry of our guilt, everyone hangs their head, publicly ashamed. Vaughn and Jennifer Brown's followers form a community of a kind bound together out of a mutual love and collective fear, meeting three times a week.

It's finally almost over. 'Hug the person next to you,' says Pastor Jennifer. 'Say: "God bless you neighbour."' It seems like all day we have been throwing our arms round each other. Next to me is a pretty, devout girl with braided hair, who stands and places her Bible on her chair. We embrace, heads on each other's shoulders. 'Say, "I love you."' We tell each other we love each other. 'Now kiss.' The girl giggles, embarrassed.

I arrived at 10am; it's after dark by the time I leave. That night, exhausted, I sleep badly, disturbed by the stern apocalyptic eye of Pastor Jennifer. In a secular society, strong blood-and-fire faith is alien and terrifying. But her flock walked out of the hall, smiling, laughing, chatting.

7

I spend time at the Battlecentre, sometimes sleeping there, sometimes joining them for evening meals with other guests, many of whom have come here for the first time, and some of whom wriggle with discomfort at what is going on around them, at the men sitting on separate tables from the women, at the babble of tongues that takes the place of grace and the singing of songs for half an hour before the food is served.

And worse, the introduction of each guest: 'This is William, who recently gave himself to Jesus.'

And then there is the table talk, punctuated by exclamations of praise from others sitting round the table. It gets a little strange.

'Thank you Jesus!'

'So. Do you have a job?'

'Bless you bro'!'

'No. I've been unemployed for, um, three years now.'

'Praise the Lord!'

Food is cheap, but plentiful. Vegetable pies, coleslaw and pasta. Apple pie and custard, made from the supply of New Creation Farm's apples. On one of the sisters' birthday she gets a sponge cake, decorated in the Army's colours: 'Jesus Lives! We all love you.'

I'm given a bed in a room shared by two older brothers when I stay over. The window hasn't been cleaned in years. A crack is held together with old masking tape. Joan, the plump sister who acts as everyone's mother, provides me with a pillow and carefully laundered sheets when I stay. One of my room-mates spends most of his time in the small room, lying on the bed. He's about fifty, and the bedroom acts as a refuge for him from the frantic, youthful bluster of the rest of the house. But communal life leaves no room for privacy. He patiently accepts his new room-mate. He has a small pile of books near his bed which includes *The Life of Jesus*, *44 Irish Short Stories* and *The Encyclopaedia of London*.

My other room-mate works for a computer company by day, and donates his wages to the communal purse. He sleeps in T-shirt and pants. The room has a faintly male and musty smell about it. 'I knew we should have opened the window this morning,' he says.

One Friday night in January, the Jesus Army organise an 'Eat Drink and Pray' – or 'EDP' as they call it – session in central London. They take food and hot drinks out into Leicester Square and minister to the homeless and drunks who roam around the city in the small hours. Jeff, the household's newest member, goes along to spread the word, dressed in the big baggy jeans with big red pockets he always wears.

On the bus, where they take people for food and prayer, out of the cold night air, he says to one man, 'Do you know about Jesus?'

The man swiftly headbutts him.

That night, in my small bed, I dream I am being chased. I wake shouting 'Help!', something I haven't done in years. I sit up, disturbed and it takes a minute to remember what I am doing in this dingy room. Luckily I haven't woken my two room-mates; one of them is snoring, the other lies tangled in his blankets.

Unable to get back to sleep, I walk down the three flights of wooden stairs and make tea in the kitchen. The absurdity of my double life is beginning to leave me frayed and strange.

The Battlecentre is half-way between a care hostel and a spiritual outward bound centre. The kitchen is built to cater for forty or more people. A pair of yellow rubber gloves dry on a pipe, written on them in black marker pen, 'Ruth Giving – washing up only'. I fish a tea bag out of the big jar marked 'Tea bags'.

It's just starting to get light and I hear Joan bustling down the corridor from the sisters' house. She's carrying a pile of sheets. 'One of the children . . . ah, had an accident,' she euphemises coyly as she bundles them into one of the washing machines. I make some comment about how she seems to be always working. 'Well,' she says, a little embarrassed, 'if I get it done now it leaves me more time to do all those other things.'

Joan, mother to the world, waddles off down the corridor again when she's finished. Later, after the post has arrived, she pops her head around the living-room door where I'm reading a book I found in the study about a boxer who found God. She's clutching a foreign envelope. 'You know, I get really *excited* when I see letters like this. Just to think that somewhere, thousands of miles away they've heard what we're doing, and want to know. God is working everywhere.' She smiles brightly and asks, 'Is Angola in Africa? I'm afraid I always get it mixed up with Mongolia.'

The people on EDP brought back a guest they found wandering alone round the London streets early in the morning. He spent the night here, sleeping late. He's from the former Yugoslavia, and no one can get his name right. He gets called Fidel as the closest approximation anyone can make.

Fidel escaped to London from Kosovo three months ago, arriving by boat on the south coast. He's got fresh scars on his forehead, a thin southern European face, bright olive eyes and short curly black hair. Every month he has to get his refugee status renewed. He's glad not to be in Kosovo, but has suffered badly from loneliness since coming here. He feels bored and lost in London. At lunch, he's still here. Before we sit for our meal, we sing a song, pray for a few minutes and then he, like all guests, is introduced as a friend. Everyone in the room applauds and looks at him. Afterwards, when he sits down, I notice him surreptitiously wipe tears from the side of his eyes at the warmth of his welcome.

Fidel says he's not been brought up a Christian. I wonder if he's a Muslim, but nobody asks. The pork sausages, beans and roast potatoes get put down in front of him and he hoovers them up like the rest of us. After the meal he goes off to stay in one of the other Jesus Army houses.

After lunch, I help dry up then I spend half an hour scraping the sausages and roast potatoes from the thin aluminium roasting trays that one of the brothers had originally said they'd clean before wandering off somewhere else. Even the kitchen is a place of praise. The previous night I had been washing up when somebody wandered in with a guitar and started singing a devotional tune. Within minutes, everyone had put away the dishcloths and started banging pots and pans in rhythm. The song, made up on the spot – people hollering 'You are my Master, You are my Lord,' – lasted about twenty minutes as gradually more and more people wandered in and joined us.

After lunch Jeff's there too, spotty faced, with two slightly protruding teeth, clutching a dishcloth ineffectually like he's never seen one before and relating the story over and over of how he got headbutted last night on the EDP coach. It's starting to drive me mad. He's been going on about it all day. 'I got headbutted last night. I said, "Have you heard about Jesus?" and whack!' he tells anyone who will listen. 'It didn't hurt at all, though. I thought it was going to. But it was like Jesus was like a sheet of perspex in front of me, stopping the blow. I didn't feel a thing.'

Everyone who puts their head around the kitchen door gets this story at least once. 'I didn't fight back either. A few weeks ago I'd have just laid the bloke out, but I didn't, I just stood there.'

'Well done,' says Steve 'Capes'. 'That shows you're coming into the love of Jesus.'

'Yeah,' says Jeff. 'I was going to fight with him, but I didn't. Isn't it *powerful*?'

But when he tells the story to me, he adds another incident. 'Satan tempted me last night,' he says. 'These two lads I got talking to in Leicester Square, they said, "Where are you living?" and I told them and they said, "Oh you don't want to live there. Come back and stay with us." For a while, I wanted to. I almost did. That was Satan, you see? But I came back here. I'm with Jesus now.'

His hyperactive chatter is getting on my nerves. All he wants is someone to say, yes, you did the right thing, not fighting back, rejecting Satan. Don't worry, you're safe now. There's an uneasiness behind his constant babble. He wants someone to take him seriously for once. I guess that's what brought him here in the first place.

At one point he asks me, 'What's Whacko?'

'What?'

'Whacko. All those guys I was talking to were saying, You're like Whacko. That place you're staying is just like Whacko.'

'Oh . . . Waco.'

'Waco?' says Jeff. 'What's that?'

Since he's joined, Jeff's parents have been in touch with him. They say they're worried that he's ended up in a cult, that he's being brainwashed. He protests he's fine. The Jesus Army have got him a job, working for them. He's got a roof over his head, and gets given meals. He's not drinking. The Jesus Army are going to help him sort out the mess he's in with the police, too. After all the trouble he's been in he doesn't know why they're worrying. But the conflict with them is making him feel even more insecure.

Living in the community, all your income goes into the central purse, out of which all household expenses are met. During the first two years of their membership, any capital the followers bring with them is 'loaned' to the community. If they decide to leave during this period, the money is returned at face value. After that time, their money can only be returned at the discretion of the trustees. Those without capital have sometimes experienced difficulties breaking away.

Stanton bases his concept of the common purse, once again, on texts from the Acts of the Apostles out of which he has wrestled the blueprint for the Jesus Fellowship. He believes it's all laid out for us there. His 'Flame Leaflet No. 21' spells it out. 'Wealth creation for Jesus – gaining and using money for God.' 'Jesus has triumphed over every spiritual power including mammon. We just capture the "economic power" for the cause of Jesus . . . All we own needs to be given to God. If we think of money, possessions or property as "ours", then selfishness still grips our hearts and our wealth still belongs to Satan!'

That evening Jeff is still wound up about getting headbutted on EDP the night before. He disappears. That night we have one of our regular Saturday night meetings, singing songs, reading the Bible, praying. No one knows where Jeff is. Last time anyone saw him he was going for a walk.

It turns out he's in a pub in Acton getting drunk. He was going out for a stroll when he met Yvonne, a woman who was baptised at Jesus Live! the same day as he was, and who lives in one of the other Jesus Army houses up the road, Spreading Flame. She was standing outside in the cold January wind, smoking a cigarette. 'I'm fed up,' she said. Jeff said. 'Where did you get that ciggie?'

She told him she has £20 that she didn't hand in to the communal purse. Next thing they were in the pub, half drunk, half guilty, relieved to be away from it for a few hours.

New converts pass from finding Jesus, to baptism and then to covenant in no time at all. Jeff has lurched from one extreme life straight into another. He is still reeling.

That night, while Jeff is drinking guiltily, Charlie, an older member, about forty, shy, twitchy and slightly nervy sits in the living room. He's wearing a black sweatshirt with the word 'Joshua' embroidered on it. He mentions he was in the army for six years. I tell him I'm surprised. He starts to tell his story.

Charlie was a storeman in the army. He lacked self-confidence, and never really got on with anyone. One day, while he was away from the base, his room-mates cruelly packed up his kit without asking him and moved him into the room of another soldier who wasn't one of the lads. His new room-mate turned out to be a Christian. He befriended Charlie and started taking him to meetings. But just as he was starting to enjoy the company of

179

other Christians, he was posted to Germany, which he hated because there was nothing to do except drink. Everyone used to get drunk all the time. Charlie doesn't like drink that much. Now he wanted to pursue a Christian life. He decided to get out of the army.

The moment Charlie applied to leave he was struck by a terror that he'd made a big mistake. What was he going to do? He didn't have any experience of life outside the army. Lost outside the army he drifted for years until he found the Fellowship. 'And I've never, ever looked back. Sometimes it's been so hard. Sometimes I've wanted to run away screaming from all the discipline of life here.' As far as he is concerned, the Jesus Fellowship has saved his life. He says, with emotion, 'The love of the brothers has always kept me here.'

A girl about six years old wanders into the living room wearing a yellow jersey with a cross and the words 'Jesus Army' on it. I tell her my name and ask hers. She tells me and adds, 'My mum's a Christian,' she says, 'but,' she adds with what sounds suspiciously like a hint of pride, 'my dad is backslidden.'

8

Sunday mornings everyone makes a slow start. I hear someone using the phone in the hallway outside the living room.

'Duty call,' he explains. 'My Sunday call to mum. "Oooh, he's turned all *funny* since he's been hanging round with those Christians."'

Next to the phone there's an old unused 1991 desk diary which is used to note phone messages. You can write notes for the whole household in it. Entries read: 'Michael Magnetic called.' 'Tom. Dentist appointment on Tuesday.' 'Thank-you Battlecentre. No matter what happens in court today I will love you all in Jesu's name. Bless you all – Brother Ronnie.'

Around 11am we wander up to the Age Concern centre in Acton where Steve 'Capes' hosts a service. Jeff gets up late, sheepishly. He tells me that the woman from the other house tempted him. But he's going to be stronger next time.

This morning I sit next to a young man of about twenty-five with black trainers who lives in Abundant Grace, the Jesus Army house in Seaford, near Brighton. He introduces himself with a hearty handshake and talks about the terrible heroin problem in Brighton. He tells me there are lot of gay people in Brighton too, as if it's somehow the same thing. He tells me, smugly, 'We have to set the people free.'

In front, one of the brothers wears a faded black T-shirt printed with what looks like the logo of a heavy metal band. On closer inspection, the inscription reads: 'Warrior of Christ'. The letters are pierced by a sword.

Following words backprojected on a white wall, we dance and sing to songs that sound like they could come from a TV advertising campaign, 'It's your blood that puts my faith in redeeming sacrifice/Washes me whiter than the snow.'

When we sit down, Steve begins one of the fiery sermons he delivers every Sunday. They're long monologues, lightened with jokes and darkened by criticisms and warnings of indiscipline amongst the ranks. They culminate in a lengthy hermeneutical examination of a biblical theme, with pauses to scold those whose attention flags. 'What are you doing here? Sleeping? I don't know why some of you bother to come. Some of you are so easily distracted from the Lord.'

These last few weeks we have been looking at biblical passages that are the basis of the Jesus Fellowship's covenant, the pledge that binds members to the cult. The truth of the Jesus Revolution's indisputable rightness is all spelled out in the Book.

Steve talks about the ideological death of the family. How trendy social workers say the family isn't important any more. 'I know some people are saying the family was never much good in the first place, but they're silly people, very silly people.' The congregation titter.

'In the Jesus Army, we're building families. These days it's hard to be a couple on your own. You've got to be a couple in a community, to have the strength to make it. If you come into the family of Jesus, you can make a relationship that lasts.'

The fires of conviction need constant stoking. The Age Concern shop is on Acton High Street. Couples, loaded with Safeway bags full of family shopping, peer in through the full-length windows, curious.

In the Sunday meeting Charlie is suddenly filled by the Spirit. Eyes closed, voice tremulous, he cries out: 'God wants you to put away your independency. He doesn't want independent people,' Charlie wails. 'There is no point competing against each other any more. He doesn't want individuals. He wants all of us to be together, all of us, as one. So turn your back on all those things that you hold dear to. Tear up your independence and come closer to Him.' It is a heartfelt plea. Independence never made Charlie happy.

'Yes,' shouts Steve joyfully. 'Thank you Jesus.'

Steve was a child of the 60s. He had tried Buddhism, and says he had experimented with 'hallucinogenic drugs' before turning up at a Jean Darnell charismatic rally at the Royal Albert Hall one day in 1975. He burned his rock records and became a Christian. For him we have come full circle from the individualism of the 60s. This new type of commune is a curious turn-about. In the past, he was one of the people rejecting Christianity. Now, in the 90s, he is happy in the shelter of an austere and vengeful father figure. 'Hate the old creation,' he implores us. 'Love the New Creation. Learn to cut off your old self, the unredeemed self. It's no use saying, well, I liked that bit, but I didn't like this bit. Get rid of all of it and make a new start. Get rid of your old associations. Love the new ones; the ones that are in Jesus.'

Sometimes, he says, it's terrifying giving your life to Jesus. He tells us that when he first joined the Jesus Army, the commitment scared him. Each time he drove to Bugbrooke for meetings he would pause at the town sign on the outskirts and he'd feel sick. Someone had drawn two eyes in the letter 'O's and they seemed to be the eyes of his conscience, looking at him, unrelentingly.

Later, in his sermon on the covenant, Steve breaks off from 2 Kings 10 and looks up. It is time to remind some people of the vengefulness of his God. 'There are two people here who aren't in the spirit.' A few people look around. Everyone knows who he is talking about: Jeff and Yvonne. Word has got around. There are no secrets in a small community. Everyone knows about the backsliders who squandered money that should have been surrendered to the common purse to buy cigarettes and beer. 'You're not!' he screams, high voiced. 'I can tell. Yesterday, you *broke* with your *solemn* covenant. You turned your *back*. You *know* who you are. And *today*, because of it, you're not in the *spirit*. You're drifting *away*, getting *colder*, leaving us. And it's *your* loss. *And we all know* about Ananias and Sapphira in Acts 5. They pledged to keep all things in common, but kept something back. And what happened to them?' The reference is taken from a passage that is the keystone to Stanton's concept of the common purse. In Acts 5, two followers who vow to sell some land for the disciples' common purse secretly keep some of the money back. Both are struck dead by God.

A lot of new members fall by the wayside in their first two probationary years. I don't give Jeff long. I can't see him lasting. I could be wrong, of course. Maybe it will change his life for the better, like big Tom and Charlie. But if he does leave, he'll probably be as messed up as he was before, if not more.

Later, I catch sight of Jeff out of the corner of my eye, praying fervently, muttering guilty secret prayers. He doesn't want to be lost, he wants to be saved, to be part of the new creation.

SEVEN

Stockholm Syndrome and the Seven Seals

1

In the battery of behaviourist psychological jargon that has been used to attempt to explain away the mystery of why people follow gurus is something called the Stockholm Syndrome. It has its origins in a bank siege that took place in Sweden, in which a robber armed with an automatic weapon took four hostages in a bank and held them for six days. By the time they were released, the captives had come to fear the police surrounding the building more than their captor. Observers, safe behind police lines, were astonished by this. The innocent victims seemed to have identified more closely with the wrongdoer who threatened to harm them than with the law, which was there to save them. The syndrome is sometimes used to explain the group dynamics of a cult. The threat to cults presented by a hostile outside world can increase cohesiveness amongst the members. There is, it suggests, a dark behavioural mechanism which even makes them sympathise with a malevolent leader.

What the concept of the Stockholm Syndrome overlooks is that the Swedish captives, surrounded by a heavily-armed police they could not see, whose tactics they did not know, might have had a perfectly reasonable fear of them. Maybe the greatest threat is getting caught up in the crossfire.

It was shortly before Waco burned, that Ian Haworth told me he had identified his twenty-six different methods of mind control.

After a year watching people join cults I have yet to see anyone lured in by anything other than their own hunger to believe. As far as I could see, everyone joined out of choice, though sometimes, as with the Emin or the School of Economic Science, it wasn't too clear what they were getting in to at the start. But even then, only a tiny proportion of would-be members were still involved a few months after they first joined. If they became suspicious about the things they felt weren't being told, they started to ask questions. If they got the answers they didn't want to hear, they left, disappointed.

If they stayed, it was because they wanted to, though staying on has its problems too. If it's hard for me to believe any of the things that the groups I joined told me were true, I realise it takes a lot of work on the believers' part too. Life is an endless round of meetings, prayers and ceremonies to keep the flames alive. It is all or nothing.

The problem for a few of the people I met was how to get out, and what to get out into. After all, a cult provides them with their friends, their faith and sometimes the roof over their heads, at the same time as alienating them from the rest of us. Sometimes, leaving a cult means they have to start from square one all over again. Just trying to find new friends who understand what they've been through is a hard task. Often the only people who are in any position to sympathise with what they've been through are ex-cult members who have been through similar experiences themselves.

Once they've stopped believing, they are sometimes left with a puzzle: how on earth did they ever get involved in something so apparently strange in the first place? And some ex-members, who can't believe they would ever have got caught up in something like that by themselves, begin to wonder who is to blame. The anti-cult movement often provides them with the answer some most want to hear. It wasn't their fault. They were the victims of up to twenty-six different types of mind control.

I looked at one of the books Ian Haworth told me to read when I first started out, *Combating Cult Mind Control* by Steve Hassan. It starts with a question that Hassan asks young American students when he tours the country, lecturing them about the evil of cults: 'How would you *know* if you were under mind control?' Answer:

You wouldn't. Mind control is such a subtle thing you're not even aware of it going on.

For much of the last year I have lived in guru land's self-enclosing logic. My favourite example is the group from Scottsdale, Arizona who believe they have achieved the miracle of immortality. They have a small following in the UK and go by the names of Together Forever, or the Immortals, or the Flame Foundation. They believe that by associating with people who know the secret, they can re-programme the death-wish in their own DNA. Some of them have died, but death is not a disproof. It's merely a consequence of lack of concentration, or lack of faith. As a logical merry-go-round it's on a par with 'How would you *know* if you were under mind control?'.

Almost a year after I first spoke to Ian Haworth, when he warned me that joining a destructive cult would be 'poison', I call him up again and ask him why he gave me that advice in the first place.

'Why? "Because I've done it and I'm alright?"' he laughs.

'Well yes,' I reply.

'Well,' he says, employing the Hassan manoeuvre, 'I guess I could argue, how do you know?'

Maybe I'm coming down with a bad case of Stockholm Syndrome.

The anti-cult movement is a broad umbrella, full of people trying to shine a light on the malignancy of cults for a huge variety of reasons. I've spoken to a lot of them. Some offer what they sincerely believe are hard facts, many also conduct labyrinthine whispering campaigns: 'Have you heard the rumour that [the name of the leader of one of groups I've joined] was investigated for child-abuse in the 50s? I'm not saying it's true, but it wouldn't be a great surprise to me . . .'

Some are ex-members, bitter about what has happened to them, some are families who feel they have lost a loved one, and some are Christians who see extreme faiths as a perversion of the truth. Deo Gloria Outreach and Christian Rescue come from the Christian perspective. Family Action Information and Rescue approach it from the point of view of relatives. Haworth's Cult

Information Centre is based around ex-members. Then there are individuals like David Wilshire, the Conservative MP for Spelthorne, chairman of the parliamentary group on cults at the time of the Waco siege, who see cults as power grabbers: 'Cult organisations are only interested in money, sex and power,' he announced as tanks surrounded the compound in the Texan desert.

In America, the vast network includes groups such as the American Family Foundation, the Spiritual Counterfeits Project, the Cult Awareness Network and Free Minds Inc. Everywhere now has its anti-cult groups.

Much of the advice they offer is sound, like telling concerned friends and relatives to arm themselves with as much information as they can about any particular group, and not trying to confront beliefs head on.

There is much disagreement between them about which cults are the worst, or about what the correct response to them is, but they all agree on the concept of mind control, even if they argue over the details. And in that, they have something in common with most cults. They are here to warn us about something evil that we can't even perceive with our own eyes.

Ian Haworth runs the Cult Information Centre from a secret address. When I ask why, he mentions the case of Robert Boettcher, the author of a book about Moonies, *Gifts of Deceit*, who committed suicide by jumping from a New York skyscraper. 'Maybe it was suicide,' ho-hums Haworth. 'Strange things occur.'

Haworth is a stocky man with a close-cropped grey beard, who talks in a soft Lancashire accent and is proud of his common-sense view of the world. Lord Denning and Baroness Cox are patrons of his organisation. When newspapers publish articles about cults they often turn to Haworth for his analysis of the situation.

During the climax of the Waco siege he was on Sky TV giving a blow by blow account of the conflagration. When he heard someone suggesting that the FBI had set the fire deliberately he pooh poohed the idea. His expert opinion was that the Branch Davidians would have lit it themselves. Programmed by Koresh, confronted by the overkill of an enemy who knew nothing about cults, it was the only way out: to kill themselves and their children. This, he said, was exactly what he had expected.

He prefers not to use the term brainwashing these days, but he says, 'It seems to be a relatively simple matter to be able to control another person.'

Brainwashing is the neologism coined by the US journalist Edward Hunter in 1951 to write about the thought reform programmes that had sometimes been attempted by the Communist Chinese on American prisoners of war captured during the Korean War, some of whom sometimes came to believe they had committed un-American atrocities. In his book, *Brainwashing in Red China*, Hunter described how victims were broken down, deprived of sleep and food, isolated, threatened with violence and given lengthy lectures on their political errors. The programme was real enough; but reports of its apparently terrifying success were a paranoid invention. Brainwashing was an abject failure. 'Conversion' was the temporary product only of coercion. That a tiny proportion of American soldiers became sympathetic to their captors is hardly surprising: it happens in most wars. But in the cold-war climate, dignified by a handful of psychologists who leant credence to the paranoia, it became the perfect reds under the beds scare story. To a nation who didn't understand how people could sympathise with Communism in the first place, it provided a perfect explanation: their thoughts had been reformed. Novelist Richard Condon fuelled the myth with his 1958 pulp-conspiracy story *The Manchurian Candidate*. They had come to steal our minds.

Since its 1950s genesis, the conspiracy-theory myth of brainwashing has always been conjured up to satisfy people who can't understand how others come to believe things that most of us find patently incredible.

Ed Hunter's word led to another one: Deprogramming. If you've been brainwashed, you need an antidote. This new form of anti-brainwashing was pioneered by a fundamentalist Christian appointed by California State Governor Ronald Reagan as Special Representative for San Diego, Ted Patrick. When ex-truck driver turned social worker Ted Patrick began to notice that young San Diegans were joining a new hippie free love cult called the Children of God, who talked about sex and revolution, he was outraged. 'It doesn't make any sense,' he told his wife, when he first discovered the existence of the cult. 'All kinds of crazy stuff about what's wrong with our country.'

'Maybe it's a Communist-type thing,' his wife replied.

Inspired with a missionary zeal, Patrick evolved his own brutal way of returning cult members to the American way. The father of deprogramming evolved a method of repeating the coercive brainwashing he believed was being carried out by the cults on the people he wanted to save, except he concentrated his deprogramming into a matter of days. The brutal technique has been attempted on thousands of cult members, lured away from the cults or kidnapped by deprogrammers.

Ted Patrick wrote a book about it. He called it *Let Our Children Go!* ('His enemy: the sinister cults that grip the youth of America,' blares the jacket of the paperback edition. 'His method: fight fire with fire.') It's a catalogue of obsession and violence. In a typical passage, he details the method by which he 'saved' one Hare Krishna member. It included locking him up, chopping off the *sikha* knot of hair on the back of the victim's head, tearing up pictures of Prabhupada in front of him, blaming him for all the trouble and expense his father was going to by hiring Patrick, and outright physical violence. To fight madness you use madness.

'Deprogramming,' sighs Ian Haworth, warily, 'is a red hot potato. Everyone that's prepared to stick their necks out and criticise cults will be tarred with that brush one way or another.'

He has a point. In the war of cult vs. anti-cult, people resort to any weapons. In 1976 a shadowy organisation called POWER (People's Organised Workshop on Ersatz Religions) emerged in London and published a book called *Deprogramming: The Constructive Deconstruction of Belief: A Manual of Techniques*. The mind control techniques they gleefully advocated were 'shame inducement through nudity', 'food termination', 'destruction of Holy works' and 'aggressive sex', which, the book went on to explain, 'the subject often confuses with rape'. It was a hoax designed to discredit the new anti-cult movement by tarring them with the brush of fanaticism. It worked. Many concerned about the new growing anti-cult movement believed it was a real document and added it to the case for the prosecution. We are in a hall of mirrors. Cult and anti-cult is a world of accusation, counter-accusation and half-truths.

These days, though, Haworth advocates what is often called 'exit counselling'. The counselling is the same as deprogramming, he says, it's just you don't actually grab people off the streets to do it. 'There's very little difference between the types of counselling. It's *how* the cult victim comes to be sitting in front of the counsellor.'

Leaving a system of beliefs that for a while has provided you with all the answers you needed, often all the affection you needed too, can be a shattering experience.

One of the curious side-effects of deprogramming's ideology was that on occasions, ex-members turned from adoration of a cult to hatred of it. Encouraged to believe the therapy ideology of the victim and the abuser, they come to believe that they never chose to join a cult, they were simply hypnotised or coerced into it. All the complex relationships of faith, love, mutual trust that they had shared, and worked so hard at with other cult members were a tremendous, cynical lie. From the other side of the fence, once you've stopped believing, everything you did in a cult can appear to have been a sham. From a victim's viewpoint, what once felt like affection can soon look like exploitation because, as David Wilshire said, cults are only interested in money, sex and power.

Some replace their faith in the cult with a new faith, the anti-cult. It too provides a view of good and evil, an international network of relationships, and another secret, sometimes mis-understood faith.

Steve Hassan is an ex-Moonie. Ian Haworth is an ex-member of a small Canadian therapy cult, the PSI Mind Development Institute, though he was only in it for a matter of weeks after being drawn by an advert offering a four-day course guaranteed to help him give up smoking. He remembers that he was upset and numb when he left it, heart-broken about those he had left behind in it. He has been dedicated to the anti-cult movement ever since. His wife is an ex-member of the cult that started the whole anti-cult ball rolling, the Children of God.

*

The Children of God, or the Family as they are now called, are one of the strangest Christian cults to have emerged in recent years. Led by a sexually obsessive minister called David Berg – now seventy-five – who renamed himself Moses David, or Mo, they originally managed somehow to weld the 60s sexual revolution to the Jesus Revolution. Berg established spiritual contact with a thirteenth-century Bulgarian gypsy king called Abrahim. What emerged was a particularly racy end-time prophet who declared, 'Enjoy yourself and sex and what God has given you to enjoy, without fear or condemnation! . . . It's a *Revolution!* – for *Jesus! Power* to the *People! Sex* power! – *God's* power – Can be *your* power! Amen? – *Be a sex revolutionist for Jesus! – Wow!* There we *go* again! *Hallelujah!* – Are you *comin'?'*

He started recruiting hippies to his communal lifestyle in 60s California, originally calling the movement Teens For Christ. It was that movement of long-haired guitar strummers that first got Ted Patrick's back up. In the 70s the sexually explicit nature of his message shocked other Christians rigid. His 'Mo Letters', which contained the message according to Berg, included sexually explicit comic strips which even depicted the prophet engaged in sexual encounters. One letter showed a woman squatting over a man, holding his penis. 'Receiving Jesus is like going all the way . . .' The frantic sexual commotion of the period became a holy quest: one of the 'Mo Letters' was headlined, 'Come on Ma! Burn your bra!'

The anti-cult movement loves to hate the Children of God. In fact the first formal anti-cult organisation was the Parents' Committee to Free Our Sons and Daughters from the Children of God – FREECOG. They scanned Berg's writings for any hint of perversion. It wasn't impossible to find.

David Berg fitted the bill perfectly for the image of exploitative dirty old man as cult leader. In 1978 the 'Sex Cult' reached its apotheosis when Mo launched a campaign called 'Flirty Fishing' which encouraged women followers to attract men into the Children of God by seducing them. 'The only Bible those boys are likely to read is that gorgeous gal with her bosoms hanging out,' leered Berg. He dreamed up the term 'Hookers for Jesus' to describe their holy prostitution.

Marie Haworth was one of those who says she felt she had a duty to sleep with men for Jesus. She remembers having sex with a sixty-year-old Englishman in Spain every night for a week. He was ugly and fat. 'It was horrible, but I pretended to enjoy it.' Like her husband she is a vociferous campaigner against cults.

The Family don't dispute that Flirty Fishing was part of the ministry between 1978 and 1983. Gideon Scott, well-groomed spokesman for the Family in the UK, remains reluctant to criticise his guru Father David and dumbly, devotedly and defiantly unrepentant of that time, claiming that abuses of the ministry were the fault of individuals, not the system. 'We make no apologies for it. We believe it was a very fruitful way of witnessing and showing God's love to other people. And it was.'

But of course, as the hippies grew up, the boundaries they were trying to abolish crept back in, as they have done everywhere in the post-peace 'n' love hippie world. The Family is now totally unrecognisable from the wild image that grew up around it. From 1985 the movement began establishing a set of regulations for sexual behaviour that are now as strict, if not stricter, than in most British families. Though they believe there is nothing sinful in sex outside of marriage, in their tightly knit communities they do not condone any sexual activity in children under sixteen. Members over the age of twenty-one are banned from sexual relations with anyone under that age, unless the relationship was already formed before they reached twenty-one. Members found maliciously contravening these rules are expelled.

Oddly enough, it was only once it had established its 'hands above the blankets' attitude to sex that the Family found itself most violently accused of systematic sexual abuse in a series of news reports that were inspired by anti-cult organisations. A number of raids were mounted by police world-wide, taken in by a whispering campaign that alleged that the Family were practising systematised child abuse, encouraged by the randy Father David. A climate of international panic about systematised child abuse made the new demonisation of the Family by the anti-cult movement easy to believe.

On 27 October 1989 eighteen children were taken into state custody in Buenos Aires, Argentina, and examined medically and psychologically for signs of child abuse, triggering a series of massive raids on Family households around the world. At least 475 children were taken into care in Argentina, France, Australia and Spain. At least a further 200 children have been examined by child-care authorities in America and elsewhere. Statistically, one might expect some evidence of child sex abuse to emerge in such a number. At the time of writing, not a single officially proven incidence has been found. With a certain justification the Family claim it is they and their children who are being abused by the anti-cult movement.

At 6am on 29 January 1991 the hysteria touched Britain. Police squads arrived at Family households in Barnet and Pinner following stories in the press that the houses harboured child pornography. Despite kicking down the door of the Barnet household in their eagerness to arrest members of the 'sex cult', the police found nothing.

Ian Haworth is exasperated by the authorities' lack of success. The children whom he believes are the victims refuse to testify against their parents. He believes they too have had their minds controlled. It is a cover up. 'For every ex-member who says this is what they did to me, the cults produce fifteen that say it's a lie.'

He complains, 'Who do you believe?'

No witches have been found. But the witchhunt against the Family continues.

In February 1994, Ian Haworth tells me dramatically on the phone: 'We've just gone public on a story about material we've managed to get hold of from the Family.' He says there's a story in the *Daily Telegraph*, and he's on BBC local news soon too.

The article on page seven of the *Daily Telegraph* is headlined: 'Cult Followers Told Be Ready To Die Soon'. 'A religious cult has told its 500 British followers they must be ready to die for their faith. A secret document circulated by the Children of God organisation tells its members they are so badly persecuted, "there is no way out but up." Followers are told their deaths would be "promotion" and would make them "martyrs". Mr Ian Haworth of the Cult Information Centre said, "In the aftermath of Waco, I find this very chilling and I am very concerned for people in that group, especially children growing up in that environment."'

A few days later I switch on BBC South-East: 'Good evening. We start tonight with the growing concern surrounding a religious cult that is telling its members to prepare for death.'

A woman billed as ex-member Christine Cordon testifies that she would have committed suicide if Berg had told her to: 'I would have done it with a smile. If he thinks his life on earth is going to end then who knows what will happen to his disciples?'

What neither report mentions is that the quotes are taken from a long letter written by David Berg that is actually almost two years old, penned long before the death cult scare was stirred up by Waco. It talks only generally about the notion of end-time, which his group have always believed in, and from which Haworth has extracted his latest absurd scare story. The Family believe that suicide is a sin. What the BBC reporter also seems to have failed to discover is that ex-member Christine Cordon, who spent five years in the Children of God and took the name of Sephorah, more frequently goes under her married name these days, which is Marie Haworth. She is the wife of the man who fed the press the story in the first place, the man who has been fighting his own eccentric war against the cults for years. The madness goes around and around.

Ian Haworth, filmed in his office, intones on my television, 'I fear the worst. I fear we may have another David Koresh on our hands. Another potential Waco.'

When people think of cults they think of two geographical locations comfortably far from Britain: Jonestown in Guyana, and Waco in Texas – two Armageddons in which, indisputably, almost a thousand people died terrible, agonising deaths.

The fear of cults is a strong one, incomprehensible to those secure within them. They don't understand how the cult they are in has become a bogeyman for grown ups, coming to take your children away, preying on the innocent and the vulnerable, a giant nightmare figure waiting around the corner to pounce. They are the mind-benders, anti-cult groups say, over and over again.

There is another side to this fear of cults. Not only is there an infectious brain virus that spreads unchecked, taking over innocent victims, but there is also another dark hungry space in all of us that is waiting to be exploited. All of us, the anti-cult logic says, are credulous; capable of being sucked into these mind traps. There is a vacuum in our souls which can be exploited by the cynical. Such a dangerous force obviously needs a violent response. Sometimes it even needs tanks, tear-gas and guns to control it.

2

Derek Lovelock is a member of a cult which no longer exists. It has been wiped from the face of the earth. Now he lives with his mother in a grey post-war semi in Withington, Manchester, confused and lonely. He still has terrible nightmares.

He sits on a green velour armchair in his mother's back sitting room, drinking weak coffee. The walls are covered with framed images of Jesus crucified, plates with poems that start 'To Mother', and photographs of his recently deceased father taken when he was serving in the RAF during World War Two. His father was from Jamaica, but he inherited his mother's fair complexion. She is a Brummie. His parents met in a Birmingham dancehall during the war.

On a table in the corner sits Derek's Bible. It's huge, and the page edges are brown from being handled. He bought it for £32 when he was a member of the Seventh Day Adventist Church.

Derek almost died the day he was born, on 13 August 1955, when he emerged from the womb with his umbilical cord wrapped around his neck, the fifth child in a family of nine. When he was eight he fell into the canal at Hulme and almost drowned. His family were C of E, and sent him to Sunday School for a while, but it wasn't until the age of fifteen, when a younger brother died of a brain tumour, that Derek's obsession with the meaning of death began to take over his life.

It started as a fear of his own mortality. Feeling that he'd cheated death twice already, he became afraid of dying without knowing God. Wherever he was he would suddenly find himself thinking about it. He couldn't get it out of his head. 'I used to go to nightclubs,' he smiles, 'and I'd be thinking about God. I don't know why. Sometimes I would be standing there thinking, "If God came, what would my position be?"' He remembers reading Revelation 6 as a teenager: 'And behold a pale horse: and his name that sat on him was Death, and Hell followed with him.' The passage scared him.

After school he tried an apprenticeship as a gas fitter, but didn't stick it. Later he worked in a bakery, but the three years he spent with Tesco's was the longest he managed. He tried out various churches too. He tried Catholicism, Methodism and the Baptist church, but none of them seemed to be offering a religion strong enough to enable him to feel the presence of God.

Then in 1984 a friend suggested he come along to meetings being held by the Seventh Day Adventists, an American sect which had survived what it called 'The Great Disappointment' when the second coming its leader, preacher William Miller, predicted had failed to arrive in 1843. The meetings were about the Book of Revelation, the apocalyptic vision of St John the Divine. For the first time Derek found a church whose millenarianism made sense of his fear of impending death. He went to church on the Saturday and attended meetings on the Sunday. He received a second baptism.

For a while Derek was impressed by the devoutness of the Adventist church. They kept the Sabbath holy as Derek believed it was decreed in Genesis. He married a Jamaican woman from the church called Joy-Anne, and they had a baby, Aden, but the marriage foundered and Derek moved out. He found that the church wasn't providing all the answers he was looking for. He was worried about whether his family and his friends' souls were going to be saved in the second coming. He looked to the Bible and the church for clear answers, but couldn't find any. He needed to be sure of God. Sometimes it seemed to him that the church was just a glorified social club.

Sometimes he would join them, evangelising door-to-door, selling the Adventists' books. It made him feel uncomfortable, like a salesman. The books were well bound, expensive – often more expensive than he felt people could afford. When he went with other church members he thought they were more interested in selling books that could cost almost £100 than in saving souls. They would offer books as if buying them alone could bring salvation. If people were interested he would occasionally hand out paperbacks for free, then pay for them out of his own pocket.

Then on 29 January 1988, a few weeks after splitting up with Joy-Anne, Derek was run over in the street. All he remembers is getting off the bus on the way to work. He woke up after eight days in a coma, in an intensive care ward, having been given a 50-50 chance of survival. He had head injuries, a punctured lung, fractured ribs and a dislocated shoulder. At first the severe pain he was in tested his faith. He blamed it on God. He wanted to die. He lay on his bed, saying to himself angrily, 'Why did You let me go through all this and spare me?'

But as he convalesced, this third escape from death only strengthened his conviction that God intended something for him. He had been spared. The meaning of death became even more of an obsession. Six months after the accident he had abandoned going to the Adventist church when a friend persuaded him to give their Sunday meetings one last try. A young Adventist called Tony McCalla was giving talks. Reluctantly, Derek turned up, and something extraordinary happened. At one of the classes he overheard McCalla saying that the Holy Spirit was female. The sureness with which he spoke this fact amazed Derek. He buttonholed the lecturer and asked him to explain. McCalla pointed out three passages in Proverbs which revealed the gender of the Holy Spirit. This sort of Bible exegesis was something Derek had never come across before. He asked where McCalla learned this from. 'A man called David Koresh,' answered McCalla.

Derek Lovelock was one of the thirty-three Britons in the compound at Waco, Texas when the tanks came in.

David Koresh, born Vernon Howell, was the leader of a strange sect known as the Branch Davidians, an offshoot of the Seventh Day Adventists which had prophesied the second coming in 1959 at Mount Carmel, Waco, Texas. Another Great Disappointment. Hundreds of Davidians who had bought land at Carmel, the site of the second coming, or paid tithes to the sect, filed lawsuits against it. The sect Howell joined was in total disarray. Howell, who believed he had the gift of prophecy, simply took it over after an absurd struggle with the previous would-be leader George Roden.

George Roden was insane, bubbling over with the wild apocalyptic fervour that infected the Davidian sect, and which attracted the death-obsessed Derek Lovelock to it. In 1986 Roden, believing himself to be Christ, had dug up the twenty-year-old coffin of one of the followers and attempted to resurrect it three times. The following year Howell had assumed the leadership of the Davidians, and several followers, dressed in camouflage fatigues bought at the local K-Mart, had driven Roden off what they considered to be *their* land in a forty-five-minute shoot out. This, after all, was Texas. Vernon Howell was arrested peacefully and tried for attempted murder. He was acquitted, largely because Roden was so obviously mad. When asked to describe his occupation he told the court he was a farmer, a minister and a Presidential candidate. When asked if he was the Messiah, he replied: 'Thou saith it.'

When Vernon Howell took charge of the Mount Carmel community it started to grow. Vernon, believing that he was a prophet of God, changed his name to David Koresh. From 1988 members of the Waco community began visiting Britain in search of new converts. Koresh himself came, staying at the London flat of convert Victorine Hollingsworth and lecturing to students from the Adventists' theological training centre, Newbold College in Berkshire. One of the students who soaked up Koresh's teaching was Tony McCalla, who later spread the message to the Adventist following in Manchester. Other disciples visited Manchester too, including American Stephen Sneider and West Indian Briton John McBean. Both died in the fire. Janet McBean, John's sister, was one of those who attended Koresh's intense Bible seminars when he came to Britain. She derides any notion that the British followers were anything other than eager followers. There was no coercion, no brainwashing. They came, like the disciples of Jennifer and Vaughn Brown in Tottenham, from a religious background that was already steeped in the apocalyptic: 'We were *not* spellbound by David. We were intelligent people who asked intelligent questions,' she says. 'All of us came from the background that this world was going to come to an end very soon, that God was going to do something catastrophic. Exactly what, we didn't know. We were young people,' she says sadly. 'We were searching.'

Faced with the certainty of Koresh's faith, Derek began to experience his disbelief evaporating. Everything began to add up for him. McCalla darted backwards and forwards through the Bible with him, uncovering passages that spoke of the impending Armageddon, of a mountain that would attract the nations of the earth in the latter days. It was exciting. 'This was like a blindfold being taken from me,' smiles Derek. In 1990 he decided he had to see this man for himself and boarded a plane for America.

The first time he met Koresh was after a long flight from London to Dallas, and a 180-mile trip through Texas to the ranch where Koresh and his followers lived. Tired from the journey, Derek was shown a single bed in a bare male dormitory where he would sleep and given a meal of half a water-melon and a bowl of the ranch's staple diet, popcorn. After the meal Koresh appeared, dressed in a white T-shirt, jeans and trainers and said, 'Tell the new guys, can I have a word with them?' That night Koresh lectured the newcomers for an hour, maybe two. Even after the long journey, Derek was eager to hear everything that was said. Koresh chose Revelation, and the subject that obsessed him – the Seven Seals of Revelation 5. 'Who is worthy to open the book and to loose the seals thereof?' According to Koresh, the mysterious book locked with seven seals was the final mystery of the Bible. Verse 5 announces that the only man worthy of opening the seals was the Lamb, the 'root of David'. Koresh believed he was that Lamb.

Derek introduced himself to Koresh, he shook his hand. Like Janet McBean, he was capable of doubt. He wasn't sure whether Koresh was the Lamb of God or not, not yet at least. Still obsessed with whether his friends and relatives would escape damnation, he asked if his son, Aden would be saved. 'You bet,' said Koresh.

For two weeks, Derek attended Koresh's Bible classes. They lasted up to ten hours at a time. 'When he spoke,' says Derek, 'I sensed a higher authority than man.' Koresh had an impressive knowledge of the Bible, dipping back and forth through the chapters, from Isaiah, to Matthew, to Ezekiel, and back, as always, to Revelation. For the first time the Bible began to make real sense as a whole to Derek. 'David Koresh answered almost all my questions just by being there and explaining it,' says Derek now. 'He was a fantastic man.' The intense Mancunian would ask Koresh about the passages that troubled him. Like Revelation 13: 'And I beheld another beast coming up out of the earth: and he had two horns like a lamb, and he spake as a dragon.'

'What does the lamb-like beast represent?' asked Derek.

'I am the beast,' answered Koresh. 'You are the beast. Man. That's what the beast is.'

Sometimes Koresh didn't even use the Bible, he just spoke prophetically, delivering his personal cosmology about how the sun and the soil were made up of matter and anti-matter in relation. At the time it made perfect sense, though when he tries to explain it now, several thousand miles away in Manchester, Derek falters: 'I can't actually remember,' he admits.

When the time came to leave he approached Koresh again and asked, 'What shall I do now, David?' Koresh answered, 'Fear God.'

Life back in Manchester was oppressive. Derek sat in his bedsit and read his Bible. He was bored. At Waco he had felt in the presence of God. Eighteen months after returning to Manchester he bought a ticket to Dallas and went back to live on the ranch at Mount Carmel.

He found the place thriving. What had looked like a house before had now grown into something that looked from a distance like a hotel in the middle of the desert. Numbers had more than doubled and the community was now ninety-strong.

Derek Lovelock is quietly spoken and shy. He often holds his hand in front of his mouth as he talks. But he becomes animated when he remembers the months he spent at the ranch. It was the happiest time in his life. 'We were one big family,' he says. 'We all believed in the one belief, and agreed on the same points. We were all one community.'

Life there was not easy. The community maintained the strength of its beliefs through its isolation. Sanitation was basic and food was unexotic. Few in the compound had jobs in the outside world, so it survived on very little income. Mostly the believers worked building the compound itself.

Derek would rise at six in the morning. At half six they would have breakfast of millet and bananas, or popcorn and apples. Sometimes there were cornflakes. From around eight they would work in all weathers building the halls and dormitories that would soon be burned with their builders inside. They dug a swimming pool. Derek felt he was serving God by his work. He took special pride in helping to build the gym and the underground storm shelter, a common enough construction in an environment where tornadoes could flatten buildings in seconds. Later the FBI would talk of 'bunkers' built under the compound.

At twelve they'd break for lunch then carry on working until about seven when they ate supper. 'What the Americans called *dinner*,' he laughs. After the meal Derek used to hope that Koresh would be leading one of his Bible study sessions. If Koresh was giving one it could go on for hours, starting at eight or nine and occasionally going on until three or four in the morning. Later these were widely described as brainwashing sessions, lowering the resistance of the listeners by depriving them of sleep. Derek finds the idea preposterous. People were free to leave them, but they *wanted* to stay. 'I remember once I fell asleep during his study. He said, "Derek, don't go to sleep during my study. Go to bed." So I did.'

Derek thought the desert was beautiful. There were three lakes in the area. Some days they would go fishing there, catching eight-pound carp. On free days Derek would mess around on the motorbikes and the go-karts that were lying around the compound. After the greyness of Manchester, the wide Texan landscape was a miraculous place. One icy day it rained hailstones as big as golf-balls, smashing car windows. He picked up one of the stones, amazed at the intricate patterns the ice made.

Then on 28 February 1993 heaven came to an abrupt end. Two mysterious chicken trucks appeared from nowhere, driving towards the compound. They were meant to be a disguised vanguard to a carefully planned military operation. 'It was obvious, really,' recalls Derek now. 'Even if you saw the two chicken trailers you thought, what are two chicken trailers coming down here for? And then one of them pulled up right in front of the front entrance and they jumped out, screaming and firing . . .'

The Bureau of Alcohol, Tobacco and Firearms – the ATF – who were raiding the ranch to arrest Koresh for firearms law violations, initially claimed that they were ambushed, but have since admitted that they lied about many of the events surrounding their inept raid on the ranch in an attempt to cover up the scale of their errors. According to Lovelock, the first shots were fired at the compound's dogs by the ATF team. Four dogs were shot. 'I think one of them was pregnant,' remembers Lovelock vaguely. Dick DeGuerin, Koresh's lawyer, believes Koresh went to the door saying, 'Let's talk,' but was fired on. All hell broke loose.

Something like 12,000 rounds were loosed off that day in the firefight between the gung-ho cultists and the ATF. At the end of it, four ATF men and six Davidians were dead. Derek Lovelock saw Koresh, shot through the wrist and the waist, still talking on the phone, being nursed by Briton Zilla Henry, who later perished in the fire. He found another victim in his dormitory. Winston Blake, another British cult member, was lying on the floor with half his head blown away by a bullet.

The shoot-out was the result of a catalogue of madnesses. Texan gun culture allows almost anyone access to lethal weaponry and the right to defend themselves with it. Koresh was a survivalist, who felt that even Texan gun laws were restrictive. But the biggest insanity of all was the huge military operation mounted by the ATF against the cult, the biggest ever in their history, to arrest one man on the pretext that he was allegedly in unlawful possession of illegal machine guns and explosives in violation of Title 25 United States Code section 5845 (f).

One of the many who were astonished by the overkill of the raid was former McLennan County District Attorney Vic Feazell. The last time he had had to arrest the guru David Koresh – for his gunfight with George Roden – he had simply had a colleague phone Koresh up and tell him they were coming to handcuff him.

'*We* had no problems,' he recalls, proudly. 'They were extremely polite people.' The difference was that Feazell and the local sheriff went to Mount Carmel to arrest someone they characterised as an eccentric local religious leader. The ATF went to arrest someone they characterised as a sadistic, power-crazed cult psychopath.

Each, curiously, met the man they expected.

Cults' paranoia about the outside world feeds on the outside world's paranoia about cults which feeds on cults' paranoia. It's a dog chasing its own tail. But the paranoia about the suicide cult which Ian Haworth earnestly invokes in the news clip about the Family is, at least, based on an irrefutably real event: when the People's Temple embraced the unimaginable horror after apparently being ordered to die by Jim Jones.

There is no disputing the insane intensity of the moment, fifteen years before Waco in 1978 when Jim Jones and 913 of his followers died, mostly drinking Kool Aid laced with cyanide. You can listen to the mad, collective fervour whipped up amongst the 900 that drove them to kill themselves; it's captured on the ghoulish tape that exists of the cult's last few minutes on 18 November 1978: 'We've made that day,' cries the voice of one of those about to die. 'We made it a beautiful day. Let's make it a beautiful day.'

You can hear the sound of adults screaming and children sobbing. 'Take our life from us,' shouts Jim Jones as his followers drink the Kool Aid. 'Take the potion like they used to in ancient Greece and step over quietly. Because we are not committing suicide – it's a revolutionary act.'

Some survivors talk of guards, ordered to shoot those who tried to escape. Others seem to suggest that nearly everyone there wanted to die. One survivor remembers that when a woman challenged Jones's demand that they all drink the potion, she was shouted down.

For months before the suicide the cult had become obsessed with the notion that the world was closing in around it. They had rehearsed the suicide together, on what were called 'White Nights'. As they shut down their own communication to protect themselves from the pollutions of the outside world, wild rumours started to circulate. The Ku-Klux-Klan were marching in San Francisco. Los Angeles had been abandoned because of earthquakes.

Reports of what life at Jonestown was really like are mostly bafflingly contradictory. Months before the catastrophe defectors from the socialist Christian utopia said that disease was rife, food was scarce, and Jones was a mad despot who stationed armed guards around the site, who drugged dissenters and who punished children by throwing them into the well – eerily exactly the same punishment that David Koresh was later accused of doling out to miscreant children at Waco.

But dozens upon dozens of letters from the encampment simultaneously depicted it as a fantastic pre-lapsarian tropical paradise – an abundant and beautiful clearing in the jungle.

If the testimonies of those defectors are true, then the letters from Jones's followers can only be the product of coercion or brainwashing. That would be the sole way to account for the immense gulf between them.

Both descriptions of Jonestown were, in their own way, deranged. There are quieter, less dramatic descriptions, from those who were happy there in spite of privations and occasional health problems, and which also painfully chronicle the isolated community's descent into collective terror and psychotic paranoia as the uncomprehending world closed in around them.

Five days before they committed that horrifying act which Jones somehow managed to call revolutionary, a delegation called Concerned Relatives arrived in Guyana, the culmination of a long and bitter campaign against the cult. Fuelled by anti-Jones testimonies from ex-members, the delegation arrived accusing Jim Jones of 'employing physical intimidation and psychological coercion as part of a mind-programming campaign aimed at destroying family ties, discrediting belief in God and causing contempt for the United States of America.' Hysteria was shared by both sides. A cult which believed the whole world outside was bent on destroying it was presented with the perfect confirmation of their dementia. The myth of the brainwashed helped, in the end, to kill them.

Afterwards, slowly and painfully piecing together their own

lives, one of the leading voices among the ex-members declared: 'The thing we have learned is not to blame ourselves for the things Jim made us do.' It was the voice of the anti-cult movement: ultimately only the guru is to blame for what a cult does, and for what society does to it in return.

The notion of the suicide cult, the most evil cult of all, was born in the minds of the anti-cult movement. In an interview with *Playboy* the next year Ted Patrick, the father of 'deprogramming' declared that the incidence of suicide cults was going to spread 'like wildfire'. The anti-cult movement started to warn of the next catastrophe, just as Ian Haworth is warning us of the impending mass suicide of the Family.

In the pavilion at Jonestown where eighty of the dead were discovered, sprawled grotesquely on the ground, hung one of the many political and religious mottoes of this new utopia. It read, with superbly clod-footed irony: 'Those who do not remember the past are condemned to repeat it.'

3

On a giant TV screen in the complex, powered only by a generator after the FBI had cut off the electricity, Derek Lovelock watched, astonished, as news reports related the horror of life in the compound. They said that Koresh had stockpiled enough arms to start a war and formed his own Praetorian guard which surrounded the site. He had been planning to attack the local community. Children inside the compound were routinely beaten with a paddle by Koresh until they bled, or thrown into cess pits. He took drugs. There was sexual abuse too: Koresh forced the husbands in the encampment to hand over their wives to him to sleep with. And their children too. The most damning allegations of all were that Koresh was sexually abusing girls as young as eleven. 'I felt frustration and bitterness, because the manipulation that was going on was totally wrong. We didn't have no chance to speak to the media. There was just one line to the FBI. It was pretty awful when they said we were going to kill the children . . .'

Derek Lovelock says he never saw anything remotely like what was being described by the newsmen take place in the compound. No child abuse; no 'paddling of children' by Koresh. Children *were* occasionally beaten with the infamous paddle that featured in the child-abuse allegations, but only by their parents and then only within what Lovelock saw as reasonable limits. He witnessed no drug taking by Koresh; no sleeping around, no harem of women for David's exclusive use.

'He is a compassionate man,' insists Derek. 'A very caring compassionate man.' He uses the present tense. He sits, unshaven, in his living room wearing a blue sweatshirt for a Texan football team, the Dallas Cowboys. Emerging from the right sleeve is the large scar that covers his right arm. He got it battling his way out of the burning ranch.

'They got the wrong idea. They say he said he was Christ. He never said he was Christ. He actually said he believed that he himself was sent to give a message for this time, but he didn't say he was Christ. They got everything totally wrong with him. They said he was mean. They said he had all different wives and children. The only wife he had was Rachel, and he had three children and they all got killed in the fire. They said he was a religious guy and shouldn't go to gun shows, but everybody does in Texas. They said he was an evil person . . .'

Once again, the gulf between the testimonies is unbridgeable. Could a quiet, devout, God-fearing man have failed to notice events on the scale depicted in news reports, both during the siege and subsequently? Maybe it is possible, even likely, that Derek, as a devoted believer in Koresh, may have missed witnessing, or overlooked some abuse. But then he wasn't looking for it.

The ATF planned the raid on Mount Carmel convinced they were dealing with a deranged psychopath. Part of the reason was that they built up their picture of what was going on in the cult on the basis of the testimony of ex-cult members who had come to believe the cult was evil. It was an ex-Davidian, Marc Breault, who told the ATF before the raid that Koresh would never submit peacefully. He claimed that Koresh was training his own armed guard. Breault had at one time been a rival for power, but was squeezed out in a power struggle with Koresh.

Another source is stranger. On the US news show *Up to the Minute* a deprogrammer and convicted jewel thief, Rick Ross, boasted that he had 'consulted with ATF agents on the Waco sect and told them about the guns in the compound'. He said he knew this from an ex-Davidian he had deprogrammed. Treasury records confirm that the ATF consulted Ross.

David Block had lived on the compound, but had been deprogrammed by Ross at the house of Priscilla Coates of the US anti-cult group Cult Awareness Network. Cynthia Kisser, executive director of CAN, praises Ross as 'among the half-dozen best deprogrammers in the country'.

After his deprogramming David Block chose a familiar route, taking the anti-cult movement as his new faith. On 25 January 1993, one month before their massive raid, Block told the ATF that Koresh was designing special guns for use on the compound.

When the ATF compiled a list of arms bought by Koresh they were horrified to find he'd recently purchased $200,000-worth of guns and explosives. It all fitted the picture that was being given to them by their ex-cult sources. What they may have overlooked was that, for the cost of a $30 licence, Koresh was a registered arms dealer. Survivors say that at the time of the raid there weren't many more arms on the site per person than there were on most Texan farms. It was Koresh's income from arms sales at the many Texas arms fairs he attended that had helped fund the utopian dream he was building in the Waco desert. It clothed and fed his followers, few of whom did any paid work, and many of whom, like Derek Lovelock, were not eligible for a work permit.

Three days after their disastrous raid on the compound, a senior ATF official justified the fiasco. They had had to act decisively because 'either they were going to come out and attack the citizens of Waco or do a Jonestown, which was why an operation was staged that placed our agents between a rock and a hard place. Our information was that was how bad it was . . .' Bemused locals wondered what they were talking about. Why didn't they just arrest Koresh on one of his regular journeys into town?

The ATF also found ex-members providing ghoulish tales of sex abuse which convinced them that they were dealing with a scale of evil they'd never encountered before. Again, Koresh may have been guilty of child abuse. But the ATF, an agency with no special expertise in this field, took the ex-member testimony of child abuse on board unquestioningly in their assessment of the cult as a Satanic blot on the Texan landscape.

Curiously, following allegations in the local Waco *Tribune-Herald* before the gunbattle, welfare workers visited the compound and were unable to confirm any child abuse.

Later, during the siege, the White House claimed it had 'mounting evidence' of physical and sexual violence against children. More recently it has climbed down and admitted that it had no evidence at all.

In the early days of the siege, after eighteen of the thirty-eight children had been released from the compound, the regional director of Texas's Child Protection Services whose counsellors had examined the children noted, 'These kids are in good shape. We were surprised.'

Evidence of child abuse remains controversial. Facts evaporate, or are burned to a crisp. Cults claim the outside world is impossibly corrupted. Anti-cultists see evil at work in cults. Once more, we're in the hall of mirrors.

When the siege hardened, the authorities, their imagination fuelled by the myths spread by the anti-cult movement, came to believe they were dealing with a 'suicide cult'. Once again, their fears created the monster they expected to meet.

As the siege deepened, the frustrated FBI became further angered by Koresh's use of local media to broadcast his messages in return for promises that he would come out. He didn't come out. They shut down communication with the cult. Instead they played the sound of rabbits being slaughtered over loudspeakers. They waited with assault rifles poised. Tanks arrived on huge juggernaut tank-transporters.

I sit in Derek's living room. His mum puts her head round the door: 'I'm Derek's mum,' she says brightly.

She wears bright pink lipstick and an electric blue jumper. 'I'm just going down the shops.' Derek smiles at her, nervily. I try to imagine this meek, ineffectual man in the middle of a compound in Texas, surrounded by tanks and assault weapons, all pointing at him.

David Koresh announced that the group would surrender when he had completed writing a document that would unlock the Seven Seals. Whether he intended to, nobody knows. He had already broken his promise to surrender more than once. Why should he keep further promises? He was surrounded by the Lamb-like beast. During the siege David Koresh told Derek that the United States forces of control were the evil that looked like a lamb but spoke like a dragon. Revelation 13. Even loyal Derek admits that the strain of acting as the figurehead of nearly a hundred followers was beginning to tell on Koresh, long before the ATF appeared.

On a Monday night, fifty days into the siege, the FBI sent in a typewriter ribbon to allow Koresh to continue typing out his final exposition of the Seven Seals. That night he sat up with cult member Ruth Riddle. She typed out Chapter One, his unlocking of the First Seal. He prefaced it with a thirteen-verse poem entitled 'Eden to Eden', an allegorical account which wove the siege itself into Koresh's belief that only by recapturing the spiritual, feminine side of his soul can Adam return to Eden. Verse two of the poem appears to describe his vision of the siege in mawkish, awkward rhymes: 'Love birds yet not of feathered creed, Shot down for gambled play, And caged a far distance betweenst themselves, For the hunter felt it best that way.'

The next morning Derek was woken at 5.45am by the sound of tear gas canisters smashing through the walls. He managed to get his gas mask on in the dark, and made it to the canteen. Parents were trying to protect children whose masks didn't fit from the worst effects of the gas by wrapping towels round their masks. A second tear gas assault started and they heard tanks punching holes into the sides of their buildings. After half an hour Derek's gas mask failed and his eyes and throat started to burn. The building was full of screaming people, huddled in groups. Derek made it to the chapel and was praying there with about ten other people when a tank smashed a hole in the wall. He saw a stairway collapse, and roof-beams falling, which Derek bitterly complains made it impossible for many of his friends to escape. They wanted to escape. Nobody wanted to die. Everyone was already terrified out of their minds, when he heard someone shouting, 'Fire!'

It all happened in a few minutes. Derek stood petrified in the chapel, choked by smoke and tear gas, looking at the hole left by the tank. If he made a run for it, would he be shot by the forces outside? Then the room exploded into fire, burning his entire right forearm. He dashed for the hole and emerged with his hands up.

Meanwhile, back home in Britain, Ian Haworth was telling Sky TV viewers that this was exactly what he had expected to happen. The cult set the fire themselves. They were programmed to do it.

Nine months after the fire, Derek's arm is badly scarred. It's hard for him to sit through it, but he's watched the fire on the video several times. He thinks the FBI, the agents of the devil, set the fire. He has seen a sequence he firmly believes shows fire spouting from the barrel of one of the tanks. The lamb-like beast that speaks like a dragon. He thinks an agent filmed clambering over the roof may have been setting light to the place. 'He just walks away,' he says sadly. 'I don't think I can forgive them.'

Roughly a third of the people in the Waco compound were British. At no time during the incident, or even after it, did the Foreign Office make any attempt to investigate what was really happening to the British citizens trapped on the ranch. Bernard Everett, the British Consul General in Dallas told the press: 'Clearly it is a very delicate situation. Clearly the raid did not go as planned and a number of people were killed, including police officers. Our concerns about the welfare of British citizens have been more than adequately conveyed, but it is not my role to criticise American tactics.'

Derek Lovelock's British passport went up in flames along with his friends, but it appears that he had long before waived his rights to be treated like a British citizen by being a member of a crazy cult.

When he emerged from the building badly burned, arms raised, knowing that his friends were dying behind him, they checked him for guns and restrained him with plastic handcuffs so tight they cut into the burns. He remembers a soldier shouting at him, 'God damn you, you will go to prison for ever!'

He was strip searched and all his clothes, down to his shoes and underpants, were taken away. He was then told to put on a thin orange shirt and trousers. That morning the wind was blowing from the north, bringing a cold Canadian air. He was marched to the ATF tent, shivering, where a medic bandaged his arm.

He was searched again at Waco jail. Somebody took him into a room, pulled down his trousers because his arms were still shackled, and told him to bend over. 'What are you looking for?' he asked. 'Drugs,' they answered. The FBI were still looking for something they understood which would explain this episode of craziness. Whey they pulled his trousers back up they left his flies undone. Handcuffed, Derek couldn't do them back up again.

There are thousands of photographs of Derek taken by press photographers that day, arms and feet in chains, wearing the absurd orange suit, dazed and horror-struck, as the prisoners were escorted into the town of Waco. He says he felt like an animal at market, herded from stall to stall.

The authorities took his fingerprints so many times he lost count. And they took photographs of him too for their records. 'Stand here. Turn this way. Turn that. I was thinking . . . this *is* the beast.'

Derek spent 200 days alone in a prison cell in McLennan County Jail Waco. He was never charged with any offence, but held on the grounds that he was a material witness. His lawyer believes that the method of imprisonment was deliberate; the authorities still believed that he would crack under solitary confinement and give damning evidence against his friends who had been charged with conspiring to murder ATF agents. In the end, much to the American government's embarrassment, nobody was convicted with murder.

The last time Derek saw his father was when the family came to the jail on a visit from Manchester, sponsored by the press. In

October 1993 he was told that his father had died. The news destroyed him. Insane with grief, he smashed furiously on the door of his cell until the guards came and shackled him with chains. Soon afterwards, still with no explanation, the authorities released him to return to Manchester for the funeral. Despite his lengthy imprisonment, he never stood trial for any offence.

He found himself standing outside the court in a pair of ill-fitting grey jeans and a shirt given to him by the prison, because all his own clothes had been destroyed. They gave him a pair of plastic sandals, but no socks. Luckily he knew the number of another Davidian who had been released and phoned him at the hotel where he was staying. He came and picked Derek up, gave him a meal, found him some clothes and helped him get the earliest flight home for his father's funeral.

His humiliation wasn't over. After the flight to Gatwick via Houston and Dallas, the immigration officers took a look at the document provided by the British Consulate to replace his destroyed passport and started to question him about whether he was coming back to start a Branch Davidian cell over here. He missed his father's funeral by two hours. The funeral card sits on top of the mirror above the gas fire, propped against the grey wallpaper.

Sometimes faith appears like a curse, especially in the eyes of outsiders who can never totally comprehend the depths of true belief. Derek, of course, still sees his faith as a blessing, as have hundreds of others I have met over this last year, who believe in fantastic things.

To the newspapers Waco was a world not of real faith at all, but of hypnotists and zombies. Faiths often appear extraordinary, but by their nature they always escape simple disproof; unlike newspapers which can more easily be shown to be wrong. The newspaper reports at the time of Waco were more often than not wholly inaccurate. Reporters were drawn into reproducing a picture of the cult which was easily recognisable, because it seemed to fit the pattern, but was also deeply misleading. The weird territory that gurus and cults map out is a world away from the press reports that screamed 'Mesmerised by a Messiah of Death', that help to arm the borders between cults and the humdrum workaday world the rest of us live in.

A week after we meet, Derek calls me. 'I just want to make sure I got over that David was a compassionate man,' he says. He's been thinking about writing a book. Do I have any idea of who might want to publish his story? I tell him I'll think about it, and feel guilty after I've put the phone down, because I should probably have told him that no one would want to print an eye-witness book about how David Koresh wasn't a mad despotic guru. David Koresh: quite nice really. I don't really believe Koresh was blameless either.

Derek's leading an aimless life now. He doesn't go to church any more. Relations between him and the Adventist church he used to attend have been soured. He's angry that during his seven months in prison, none of them wrote to him. Instead he thumbs through his big Bible, turning most frequently to his favourite part, the Book of Revelation which scared him so much as a child, but which now comforts him. It tells him, as Koresh predicted, that his friends are waiting under the Altar of God, as written in Revelation.

He misses them. Spiritually he believes they are saved, but he feels lonely without them. He still believes that everything David Koresh said was true, and feels privileged that he was one of those chosen to meet him. He believes that Koresh was a messenger of God, the Lamb of God, destined to open the Seven Seals and bring about a new kingdom on Earth, who had taken God's name, Koresh. His friends died with His name on their lips. Every dying man, Koresh told them, exhales the name of God, 'Koresh', in his death rattle. He doesn't understand why God chose him, yet again, to come so close to death, but to escape it.

We are at the time of the Fifth Seal. Soon, the Sixth will open and a rider on a white horse will come, with the four horses of the Apocalypse. The rider's name is Death, or Koresh, and God's army of two hundred million will come riding behind. He believes that the prophecy, which Koresh made clear to his followers, will be fulfilled within the next four years. The seals will be unlocked, and the new Eden will be established on Earth.

Until then he's waiting. Sometimes he thinks people are staring at him in shops and on the streets. He wonders if they're saying, 'Oh look, there's one of those devil worshippers, those cult guys. Waco guys.' He jogs and lifts weights like he used to do with his friends in Texas.

ACKNOWLEDGEMENTS

I'm grateful to many people who helped me with this project. Dr Bob Towler, Kathie Walsh and Jennifer Jeynes of INFORM – a non-sectarian organisation devoted to the study of 'New Religious Movements' based at the London School of Economics – provided much needed assistance. Though they may well not agree with some of the content of this book, I would recommend anyone who needs independent advice on cults to call them on 071 955 7654.

Dr James R Lewis of the US organisation AWARE kindly provided vital background on the Waco siege. A vast amount of information on the organisations I studied was gleaned from the writings of Dr Eileen Barker. I also relied on work by Dr Paul Heelas (Exegesis); Hounham and Hogg (SES); Larry Shinn and Kim Knott (ISKON); Shiva Naipaul (Jonestown), and Nick Davies's Guardian report "Lost in America" (Waco).

Others who provided much appreciated advice, assistance and encouragement include John Allen, Jane Carr, Joy Caton, Andrew Chapman, Val Dunmow, Chris Heath, Tom Hibbert, Richard Lowe, David Keeps, Wade Mansell, Jane McMorrow, Grace Packman and Jane Sand.